HISTORY & FEMINISM

A Glass Half Full

The Impact of Feminism on the Arts & Sciences

Claire Sprague, *General Editor*
New York University

HISTORY & FEMINISM

A Glass Half Full

Judith P. Zinsser

Twayne Publishers • New York

Maxwell Macmillan International
New York • Oxford • Singapore • Sydney

Twayne Publishers
Macmillan Publishing Company
866 Third Avenue
New York, New York 10022

Maxwell Macmillan Canada, Inc.
1200 Eglinton Avenue East
Suite 200
Don Mills, Ontario M3C 3N1

Library of Congress Cataloging-in-Publication Data

Zinsser, Judith P.
    History and feminism : a glass half full / Judith P. Zinsser.
        p.   cm.—(The impact of feminism on the arts and sciences series)
    Includes bibliographical references and index.
    ISBN 0-8057-9751-3 (hc: alk. paper).—ISBN 0-8057-9766-1 (pb: alk. paper)
        1. Women's studies—United States.   2. Women—United States—
    Historiography.   3. Education, Higher—United States.   4. Feminism—United
    States.   I. Title.   II. Series.
    HQ1181.U5Z56   1992
    305.4'07'073—dc20   92-28707
                                                                                                CIP

The paper used in this publication meets the minimum requirements of American National Standard for Information Sciences—Permanence of Paper for Printed Library Materials.
ANSI Z3948-1984.∞™

10   9   8   7   6   5   4   3   2   1

Printed in the United States of America

CONTENTS

FOREWORD

After more than two decades of feminist thought and action, it is time to stand back and assess what has been happening to traditional modes of research and evaluation in the universities. The Twayne series on the Impact of Feminism on the Arts and Sciences represents one contribution toward such an assessment. It addresses the complex questions as well as the uncertainties and possibilities that are raised by the meaning of feminist impact. Which disciplines can claim to have been altered as a result of feminism? Which cannot? How can we measure feminist impact? What biases or gaps in scholarly thought are still there? Are we creating new ones? Has a gendered approach developed in the field? What are the major areas of resistance to change?

The scope of the series is ambitious. Over the next several years, we envision the publication of volumes on anthropology, art history, bioethics, biology, classics, education, economics, film, history, law, literature, music, philosophy, political science, psychology, religion, sociology, and theater. These volumes will not follow a uniform format or approach. We anticipate that each one will combine the virtues of accessibility with original interpretations of central issues of gender, genre, methodology, and historical perspective. These are the questions that feminism has explicitly and implicitly unsettled in every field of knowledge, forcing us all to reconsider how we learn, how we choose what we learn, and how we change what and how we learn. We hope that the series will be both charting change and making it happen.

With the launching of the first two volumes, *History and Feminism*, by Judith P. Zinsser, and *Biology and Feminism*, by Sue V. Rosser, the series has become a reality. These two volumes make exciting inaugural companions, for history and biology, apparently so far apart, in fact raise similar crucial methodological questions about an ideal of "objectivity" based on value-laden data. They provide a much needed synthesis of feminist thought and efforts at change in the academy. They do not segregate the theoretical from the practical. The place of women in the profession, the politics of the profession, the lives of practitioners, the design and staffing of courses—these matters are not peripheral to an evaluation of the impact of feminism on a particular profession. The awareness that there are feminisms but no single, monolithic feminism is axiomatic to both volumes as it is to the series as a whole.

Zinsser's study demonstrates with force and clarity the continuing androcentric character of the practice and teaching of history. It suggests, furthermore, that despite visible changes in outlook, curriculum, and the representation of women in the profession, women's history still occupies a marginal place. If this is true for history, it is even more true for biology.

Women are still not very visible in the biological or physical sciences as students or professionals. Yet women's health and reproductive issues, now at the center of national debate, did, in Rosser's words, unite ''biology and feminism at the rebirth of the women's movement in the twentieth century.'' Rosser's critique of so-called ''scientific method'' and its androcentric bias demonstrates that the interaction between biology and feminism continues to be unequal and ironic, for while biology as a field has significantly affected feminism, feminism has had very little effect on biology.

Both authors see positive change as a continuing possibility, Zinsser with her assessment of a new approach to history represented by grassroots initiatives, Rosser with her discussion of ecofeminism and the possibilities inherent in a strengthened interaction between biology and feminism.

Claire Sprague
Series Editor

ACKNOWLEDGMENTS

Those of us who write works of synthesis by definition incur debts to many colleagues. In what must seem to be very long endnotes I have attempted to credit all those whose ideas and information I relied on in the construction of my narrative. I hope that what I have told does justice to their analyses and experiences. Other individuals made special contributions, which it is now my pleasure to acknowledge.

Without meaning to be, the members of the Rutgers University History Department became true partners in the writing of this book. They gave me many kinds of support including funds for my research in California. Rudolph Bell, Phyllis Mack, and Muriel Trager Clawans were always ready to listen and to suggest solutions to an odd assortment of problems and concerns. Martin Bunzl (from Philosophy), Lora Dee Garrison, John R. Gillis, T. J. Jackson Lears, and Deborah Gray White read all or part of the manuscript and gave me useful perspectives and the advantage of their writers' sensibilities. Suzanne Lebsock recalled experiences, culled files of minutes and correspondence, and kept me from being discouraged by the complexities of living memories. Bonnie G. Smith spoke with me about national history testing and her own work on women historians; she challenged me to clarify and refine important aspects of my analysis. Carol Helstolsky, Suzanne Kaufman, and the other members of the Women's History Seminar, made the first comments on chapters and helped me believe that this study of the interaction between feminism, the historical profession, and history could be done.

One of the reasons I wanted to undertake this project was the opportunity it would give me to draw on my experiences as a reporter. I can now thank those whom I interviewed for their patience with my questions and with my renditions of their responses: Berenice A. Carroll, Sandi E. Cooper, Jane S. DeHart, Pam Elam, Alice Kessler-Harris, Bette Morgan, and Hugh Van Dusen. Mary S. Hartman and Amy Swerdlow also allowed me access to documents and tapes that brought descriptions of the 1970s to life. Despina Danos at Educational Testing Service gave me a mini assessment course, answered my queries, and arranged for me to see recent history examinations.

In California, Molly Murphy MacGregor, Mary Ruthsdotter, Maria E. Cuevas, and Bonnie Eisenstein of the National Women's History Project took special time for me and made moving back and forth between their very active present and the past beginnings of their organization possible. Elizabeth Bock generously let me use her collection of materials relating to the early years of the women's movement in Sonoma County.

A number of other historians were key to the completion of the book: Noralee Frankel and Temma Kaplan helped me with files of minutes and correspondence, recreated memories, and then commented on what I had made of the whole story. Angela V. John and I resolved a conflict over the historian's "prime directive" at a critical moment in my writing. Claudia Koonz saved the tone of the first section when she turned "traditional historians" into "traditional histories." Dorothy O. Helly not only encouraged me to accept the commission for the book, but also convinced me that returning to graduate school was a logical next step in my career.

In the book's first summer, Angelyn Olson thought nothing of organizing interlibrary loans from the mainland for a visitor to Vinalhaven. In its third summer the island's writers group gave their approval to the unorthodoxies of the last chapter.

My editors, Claire Sprague and Carol Chin, shared my excitement with each completed section, and kept me focused on what the reader needed to know. Melissa Solomon gave extra encouragement in the last stages of the process.

Some of my friends took time from their own work to comment on drafts of various chapters and helped me to clear up and enliven the prose: Margot K. Jones, Louise Yelin, Hilary Ainger, and Nancy Partner. Others, like Antonia M. Grumbach, Jane Marla Robbins, Katherine J. Zinsser, and the members of my Seventy-third Street family, helped me to take my strengths and skills for granted.

And most important: without Murray D. List, Ph.D., there would have been no books; without my daughter, Sarah K. Lippmann, there would have been only selfish reasons to write so long and so hard about women.

Judith P. Zinsser
New York City

I

MEN'S HISTORY

The women's history titles that fill the shelves in bookstores, the women's history courses listed in university catalogs did not exist before the 1960s. In the previous decades only a handful of scholars had valued and given significance to women's activities and perspectives. As one twentieth-century historian described it: "the subject matter of history is always men in the midst of other men—men in collectives and groups."[1] Simply, women were not viewed as an integral part of the historical record. The vast majority remained silent and invisible, their history subsumed under general descriptions of men's lives. The few women who did appear had predictable roles as the mothers, daughters, wives, and mistresses of famous men. Extraordinary figures like the queens of sixteenth-century Europe or the nineteenth-century reformers in the United States, active agents in their own right, fared no better. Though sometimes praised for having successfully assumed male roles, traditional, patronizing phrases and denigrating stereotypes abstracted and diminished even their exceptional personalities and experiences.

Forcing acknowledgment of this "time-honored neglect," as Gerda Lerner has called it, and of the distorted memory of women's lives, represented the beginnings of feminism's impact on history. This process of recognition went slowly. There had been "a few stirrings of interest in the history of women . . . here and there," remembered Anne Firor Scott. But it was the new-found feminism of the 1960s that "inspired many young historians to take up the challenge" to reclaim and to give form to women's past.[2] These feminist historians of the late 1960s and 1970s in their first articles and books provided new perspectives on the famous queens and admired reformers already mentioned in the pages of existing histories. They then turned to the reconstruction of the lives of everyday women, to those who constituted the majority of humanity throughout historical time.

In discovering and writing women's history, feminist scholars challenged every aspect of the historian's craft. Now, over twenty years later, the questions

3

they raised about historians' methods and perspectives, the changes they required, have become so commonplace that it is perhaps difficult to imagine what history was like before. Who were the historical participants? What did they do? Who became significant and what was valued? In short, what did history sound like?

1.

TRADITIONAL HISTORIES

GREAT HISTORIANS

Come back in time. Imagine it is the 1960s when every college history major took a course called "Great Historians," or some variant of that title. Walk through the reserve section of the library. There are the acknowledged masters of the discipline from the Greek historian of the Peloponnesian War, Thucydides, to the nineteenth-century historian of the Renaissance, Jacob Burckhardt. Take one of their books in your hand. Open the pages of Francis Parkman's *Pioneers of New France*. He described the historian's task to his nineteenth-century readers: "Faithfulness to the truth of history involves far more than research, however patient and scrupulous, into specific facts. . . . The narrator must seek to imbue himself with the life and spirit of the time . . . He must himself be, as it were, a sharer or spectator of the action he describes."[1]

Imagine discussing statements like these, the writing styles, sources, and theories of causation. Be ready to debate whether history is "art" or "science," belongs to the humanities or the social sciences. Or just glance through any one of these traditional histories for the sheer pleasure of the carefully crafted analytical narrative. Share in the spectacle. Allow yourself to be caught up in what historians like to describe as the "drama of history."[2]

The immediate reaction of a feminist to these "classics," whether an eighteenth-century work like Edward Gibbon's *Decline and Fall of the Roman Empire* or Jules Michelet's nineteenth-century *History of France*, is to the sheer maleness of the concerns, the content, and the personalities. The orientation might be political, economic, cultural, or intellectual, the history might be written from the perspective of one culture or many; but whatever the approach, this was the study of man. Voltaire, the French eighteenth-century philosophe, explained to his readers that it was "the spirit of men in the most enlightened age the world has ever seen," the "heroes," and "the men of taste," that inspired his enthusiasm for the era of Louis XIV, the subject of his cultural history.[3] In Arnold Toynbee's study of the rise and fall of civilizations, a monumental six-volume work published after World War II, the "individual" was "he," and the sweep of history, his: "Ever since Man's passage from the lower to the Upper Paleolithic stage of technological progress, the Human Race had been Lords of Creation on Earth . . ."[4]

In addition to gender, other factors limited the choices these scholars made about whom to include and what to value. As E. H. Carr, the twentieth-century historian, explained: "History is concerned with those who, whether victorious or defeated, achieved something."[5] "Achievement" for a historian like Carr was by definition political. Men, and only a few men, the Napoleons and the Franklin D. Roosevelts, were seen to dominate politics and thus all of the significant events of their time. Other individuals, groups, races, and classes merely reacted. In this way history became a selective drama, "a world in which the historian [and the reader] may delight in consorting with princes," with "those exceptional beings who occasionally emerge and who often are the masters of their own fate and even more of ours." When these scholars "speak of 'general history,' " the French historian Fernand Braudel explained, "what they are really thinking of is the intercrossing of such exceptional destinies."[6] The reason for this systematic exclusion of all but these "exceptional beings" seems simple to understand now. The writers of the traditional histories (whether female or male) saw no difference between the history of the men they chose to write about and everyone's history. So, they omitted most men from their narrative and rarely mentioned women at all.

In the few instances when they did describe women's experiences, their analyses became distorted. Their narratives reflected more of contemporary prejudices about the female than the historical evidence of women's past. The authors of the traditional histories, though living in different centuries, shared the same positive image of the masculine, a set of superior, dominating characteristics. The feminine by definition was the opposite, a collection of inferior, negative qualities.[7] A brief survey of some of the "great historians" from the eighteenth to the twentieth centuries shows the ways in which the realities of women's past disappeared in the denigrating, stereotypical portraits painted of individuals, and in the rhetorical uses made of women in the abstract.

Voltaire in his history *The Age of Louis XIV*, wrote of individual women, the queens and regents who ruled in the seventeenth century. Females in his world were by nature weak, malleable, slaves to those they loved. Given political power they abused it. Anne of Austria's passion for Mazarin gave him "such dominion over her as a clever man may well have over a woman born with sufficient weakness to be ruled and sufficient obstinacy to persist in her choice."[8] Even the Queen Regent's piety identified her as subject "to the common frailty of women," and made her less fit to rule, for piety, according to Voltaire, was "closely allied with love, with politics and even with cruelty."[9]

Parkman also believed in women's inferiority, their susceptibility to influence, and thus their inability to rule. He saw the seventeenth-century French court pervaded with false religion, "a fashion" "fanned by the Jesuits" with Marie de' Medici, the mother of the king, the most perfidious adherent. Parkman described her as the "coarse scion of a bad stock, false wife and faithless queen, paramour of an intriguing foreigner, tool of the Jesuits and of Spain."[10]

By way of contrast, a successful woman ruler was an anomaly, extraordinary, unlike other women, admired because of her likeness to a man. Burckhardt in his *Civilization of the Renaissance in Italy* gave his highest accolades to women like Caterina Sforza who "had the mind and courage of men." Called "Virago" by her contemporaries (from the Latin *vir*, man), for Burckhardt she stood in stark contrast to the typical weaknesses of "womanhood" because of her "energy," "beauty," and life "full of danger and opportunity."[11]

Women rulers in tragic circumstances also merited praise in these older histories. But it was their loss of power, not their exercise of it, that was noteworthy. Gibbon, the eighteenth-century English historian, admired Queen Boudica, warrior leader of the Iceni, though she succumbed to the "steady progress of Imperial generals."[12] Voltaire complimented Sweden's seventeenth-century Queen Christina even as he reminded his readers of woman's more appropriate environment. She "renounced a throne of which she was worthy in order to live at peace and in tranquillity."[13] In the hands of Michelet, the nineteenth-century French historian, another praiseworthy woman, Joan of Arc, "La Pucelle," "The Maid of Orléans," became a powerful model for the sainted heroine, abstracted by her perfect qualities and by the concentration on her death rather than her life. In his history this early-fifteenth-century peasant lost her identity as an actual young woman and merged with his image of France.

Michelet, known for his powerful descriptions of women, did give the facts of Joan's rise to prominence and told of her military skills. His primary goal, however, was to portray the drama of her sacrifice not the complexity of her life. Captured and imprisoned, Joan became the central figure in a grand tragedy. During her interrogations she was a "young soul," "the unfortunate, rejected by the visible, abandoned by the invisible Church, by the world, and by her own heart." Joan ceased to be significant as an individual. "Her cruel fate," he explained, "was inevitable," "and—we must say the word—necessary." The trial, the suffering, and the burning at the stake, meant "purification," and gave her immortality by the dispelling of shadows that "would have interposed amidst the rays of glory which rest on that holy figure: [otherwise] she would not have lived in men's minds the MAID OF ORLEANS."[14] Michelet then made the gentle, pious, female martyr his idealized vision of France: "The saviour of France could be no other than a woman. France herself was woman having her nobility, but her amiable sweetness likewise, her prompt and charming pity; at the least, possessing the virtue of quickly-excited sympathies."[15]

Later in his history Michelet abandoned this winning, girlish image of the nation. His country's subsequent greatness in the seventeenth and eighteenth centuries could not be attributed to feminine qualities. It was as if France changed gender. For Michelet only the masculine could explain the later "unity and personality of our mobile land." He noted that women had been excluded from the royal succession, thus the "male element . . . remained the same, preserving identity and spirit, and perpetuating traditional feelings."[16]

In the twentieth century, Arnold Toynbee in his *Study of History* indulged in the same kind of glorification of "maleness" with even more denigrating implications for its opposite, "femaleness." He mentioned only a few women by name and all, with the exception of Anna Comnena, the twelfth-century historian of the Byzantine Empire, were defined in relation to men. Most were described with stereotypical phrases: Olympias, Alexander the Great's noble mother; malicious "mischief makers" like Helen of Troy, the Frankish queen Fredegund, and Rosamund, Henry II of England's mistress.[17]

In fact Toynbee revealed more of his view of women by implication than by explicit use of examples. His "civilizations," the heroes of his history, melded with an unstated image of "man" representing all that Toynbee deemed admirable in the human spirit. Thus, the developments and the qualities that weakened these civilizations came to be embodied in an opposite force, the female, as manifested in an all-pervasive, seemingly uncontrolled sexuality. Toynbee identified these failing civilizations with "promiscuity," a general phenomenon of "the souls of men" in "disintegrating societies."[18] Worship of women goddesses like Isis and Ishtar was one aspect of this weakness. These religions "spread over the Roman Empire, and by saturating the European peoples with alien ideas of life undermined the whole fabric of ancient civilizations.''[19] In describing the twentieth century Toynbee made the story of Circe's seduction of Ulysses' men a metaphor for the modern day uses of leisure time: listening to radio and television was equivalent to being "penned in Circe's sty.''[20] Even worse from his perspective, "vulgarity" characterized this new age, a society given over to unreasoned breeding. "Western Man," he explained, had lowered everyone's standard of living with the "worship of family fecundity.''[21]

The identification of women with latent, potent sexuality was not a new phenomenon in twentieth-century historical narrative and analysis. The association had a long history of its own. It animated Gibbon's *Decline and Fall of the Roman Empire* in the form of a host of cruel, sexually manipulative empresses. The images of sisters, concubines, and wives murdering rivals' sons, poisoning lovers, and cuckolding husbands filled the pages.[22] Gibbon used all of his descriptive skills in his portrait of Theodora, wife of the sixth-century emperor, Justinian. To him she was first and foremost a prostitute with amazing sexual stamina—able to handle 10 of her guests and 30 of the enslaved men serving them in a single evening. She held the emperor with her body and therefore spent "her private hours . . . devoted to the prudent as well as grateful care of her beauty.''[23]

In the nineteenth century, Michelet in his history of France saw this female force both in the abstract as "woman," and in particular women, as quintessential evil seductresses. Michelet described the twelfth century as one in which because of Christianity "woman reigned in heaven and on earth. She is seen interfering in the things of this world and ordering them." He believed that the established Church also feared woman's apparent dominance for: "Man knew himself to be weak and tender. He kept her [woman] at a distance; the more he felt his heart sympathize with her. Hence, the hard, and even contemptuous expressions, by which he strives to fortify himself against her power.''[24]

Eighteenth- and nineteenth-century historians could also imagine the opposite stereotype, the circumstances in which women's sexual attractions, their potential grace and beauty, could bring man happiness and would be cause for praise rather than condemnation. Just as they used the caricature of the "bad" woman, so they perpetuated the ideal of the "good" woman. Voltaire presented his ideal female. He complimented royal wives and mistresses for their "charm and gentility of manners," for their ability to amuse, and their "pleasing and vivacious conversation." He found Madame de Maintenon "a woman of easy temper," who lightened "the burden of affairs" for the older Louis XIV now more interested in her "companionship" than her sexual skills.[25]

The Renaissance woman of Jacob Burckhardt's history best exemplified this stereotypical image of the "good" female. Believing "that women stood on a footing of perfect equality with men," that "female emancipation . . . was a matter of course," he then proceeded to describe a constrained world very different from men's. An individual, like the courtesan Imperia, might become "a woman of intelligence and culture," but only in the service of the privileged males of her circle. Women were to be the modest, attentive, moral counterparts to their active, vital male family members. "Their function," Burckhardt explained, "was to influence distinguished men and to moderate male impulse and caprice."[26]

This ideal of women's lives given over to the service of men found an extreme expression in Parkman's history of the frontiers of New France. The Ursuline nuns sent to establish hospitals and schools had "an ability, a fortitude, and an earnestness which command respect and admiration."[27] Of those in Montreal he wrote, "The nuns died, but they never complained."[28] The Native American women and the wives of the European settlers had no other life but for their men. Huron women became "shrivelled hags, hideous and despised;" their lives "had no bright side. It was youth of license, and age of drudgery."[29] The young French peasant women fared no better. Brought to the king's colony to marry, paid bounties for births, isolated in remote forest settlements, they were described by a priest: "Wild-looking women, with sunburnt faces and neglected hair, run from their work . . . while half-savage children . . . bareheaded, bare-footed, and half-clad, come to wonder and stare."[30]

POPULAR TEXTBOOKS

Some have urged that readers accept such pictures of women's character and experiences as the innocent product of "old fashioned" history. Defenders argue that the "great historians" merely wrote as representatives of their times. They could no more free themselves from cultural stereotypes and gender expectations than any other men or women of their time. What then of the more recent past, of histories written in the 1960s? What kinds of images and accounts of women's lives appeared in books meant for a more general readership?

Take for example, three of the most popular college textbooks of the 1960s, each by eminent historians. Contemporaries praised R. R. Palmer's and Joel Colton's *A History of the Modern World* for the integration of intellectual history with the political narrative. Thomas A. Bailey's *The American Pageant* was often chosen for courses because of the wonderful attention to descriptive detail. William H. McNeill's *A World History* remains unique in its analytical sweep and broad erudition. Yet a feminist would be disappointed in the three texts. These historians no more escaped the traditional premises than had the scholars of earlier times. Each author made the same assumptions about the universality of men's experience and came to the same focus on men's political activities. When they did mention women in general or describe the activities of individuals in particular, the pictures of women's past and the images projected remained unchanged. They accepted the traditional definitions of feminine and masculine traits of character; they perpetuated the ancient stereotypes of "good" and "bad" women; they utilized the same subtly denigrating abstractions.[31]

The process by which most women's experiences were neglected or distorted in these modern studies of the world evolved much as it had in the older, classic works. McNeill unabashedly described his book as a "history of mankind." He gave his readers a grand vision of successive male-created civilizations, a world always in balance as one "center" of culture rose and another receded. In this sweeping account of "mankind's past" he found only one significant female, Catherine the Great of Russia, a woman who played a traditionally male role.[32]

Though McNeill omitted virtually all individual women from his world history textbook, he used them for his illustrations, traditional representations of the female and all that it could connote in Western culture. David's "Market Woman" and Daumier's "Women in a Third Class Railway Carriage" gave him his pictures of the noble, poor, victimized members of the lower classes. Other plates drew on familiar, negative images of women's qualities: the "slender aristocrat delightfully decorative and sweetly debonair" contrasted with his earnest male burghers; two busts of women showed the deterioration of the Greco-Roman civilizations in the "towered and patterned curls" of one matron and the "strong and haughty face" of the other. He chose a female figure from an Indian temple to exemplify the sensuality of Hindu culture.[33]

Palmer and Colton and Bailey were not so cavalier as McNeill in their statements of purpose. Palmer and Colton formulated a broad definition of history in their preface, including "matters of many kinds." Their focus, however, remained clearly on men's lives and the familiar political achievements and economic developments of the European past.[34] Bailey also began by acknowledging varied approaches to history, but concluded that "the most clearly identifiable channel" of his textbook was "the political one." And although Bailey wanted his readers "to come away with a deeper appreciation of the hardships and contributions of the men and women who built America," the contributions he valued were most often men's, not women's. For example, he hoped that his narrative of United States history would enlist from his readers "a sympathetic understanding of the problems confronting our statesmen."[35]

Neither were these historians so dismissive as McNeill of women's lives. They included in their textbooks individual women who had been close to powerful men, and many of those who sought, or were allowed to assume male roles. Even so, the references to women and the stories of women's experiences reenforced the old gendered prejudices. By implication and by explicit example their survey histories replicated the traditional definitions of feminine and masculine qualities and of women's and men's proper relationship.

Palmer's and Colton's careful use of adjectives and descriptive phrases made it difficult for readers to respect the European women whose lives intersected with men's as mothers, wives, and mistresses. "The buxom Anne Boleyn" displaced Catherine of Aragon in Henry VIII of England's affections. Jean Jacques Rousseau's companion had more sentences but with the same effect. Palmer and Colton explained that Rousseau's "sex life was unsatisfactory; he finally settled down with an uneducated girl named Thérèse Levasseur, and with her mother, who kept interfering in his affairs." The female individuals significant in the Russian Revolution received the same negative treatment. The Tsarina Alexandra was described as a "superstitious woman much given to consultation with necromancers," whose antics made the "private life of Louis XVI and Marie Antoinette" "less primitive" by comparison. Nadezhda Krupskaya, Lenin's wife, was dismissed with the story of their meeting: "She already belonged to a circle of argumentative Marxists."[36] The English suffragists remained nameless in the text and received scant coverage despite their actions in the political sphere. A few sentences described their forced feeding and imprisonment, all brought on by their own ill-considered actions. "Despairing of ever getting the men to listen to reason [they] resorted to amazingly 'un-English' and unreasonable arguments."[37]

In contrast to these brief mentions of big-breasted, irrational women, Palmer and Colton devoted paragraphs and pages to the eighteenth-century European rulers, Catherine the Great of Russia and Maria Theresa of Austria. It is evident, however, from their language that traditional ideas of male and female qualities still dictated much of their analysis. Palmer and Colton acknowledged Catherine the Great as "one of the main builders of Russia." Given their disdain for the feminine they suggested that her success came because of her masculine traits: she was "unscrupulous," "mannish, hearty, and boisterous." She "wore out a succession of many lovers, mixing them freely with politics." "Her intellectual powers were as remarkable as her physical vigor"—for a woman, they implied.[38]

If Palmer and Colton believed that Catherine the Great succeeded because she behaved like a man, it was the stereotypically feminine that they noted in their description of Maria Theresa of Austria. On the one hand, they called her "one of the most capable rulers ever produced by the House of Hapsburg." On the other, they wrote an admiring physical description: "graceful and attractive as a young woman, buxom and motherly as she grew older." There were men's responses to her: "affectionate loyalty from her assistants," acceptance of her domination by her husband and sons. Their final tribute recalled some of the oldest images of female behavior. "She knew how to use so-called feminine wiles, charms, moods, and even outbursts of tears to gain her ends. She once remarked to her husband, Francis of Lorraine, that the singer they had just heard at the opera was the greatest actress that ever lived. 'Except yourself, Madam,' he replied, with a freedom permitted to the husbands even of queens."[39] The apocryphal tale, the husband's retort, reasserted the proper relationship between the sexes and put an empress in her place.

Bailey in his history of the United States mentioned even more individual women prominent in their own right. He treated them, however, no differently than Palmer and Colton had. As in the European text, the descriptive language and the choice of facts reenforced ancient stereotypes and denigrated women's perspectives and experiences. For example, Anne Hutchinson, the seventeenth-century religious dissident, became "an intelligent, strong-willed and talkative woman, ultimately the mother of fourteen children." It was the "dusky Queen Liliuokalani" who opposed United States efforts to annex and rule Hawaii.[40]

These brief references seem relatively complimentary in comparison to the way in which Bailey wrote about nineteenth-century women feminists and reformers, a group with a whole chapter devoted to their history. In addition to physical description and comments on their fecundity, Bailey used veiled humor and irony that diminished the significance of their activities more subtly but no less effectively. For example, he entitled the chapter on their lives "Petticoats in Revolt." He described the most outspoken as "arresting characters," "a belligerent bevy of female agitators." He quoted a contemporary derisive rhyme about the feminist Amelia Bloomer; portrayed Mary Lease, the Populist speaker, as "a tall, mannish woman," "the queen of the 'calamity howlers,' " and "Mrs. Carrie A. Nation," as a "muscular and mentally deranged Kansan . . . [who] brought disrepute to the prohibition movement by the violence of her one woman crusade."[41] The suffragists became "the fighting feminists," "sprightly," "austere"; one was noted as a "Quakeress," another as the mother of seven children. Any serious understanding of their ideas and accomplishments was vitiated by his decision to make a contemporary riddle part of his account: What is a suffragist? "One who has ceased to be a lady and has not yet become a gentleman."[42] In fact, he suggested that nineteenth-century women in the United States had no need for a feminist movement: ". . . though legally regarded as perpetual minors, [they] were in a relatively good position. They were probably better treated than in any country of Europe, partly because of their scarcity in frontier communities. . . . Few American husbands were brutes; and the softer sex had quiet and time-tested ways of protecting itself, regardless of the law."[43]

For Bailey, those of the "softer sex" who remained "ladies," the women reformers who exemplified appropriately feminine activities and concerns, merited favorable descriptions. Even so, he continued to give more details about their appearance and their reproductive lives than their accomplishments as activists. Bailey's model heroines like "Mrs. Harriet Beecher Stowe," "a wisp of a woman and the mother of a half-dozen children," wrote books. They were discreet in their social reform efforts: "the dynamic five-foot Clara Barton, an 'angel' of the Civil War battlefields"; "the saintly" Frances E. Willard of the WCTU (Women's Christian Temperance Union); Dorothea Dix, the "quiet New England teacher-authoress," "a frail spinster afflicted with persistent lung trouble." His twentieth-century ideal was Margaret Chase Smith, "a gray-haired, attractive matron," and a Senator from Maine.[44]

Although Palmer, Colton, and Bailey included these exceptional female individuals, by and large they assumed that women's lives were described in the sections on men's experiences. When these historians did touch on women's everyday activities they fell prey to the same old-fashioned attitudes that colored their writing on wives, empresses, and activists. Europe's nineteenth-century rural women became part of impersonal forces like the "domestic system" of manufacturing when work was " 'put out' . . . to people in the country."[45] Industrialization in Bailey's history was especially harsh on nameless female victims. He imagined an idyllic rural life, a golden pre-industrial age before new inventions "confined women into industry" and "sucked" them "into the unhealthy vortex of the factory." The sewing machine, for example, drove "the seamstress from the shelter of the private home into the factory where as a human robot she tended the chattering mechanisms."[46]

Bailey, Palmer, and Colton also perpetuated traditional images of groups of women. For example, the beliefs that underlay the sixteenth- and seventeenth-century witchcraft persecutions were not "entirely unfounded," for, the European historians explained, the accused women "were nevertheless, in many cases, antisocial beings who meant no good to their neighbors." The enslaved women of Bailey's section on the antebellum South deserved separate mention as "breeders," and for their "loose morals."[47]

When it came to the contemporary period, to describing women's circumstances since 1945, not one of these historians approved of the changes. They could not escape the ancient prejudices about women's proper role and relationship to men. The overall impression they gave to the reader was of a lovely, though imperfect world, lost forever because of the ways in which today's women had claimed separate authority over their lives. Bailey accepted that the "softer sex" had been freed "from clinging-vine dependence on males," but noted that these new "careers" caused "delayed marriages and smaller families." As early as the nineteenth century the "gradual emancipation of females was reflected in a disquieting increase in the divorce rate."[48] Palmer and Colton saw even direr consequences in the creation of this age of independent women leaving the traditional life of household and children. They belittled women's need for waged work outside the home "as the supposedly more edifying labors of factories and fields." They called it "an invasion." Like Bailey they cautioned their readers about this revolution in "women's place in society" and its "transformation of the institution of marriage and the relations of husband and wife," for, they explained, with the first decades of women's participation in industrialization in the nineteenth century "family life and common morals went to pieces."[49]

As Palmer and Colton continued their description of these trends into the twentieth century, ancient sexist attitudes clouded their analysis. They had told of the unfortunate effects of women taking up waged work outside the household, but even when modern women remained in a traditional setting, the two historians saw new dangers to society. Privileged women could now control their fertility. In images reminiscent of Gibbon's descriptions of Roman empresses and Toynbee's sections on "Promiscuity," they called up the spectre of "self-indulgence," and thus suggested a world of idle women pleasuring themselves. Gone were the noble, middle-class wives and mothers happily surrounded with their children. By leaving their homes and interfering with their fertility these modern women created "a fateful paradox," a declining birth rate in just those elite cultures and among those special classes and races that by implication these gentlemen scholars most honored.[50] Once again women became the cause of all men's troubles. Contemporary Eves, Helens of Troy, and Theodoras reformulated for the modern reader.

2.

CHALLENGING TRADITIONS

In the 1960s many women who would today consider themselves feminists read the standard textbooks and studied the "great historians." What surprises them now is that they never noticed what had happened. They too accepted that their history had somehow been told, that the denigrating asides and stereotypical descriptions and abstractions accurately portrayed women's lives in the past. How was this possible? How had the most respected historians, skilled researchers with sophisticated analytical approaches to the discipline, produced such simplistic images of women? How could readers, even women readers, fail to see the omissions and distortions?

To answer these questions requires an understanding of the way in which the past becomes "history." When we open a history book we encounter certain people, in a certain place, living through time. One picture, one fact, one detail from these lives, will not be enough. To be history there must be a sequence of events and many interactions between groups and individuals. There must be a sense of chronology, a sense of change, a sense of purpose. Whether explicit or implicit, this construction and representation of the past will reflect an explanation, a way of making logical the relationships within a specific set of facts. At every point in this process, the historian makes choices among a multiplicity of events and personalities, from a wide range of possible causes. Those choices transform the past into history.

The historian's decision to write about one facet of human experience and not another gives that aspect permanence and significance. For history represents a people's, a society's, a culture's way of remembering itself. Jacob Burckhardt described history to his nineteenth-century readers as "the record of what one age finds worthy of note in another."[1] The recorded is saved, and conversely, the unrecorded is lost. Thus, the great power of historians is that with their study of documents, of oral statements, of physical artifacts, they "preside over the construction" of what the cultural historian Peter Gay has called "the collective memory." Even more important, by default, by their omissions, they preside over "a convenient distortion of an equally collective amnesia."[2]

Challenges to the narrow "collective memory" of traditional histories have been made for a variety of reasons. Burckhardt was considered unorthodox in the nineteenth century for writing about, and thus valuing, the culture and not the politics of the Italian Renaissance. In the twentieth century, historians like Carl Becker and Charles A. Beard questioned the whole process of writing history and the choices it entailed. Becker entitled his 1931 address as president of the American Historical Association "Everyman His Own Historian"; Beard called his in 1933 "Written History as an Act of Faith." With their titles they drew attention to the central problem for any researcher into the past. Becker and Beard each argued that because of the range of possible choices and interpretations all histories were suspect and all historians open to criticism for their "subjectivity," for the ways in which circumstances of their own time influenced their views of the past. These questions of historical validity and scholarly authority arise for all researchers as soon as they admit that they have selected facts for their narratives. As criteria of selection may differ from one era to another, so the representations of events may differ.

The practitioners of the traditional histories denied the possibility for such variations and insisted on their "objectivity" as scholars. They warned that approaches like Becker's and Beard's, the "relativist" position as it came to be called in the 1930s and 1940s, presaged intellectual chaos, conflicting accounts of the past in which no one history was "true," no sequence of facts self-evident, no interpretation more valid than another. By and large academic historians (both women and men) agreed with this thinking. Becker and Beard, despite their prestige and the popularity of their work, remained mavericks within the profession. The majority of scholars glossed over or marginalized criticism of choices, praise for other analytical approaches, and the efficacy of multiple accounts of events. Until the first reinterpretations of United States foreign policy in the early

1960s the decisions about how to write history, about what to call "history," and what to let fall away were clear to all of the leading practitioners and to their students. Consensus turned the controversy over "objectivity" and "subjectivity" into a historiographical curiosity rather than a challenging professional concern.[3]

Academic historians wrote with such unanimity and others read with such naiveté because they shared certain premises about the discipline.[4] First, historians defined history narrowly, deciding what was significant and what was not in such a way as to eliminate all but a few participants and certain kinds of activities, essentially, the male elite and its exercise of political power. Second, they conducted selective research, choosing as valid only those sources, methods, and analytical approaches that illuminated the lives of the elite in general and its use of public authority in particular. Third, when criticized for these choices, the authors of traditional histories described themselves as neutral and objective. They dismissed supplemental or alternative narratives as unimportant and declared their version of events as complete and accurate.[5]

"Accurate" was the important word. Some thought of their truncated history as almost scientific, verifiable, a "true" representation of reality. Also, much like a science, history was taught as a rational, logical discipline employing objective rules of evidence. Whether a scholarly monograph or a popular textbook, a traditional history appeared to present a series of answers to obviously significant questions, answers based on information meticulously researched and carefully described in a coherent and self-evident analytical narrative. The profession liked to believe "that the good historian sits before the facts with little in the way of assumptions, and the facts speak to him." Images like these made the premises seem impregnable.[6]

Given this closed system of research and analysis, to include women—or any of the groups of people previously omitted or identified only in relation to the male elite—involved more than the addition of a few sentences or paragraphs. To cure "the collective amnesia" meant changing the basic premises governing history and acknowledging the inevitable subjectivity of the historian. The profession would have to admit that "most narrative history does not quite live up to its advance billing: it is neither as comprehensive nor as 'objective' as it is popularly supposed to be."[7] In fact, the exclusive definition of history as the political experience of male elites would have to be discarded. To construct the forgotten histories, new categories of analysis, new kinds of sources, and new methods of research would have to be utilized. There would be no broadening of history and no transformation of women's history until these newly formulated and potentially revolutionary views of the discipline had been accepted.

By the end of the 1960s in the United States all of these preconditions had been met. The premises basic to the writing of traditional histories came under attack from many different sides. The methods of the social and cultural historians associated with the French Annalistes and with the European Marxist historians and demographers called into question the old choices about sources and content. From the early 1960s United States historians researched the lives of men formerly omitted or never particularized: laborers, immigrants, members of racial and ethnic minorities. These "revisionist" and "radical" historians, as they were called, along with the practitioners of many academic disciplines (not just history) reassessed traditional scholarship and discovered implicit motives. As historians, they identified subjective choices in their predecessors' works and debated the political uses made of the elitist history of the past.

Both through their writings and by their activities outside the classroom these "New Left" historians of the United States thus derided the old claims to objectivity. Purposely subjective in their approach, they articulated "the notion of the historian as actor," and advocated an explicit, political function for themselves. They were not the first to set such a task for scholars. In the Progressive era (before World War I) James Harvey Robinson, a historian of Europe, had advocated this kind of role for his colleagues. In *The New History* (1913) he asserted: "The present has hitherto been the willing victim of the past; the time has now come when it should turn on the past and exploit it in the interest of advance."[8] Much in the spirit of Robinson, William Appleman Williams trained as a diplomatic historian after his discharge from the navy at the end of World War II "because," he explained, "I really did want to try and make some sense out of what the hell was going on—the bomb and all that. . . ."[9] His critical study of United States foreign policy was considered so influential that his second manuscript, *The Contours of History* (1961), was subpoenaed by the House Un-American Activities Committee. Staughton Lynd chose to write on class and racial conflicts in the eighteenth- and nineteenth-century United States. He also directed the Mississippi Freedom Schools in 1964. In 1965 he helped to organize the first march on Washington to protest the war in Vietnam and made a trip to Hanoi with Herbert Aptheker, the historian of black Americans, and Tom Hayden, leader of Students for a Democratic Society.

By the late 1960s this powerful combination of circumstances—the sheer volume of work in fields other than political history, the stridency and persistence of the critics, the widespread popular outrage over civil rights and the increasing opposition to the war in Vietnam, violent campus protests at every major university, massive political demonstrations against the Federal government—forced new thinking. The old cries for consensus among historians no longer held the same authority. The discipline had to tolerate a multiplicity of perspectives and causal explanations.

THE 1960s

The case against the traditional histories and their premises represented the coming together of four major historiographical trends of the twentieth century. There was the new definition of history from the French Annalistes, the social and cultural emphasis of the European Marxist historians, the techniques of the French and English demographers, and the political awareness of the revisionist historians in the United States.[10] Each contributed to the opening of history to experiences other than those of the powerful male elite.

Lucien Febvre founded the journal *Annales d'histoire économique et sociale* in Strasbourg in 1929 (renamed *Annales: Economies, Sociétés, Civilisations* in 1946). Over the next twenty years he and Marc Bloch created a new approach to history. They attempted nothing less than the reconstruction, as Febvre described it, of "the whole physical, intellectual, and moral universe within which each generation . . . transformed itself."[11] Fernand Braudel, the best known of the Annales school of historians (as it came to be called) explained the way in which the Annalistes approached and reconstructed the past. His history, *The Mediterranean and the Mediterranean World in the Age of Philip II*, was a classic example of their attitudes and techniques (published in France in 1966, and in translation in the United States in 1974). Braudel let the whole region, the whole era, mould and shape the inquiry and the description that resulted. The Mediterranean basin, not dynasties or emergent nation states, economic or religious forces, was the subject of the study. He replaced traditional periodization with a threefold division of the text that reflected what Braudel saw as the three levels of the past: "a geographical time, a social time, and an individual time." In this two-volume work "events," the subject of traditional histories, became "essentially ephemeral," nothing more than "the 'headlines' of the past."[12]

To write this novel history required special skills and techniques. The Annalistes chose to benefit from all of the "human sciences," from geography, sociology, anthropology, and psychology, for example. Bloch described the approach as a "work of reintegration," by which the research of specialists "coalesce[d]" in order to create a history of the whole of human experience. History "has used" the other disciplines, Braudel explained, "to rebuild itself in a genuinely new form," a total, all-encompassing history.[13]

By the early 1960s European Marxist and French and English demographic historians had created new social histories of the lower classes. They literally turned history upside down. In books like George Rudé's *The Crowd in the French Revolution* (1959), Albert Soboul's *Les Sans-culottes parisiens en l'an II* (1962, 2d ed.), Eric Hobsbawm's essay collections *Primitive Rebels* (1959) and *Labouring Men: Studies in the History of Labour* (1968), and E. P. Thompson's *The Making of the English Working Class* (1963) groups previously portrayed as victims, or as actors peripheral to the central political narrative, became active agents of their own histories. Peter Laslett in his book, *The World We Have Lost* (published in the United States in 1964), showed how local collaborative history projects like the Cambridge Group for the History of Population and Social Structure, using demographic techniques, had "reconstituted families" and thus recreated English peasant life before the industrial age.[14]

This eclectic approach, the use of "the analytical concepts and interpretive models" of other schools of history and other disciplines, found enthusiastic adherents in the United States.[15] As early as 1957, William L. Langer, a historian of Europe, had spoken in his presidential address to the American Historical Association about using psychology in history. (*Young Man Luther*, the first biography of this sort, by the psychologist Erik Erikson appeared in 1958.) H. Stuart Hughes had already written on the uses of anthropology in history for the *American Historical Review* (the journal of the American Historical Association) in 1960. He saw a "whole new world of possibilities," and believed that he and his students were "on the verge of great discoveries."[16]

United States historians took the European approach and methods as models and wrote similar social and cultural histories for their disadvantaged peoples. Works like Herbert G. Gutman's early essays on U.S. laborers in Pennsylvania and the Ohio Valley (1959–69), Eugene D. Genovese's *The World the Slaveholders Made* (1964), and Staughton Lynd's *Class Conflict, Slavery, & the United States Constitution: Ten Essays* (1967) revealed new aspects and interpretations of familiar periods and were intended to alter the politically oriented exclusionary pictures of the country's past. In this they succeeded. Their writings broadened the definition of history and legitimated inquiry into the lives of those formerly forgotten.[17]

In addition, by the end of the 1960s, most historians had acknowledged that they could not write history without making choices and therefore could not be disinterestedly scientific in the sense originally imagined. Eminent male leaders of the profession such as Richard Hofstadter in his analysis of *The Progressive Historians* (1968) accepted periods of "consensus" as yet another manifestation of the ways in which historians' interpretations might be affected by their era.[18] D. H. Fischer wrote positively about this different image of the profession: "To write history, or even to read it, is to be endlessly engaged in a process of selection."[19] Hughes went even further in his analysis of historians' criteria of selection. These "derive," he explained, "from the historian's own value system."[20] Many believed some degree of subjectivity would, in fact, enhance their ability to explain the people and forces that they studied. E. H. Carr, like Francis Parkman nearly a century before, wrote of the "historian's need of imaginative understanding of the minds of the people with whom he is dealing."

Carr eloquently described what he called history's dialogue between the present and the past, and the historian's role as "the conscious and unconscious spokesman of the society to which he belongs."[21]

Yet for all that they accomplished in terms of new methods, new sources, and new perspectives, the leaders among these gifted and revolutionary European and United States historians remained traditional in one key respect: They failed to value women's experiences equally with men's. For example, an activist like Howard Zinn continued to describe "radical" history in masculine terms and asked "How can history serve man today?"[22] When they researched, when they wrote, the vast majority still envisaged male protagonists and believed that their depictions of men's lives described women's as well. Jesse Lemisch in his 1965 essay for the Radical Education Project of the Students for a Democratic Society coined the phrase that became the slogan for the historians of the New Left, history "seen from the bottom up." Though later he would acknowledge his omission, at the time he heard no contradiction in the proud assertion that he was writing a truly "democratic" history of "the majority," the history of "the common man."[23] When groups of women or female individuals did figure in the results of the new research, even these consciously revisionist historians portrayed their subjects in familiar gendered images and placed women in their time-honored relationships to men.

THE STUDY OF MEN[24]

Linguistics was among the unorthodox sources that Bloch analyzed for his study of *Feudal Society*. He attached great importance to language and wanted historians to use it to illuminate the meanings of past practices and institutions. The Annalistes believed that sensitivity to language more than any other skill enabled them to understand the "mentalités," the overriding cultural attitudes of a particular age. Ironically, language also first signified the limitations of the Annales school—its failure to include women in the new vision of the past. For the Annalistes, as for the historians they hoped to supersede, history was a masculine phenomenon. Bloch explained in his description of the historian's craft that "the object of history is, by nature, man. Let us say rather, men." He continued: "The variety of historical evidence is nearly infinite. Everything that man says or writes, everything that he makes, everything he touches can and ought to teach us about him."[25]

With their goal of an all-encompassing history, with their broader perspectives, the Annalistes should have invented women's history. They did not. Susan Mosher Stuard explained that they saw women as "other," as outside of society and related to it only because of their function. For example, Georges Duby in his *Chivalrous Society* described women as a means of exchange between families, as objects of inheritance and negotiation. Emmanuel Le Roy Ladurie included them as part of the household in his study of the community of Montaillou, but a household in which the male was the center; the female, the periphery.[26]

Throughout most of Braudel's study of the Mediterranean in the sixteenth century, populations rose and fell, nomads and immigrants passed through the pages of the *longue durée* as if women and men had the same responses and experiences. In the section on social and economic institutions peasants and silkworkers labored in neutered activities. Even witchcraft was a genderless phenomenon. Braudel made no mention of the sex of the vast majority of the persecuted. Women only appeared in the "political" section, and they were the same women included in the most traditional histories, appearing in the same roles. Braudel identified them first as daughters, nieces, sisters, wives, mothers, and only gave them their own space in the narrative when, like Mary and Elizabeth Tudor or Catherine de' Medici, they ruled as men.[27]

Braudel believed that the value of history was determined by "the extent to which it can explain the life of men as it is being woven before our very eyes, with its acquiescences and reticences, its refusals, complicities, or surrenders when confronted with change or tradition."[28] As Stuard wrote, it was these "complicities" with and "surrender" to gendered traditions that "call[ed] into question the fidelity of the Annales School to the history of the masses, in which women play so great a part. It also hinder[ed] them from creating a history that may legitimately claim to be total in its grasp."[29]

The French and English social historians did no better. Joan W. Scott explained that the new, like the old history, "as a unified story was a fiction about a universal subject whose universality was achieved through implicit processes of differentiation, marginalization, and exclusion." Forces, not female and male individuals, caused change. Gender became just one more group identity. Even an original historian like E. P. Thompson who "pulled the working class from a world of silence left women out."[30] Women remained "marginal" and appeared only occasionally in his massive chronicle of the emergence of England's modern class society: a widow, a dressmaker, a tally of female domestics, a reference to artisans claiming women's rights. Associated with "domesticity," despite their vital roles as laborers, artisans, and popular leaders, women's past remained devalued by omission, their contributions tangential to the real story of men's activities.[31]

Like their European counterparts, United States "revisionist" and "radical" historians of the 1960s, despite their broader vision, their creative scholarship, and their political fervor "tended to ignore women." As Carroll Smith-Rosenberg described their works, these experts in social history "often dealt superficially with a major segment of the population and underestimated the complexity of institutional arrangements and of social processes." Instead they and other historians researching social rather than political history continued to focus on men's experiences albeit from the new perspectives of class, race, and ethnicity. They missed, for example, Smith-Rosenberg explains, the role of women in nineteenth-century religions, that "male ministers preached to and worked with a largely female church". They also failed to mention women's colleges, "one of the major educational innovations of the nineteenth century." When women did appear, it was "mainly as members of families" and "seldom as persons in their own right." In these skewed social histories the family appeared "either as an institution divided between neuter and monolithic units of parents and children, or as an association of fathers and sons."[32]

Though the challenge to the sexist nature of previous histories did not come from even the best intentioned and most radical male historians, they did make a significant contribution nonetheless. Their research and analysis prepared the groundwork for the new generation of feminists to speak for themselves. With the acceptance of their writings, the classic premises had lost their impregnability. It merely remained for feminist historians to apply the insights of the new histories to their own subjects.[33] They began by identifying old-fashioned and revisionist histories as male stories written by men for men's purposes. They found allies among their colleagues, both radicals like Herbert Gutman and more traditional liberals like David Potter. They could use the words of the most respected male members of the profession to make their case. For example, Carl Degler, a historian of the United States, came to believe that women had been excluded from accounts of the past: "Because men have dominated society, the history they found most useful was that which depicted the activities and institutions that interested them."[34]

Feminists would not choose to "dominate" society. As historians, however, women would make different decisions about what was and was not "useful," and depict "the activities and institutions that interested them." E. H. Carr wrote that "by and large the historian will get the kind of facts he wants."[35] Feminist historians began to collect the facts they wanted. They took the old and the new methods, traditional and unorthodox sources, and constructed their own narrative, told from a consciously gendered female perspective.

In this new academic and political context Gerda Lerner's first essay advocating the study of women's past was published. This 1969 article and others like it inaugurated the process by which women's history gained adherents, an audience, and scholarly legitimacy. The creation of this revitalized and expanded field of historical inquiry would be contemporary feminism's first impact on the discipline of history.

II

WOMEN'S HISTORY

In the fall of 1969 *The Journal of American Social History* published Gerda Lerner's article, "New Approaches to the Study of Women in American History." She wrote as a feminist and as a historian with fervor and righteous impatience. Her purpose was both scholarly and political. As she explained in this and subsequent articles and books, she perceived women as disadvantaged in two significant ways. First, their history had been omitted and distorted. Second, only a few had been granted access to the profession, and once accepted, they had been passed over in the allocation of promotions, rewards, and power. Thus, Lerner believed, women historians had lived in a kind of worldly limbo, assigned to a "unique and segregate relationship," separate and yet part of "the making of history" and of "the interpretation of their own past."[1]

For Lerner and other feminist historians across the United States the 1970s became the decade for changing the scholarly and political realities she had identified. To begin, they went to their craft. Using their abilities to analyze, to write, and to speak, they discovered, valued, and chronicled women's forgotten lives. The collection edited by Berenice A. Carroll, *Liberating Women's History: Theoretical and Critical Essays* (1976), was typical of their first efforts. The topics ranged from historiography and methodology to studies of the economic and social roles of women from the seventeenth century to the present. The authors came from every part of the country. Hilda Smith, for example, was a graduate student at the University of Chicago, Kathleen Casey was at Berkeley, Mari Jo Buhle taught at Brown, Asunción Lavrin at Howard, and Nancy Schrom Dye at the University of Kentucky.[2]

With their articles, collections of essays, surveys, and monographs these feminist historians revitalized and transformed women's history. They quite literally, as Joan Kelly explained, "open[ed] up the other half of history."[3] In addition, they envisioned a broader impact. They challenged all historians to formulate new analytical syntheses, to give reality to interpretive frameworks only imagined by earlier women scholars. Together they would create a new history that would speak "in male and female voices," that would be inclusive, not exclusive, universal, not particular.[4]

3.

DISCOVERING CONTINGENCIES

PRECONDITIONS

To reject, to oppose, and to turn away from accepted perceptions of what constituted history required courage. To break the old canons of historical investigation and to discern and legitimate new analytical patterns in human experience required imagination and perseverance. Why was it those women, at that time, who transformed the "historical givens" of their professional education into what historians call "historical contingencies," and who formulated new ways of thinking about everyone's history?[5] There were leaders, individual feminist scholars, like Gerda Lerner, Berenice A. Carroll, Joan Kelly, and Natalie Zemon Davis who first articulated the doubts, criticisms, and new perspectives. But, as with other great changes, these individuals acted in concert and out of a series of preconditions that not only enabled them to see and to speak in new ways, but also made it possible for others to hear and to understand.

By the end of the 1960s historians in Europe and the United States committed to the approaches of the Annalistes, of social historians like the Marxists and demographers, and the revisionists of the "New Left" in the United States, had created uncertainty about the exclusive validity of traditional histories and their hegemony as the only visions of former times. Feminist historians have acknowledged the role of these innovative scholars in the evolution of women's history. Social historians like Joan W. Scott have written of their methodological contributions, of the way they used quantification, everyday details of people's lives, and the insights of other disciplines. Scott has praised their conceptualization of topics not usually considered historical such as "family relationships, fertility, and sexuality." Most significant of all, these historians, by choosing to write about those habitually excluded and by focusing on "social processes" rather than political narrative, challenged the very definition of history.[2] Their techniques sometimes led feminist historians to the discovery of their own alternative version of the past. Susan M. Stuard remembered: The "Annales School of history opened up new approaches to women, and they were breathtaking."[3]

Like other women in the late 1960s and 1970s, historians had to discover the relevance of the broader feminist movement to their own experiences. Three books from very different perspectives seem to have been significant in this process. The anthropologist Margaret Mead's cross-cultural examination of gender, *Male and Female: A Study of the Sexes in the Changing World* (1949), suggested that Western culture's traditional definition of family, divisions of labor, and gendered assignment of roles and functions in society were not fixed universals. She explained that other cultures made different choices.[4]

The publication in English of Simone de Beauvoir's *The Second Sex* in 1953 (French edition, 1947) caused women academics to begin questioning basic premises about what it meant to be female. In earlier eras women writing about their gender had often responded defensively to traditionally negative descriptions of "the feminine." De Beauvoir refused to argue in these terms. She moved to a new way of defining the questions. She first separated the biological fact of being female from all other aspects of a woman's existence. She then asserted that Western culture had designated certain qualities as "feminine" with all of the negative and positive connotations. Neither these qualities nor the subordination of the "feminine" to the "masculine" were innate. Having stated these premises about women's and men's lives and relationships, she focused on the process rather than the result. How did the infant become "feminine"? How is the subjugation of those who are "feminine" different from other kinds of oppression? De Beauvoir then proceeded to answer her own questions. She described the complex reality of women's lives: economically dependent like the legally enslaved, subordinate by law and custom, perpetually the "other"; yet, privileged when of the dominant race or class, seemingly pleased with the lack of liberty, seemingly complicit in their own subjugation.[5]

Betty Friedan's *The Feminine Mystique* (1963) challenged essential United States beliefs about the "the American Dream" of the 1950s. However satisfying it might be to middle-class white men, she found the reality of suburban security stifling with its kitchens full of household appliances, its supermarkets, station wagons, and the primacy of children's and husband's needs. Out of her frustration and desire for alternatives, Friedan helped found the National Organization for Women (NOW) in 1966. The avowedly feminist group had a clear political, economic, social, and cultural agenda, the realization of a different "American Dream," one based on the equality of women and men, both in the family and in the wider world of the wage earner.

Women historians have analyzed how their personal responses to such books and to contemporary activists turned into a new perception of history. The English feminist Sheila Rowbotham called it "historical self-consciousness," the moment of relating one's situation in the present to the old descriptions of other centuries. First came recognition that women were "another group whose rights have been restricted systematically by the powerful . . ."; then identification with this experience, what Sheila Ryan Johansson described as "a shared awareness of the past." This identification with other women brought the realization that an individual's problems were not unique but rather part of the "general pattern of women's existence."[6]

Once aware, feminist historians puzzled over their previous failure to see. "The ways in which academic inquiry [had] subtly subsidized" an oppressive social system now stood in stark relief. They marvelled that "until very recently not a single professor protested that historical 'truth' should be so unlike reality, not a single paying customer demanded her money back on the basis that she had paid for a history course and had been sold a male fantasy instead." Dolores Barracano Schmidt and Earl Robert Schmidt called it "academic sleight of hand," this "ability to depict a world without women, a world whose existence is clearly denied by the writers' and readers' own experiences."[7]

Discovery that the hand had been quicker than the eye brought disbelief and outrage. Linda Gordon remembered working as a young scholar in Boston. In doing her research she found Alice Clark's *Working Life of Women in the Seventeenth Century* (1919) and Rolla M. Tryon's *Household Manufacturers in the United States 1640–1860* (1917). "I thought, my God, this is incredible; these two women's history books have been available for half a century and ought to have been absolute staples for any historian." This led to "discovering how possible and shameful the suppression of knowledge is."[8] In the course of the 1960s and 1970s, like Gordon, many women historians discovered their predecessors. The writings of these older scholars—hundreds of volumes of every variety—brought excitement, raised questions, gave confidence, and in- spired action on behalf of this newly refashioned feminism.

This combination of feminist consciousness and scholarly goals was not new in the 1970s. It had motivated some writers of women's history in the nineteenth and early twentieth centuries. Elizabeth Ellet's two volumes on *The Women of the American Revolution* appeared in 1848 and formed part of the general mid-nineteenth-century effort to reclaim women's past, and to assert their rights.[9] The activists Elizabeth Cady Stanton, Susan B. Anthony, and Matilda Joslyn Gage produced six volumes of *The History of Woman Suffrage*, the first appearing in 1881, the last in 1922. Interest in church history, in medicine, in a variety of traditional and unorthodox areas of female endeavor brought more research on women's experiences as distinct from men's.

By the late 1930s a young historian could find classic studies like Lina Eckenstein's *Women Under Monasticism* (1896), Eileen Power's *Medieval English Nunneries* (1922), Kate Campbell Hurd Mead's *History of Women in Medicine* (1938), Elisabeth Anthony Dexter's *Colonial Women of Affairs* (1924), Julia Cherry Spruill's *Woman's Life and Work in the Southern Colonies* (1938), Alice Clark and Rolla Tryon's two histories of wage earning and home workers, and Ivy Pinchbeck's *Women Workers and the Industrial Revolution: 1750–1850* (1930).

By the early 1960s when historians like Linda Gordon received their training, there were the results of more recent scholarship as well: document collections on women's civil rights in the United States, a bibliography of women in colonial and revolutionary times, and general surveys such as Doris Mary Stenton's *The English Woman in History* (1957). Eleanor Flexner had written what would for many years be the accepted study of nineteenth-century feminist political activity, *Century of Struggle: The Woman's Rights Movement in the United States* (1959).[10]

Of all the predecessors of the women in the United States who wrote the history of their own sex, Mary Ritter Beard (1876–1958) had more influence than any other.[11] Like the feminist historians of the last twenty years, she was both writer and activist. From the 1930s on she was the most well-known authority and advocate for women's history in the United States. She later explained that her militancy on behalf of women came from the time she spent in England with her husband just after they were married. One night in May of 1900 the streets of Manchester filled with people celebrating the British Boer War victory of Mafeking. Beard had a chance encounter with a drunken, teenage, factory worker. This harsh glimpse of a young girl's life was Beard's moment of "historical self-consciousness." From this point on, she wrote, "I knew I must do something for women."[12] For Beard, doing "something for women" took two major forms: participating in women's labor and civil rights advocacy groups like the National Women's Trade Union League and the Congressional Union, and lobbying and writing to preserve the historical record of women's lives and to give value and authority to all that they had accomplished.

Beard first researched women's history with her husband when they collaborated on a multivolume history of the United States, *The Rise of American*

Civilization (published between 1927 and 1939). Charles A. Beard had already identified himself with the "new history" and the attempts of historians like James Harvey Robinson to give a broader economic and social dimension to the usual political narrative. Their textbook reflected this changed emphasis. Beard, herself, took pride in other aspects of the volumes as well, in the space given to cultural history, and in the detailing of women's contributions from the seventeenth to the twentieth centuries.[13]

Though easily criticized now for its white, middle-class focus, and for its failure to integrate everyday women's lives into the overall narrative, until the late 1970s theirs was the only major United States text to acknowledge women's roles and significance. Beginning with the colonial period, the Beards explained that "the participation of women in every sphere of life and labor" was "absolutely imperative to the development of European civilization in America." Women crossed the country "with children at their breasts."[14] They were reformers, educators, religious leaders, and writers, including Clara Barton, Helen Hunt Jackson, Harriet Beecher Stowe, Jane Addams, Charlotte Perkins Gilman, Mary Lyon, Emma Willard, Mercy Warren, Mary Baker Eddy, Edith Wharton, Sarah Orne Jewett, and many more. The Beard bibliography listed the extant literature on United States women's history.

While working on these texts, Mary Beard embarked on a variety of other projects designed to bring women's past lives and influence to the attention of contemporaries. In 1934 her document collection, *America Through Women's Eyes*, was published. In the same year she proposed in her pamphlet, "A Changing Political Economy As It Affects Women," a syllabus for what was essentially the first women's studies course.[15]

Beard understood that women's and men's experiences differed and that therefore the historical records and evidence of those experiences would differ as well. She came to feel a sense of urgency about the loss of documents and artifacts, for example, the diaries, letters, and photographs that made up women's history as distinct from men's. For five years, 1935–40, from an office at Rockefeller Center she worked to establish the World Center for Women's Archives. This collection, she believed, would finally prove women's significance and bring "half the human race" out of "the shadow of time."[16] There was some interest in the project at Radcliffe and Smith but it would be another generation before the two women's colleges acted on her initiative and established the Arthur and Elizabeth Schlesinger Library and the Sophia Smith Collection.

Beard's idea for an encyclopedia of women also met with no significant response. Instead, in the early 1940s the Encyclopedia Britannica asked her to write an article on women for their new edition. She chose to interpret the request more broadly. In 1942 she returned to them a complete report on the treatment of women throughout the encyclopedia. It was Beard who first used the word "invisible" to describe what had happened to women. She explained that most of their authors had simply left women out. When included, in a description of religious life, for example, the women's activities appeared insignificant. Tradeswomen's lives were subsumed under the description of men's experiences. The omission of entries about women once influential, but subsequently excluded or assigned secondary roles, as had happened to women medical practitioners, particularly annoyed her.[17] The Britannica accepted her report without comment.

Frustrated in her efforts to have others change the historical record, she took up the task herself and embarked on her best-known work, *Woman as Force in History: A Study in Traditions and Realities*, published in 1946 when she was seventy. Beard intended to write a survey of women in Western society, but much of the book reads as a narrower investigation of seventeenth-century English common law. In particular, she wanted to prove that law did not always reflect practice, and that women, despite their legal disadvantages, had made important contributions throughout history.

Beard had a second purpose in writing this book. She wanted to challenge the prevailing ideology of the women's movement of the 1930s and early 1940s. Feminists of the interwar decades, she believed, had portrayed women as victimized. Their remedy Beard characterized as advocacy for a "competitive equality" with men. She disagreed with the negative image and the solution. Beard refused to accept the idea that women could be both subjugated by men and significant at one and the same time. The concept of women as an oppressed group she described as "dogma," "one of the most fantastic myths ever created by the human mind," an idea that exercised "an almost tyrannical power" over all individuals.[18]

Her book was meant to dispel the "dogma" in two ways—by showing that women have never been completely subjugated in Anglo-American law and by demonstrating that they have made important contributions throughout Western history. She insisted in her introduction: ". . . the personalities, interests, ideas, and activities of women must receive an attention commensurate with their energy and history. Women have done far more than exist and bear and rear children. They have played a great role in directing human events as thought and action. Women have been a force in making all the history that has been made."[19]

Along the way Beard also discussed the origins of what she viewed as the unfortunate striving for equality. She wrote on early feminists like Mary Wollstonecraft in England in the 1790s, on the United States leaders of the 1848 Seneca Falls Convention, especially Elizabeth Cady Stanton and Lucretia Mott, and on their image of women as subordinated by the law. Beard saw a demand for equality, even the Equal Rights Amendment of the 1920s, as a devaluing of what she identified as praiseworthy in the female nature and of all that women had done in the past.[20] In the spirit of the radical feminists of the 1970s, she refused to take "man as the measure." Instead she glorified the "feminine" and in her most enthusiastic passages credited women with the creation of all that separated the human way of life from "that of the beasts." She described women's accomplishments as a "civilizing triumph" that "involved infinite experimentation with natural resources, infinite patience, . . . a sense of esthetics, extraordinary manual skill, and the highest quality of creative intelligence."[21] Her book, she hoped, would motivate women to "feminine patterns of action," to awareness of their "force, potentialities and obligations." Beard believed in the need for reform of society and of women's unique role in this endeavor. She wanted them once again to become the key actors in the struggles "*for* the realization of the noblest ideals in the heritage of humanity."[22]

The *New York Times* chose J. H. Hexter, a political historian of early modern Europe and a consistent critic of her husband's work, to review her book. Not surprisingly, Hexter dismissed what she had written in phrases that would continue to be used in discussions of women's history in the 1970s and 1980s. Hexter explained that this was not really history, for Beard had not written about those who truly make change. True "history" had always been, he explained, "a stag affair." More thoughtful critics have subsequently acknowledged that *Woman as Force in History* was repetitious in style, uneven in the coverage of different eras, and naive in its monolithic images of "feminine" and "masculine."[23] But as Gerda Lerner has asserted, it is still remarkable. Women historians and feminists are still working through the contradictions Beard identified and the challenges she made to traditional equal rights strategies and justifications.[24]

LEADERS

For Gerda Lerner, in fact, this was the book that brought her to the moment of "historical self-consciousness" so important in other feminists' lives. Though educated in Europe, Lerner in her late thirties decided to return to university and complete a United States bachelor's degree. There she discovered Beard's *Woman as Force in History*. She remembered: "Somehow, I was able to disregard the poor presentation, her fervent, and sometimes ill-tempered rhetoric and to connect with her central idea: that women have always been active and at the center of history." Like Beard, she responded to the apparent contradiction, what she described as the "duality of women's position in society—women are subordinate, yet central; victimized, yet active." In addition, Lerner appreciated the interdisciplinary approach and the wide variety of sources—legal documents, diaries, letters, sermon books, and literature—characteristic of Beard's history. She would follow these precepts in her own work. She called Beard "my principal mentor as a historian."[25]

Beard's appeal to Lerner seems all the more understandable as much in their lives was similar. Both married, had children, and accepted responsibility within their families and outside as writers and social activists. Already published as a novelist and short-story writer, in the 1960s Lerner turned to work with the civil rights movement and wrote the screenplay for *Black Like Me*, a radical movie in its era, that dramatized a fictional account of a white reporter living briefly as a black man in the south. Once she began writing women's history with her biography of the abolitionists Sarah and Angelina Grimké, Lerner also found herself isolated, as an older woman scholar researching an unorthodox topic. Like Beard, Lerner wanted to give historical perspective to the feminist initiatives of her day. Taken by themselves, she believed that Betty Friedan's *The Feminine Mystique* and the *President's Report on the Status of Women* (both published in 1963) left readers with images of powerless victims. As Mary Beard had rejected such portrayals, so did Lerner.[26] She too wanted to use history to show women as active participants and their roles as significant despite their unequal circumstances and subordinate status. Rather than chronicling women's disadvantages, Lerner posed alternative questions. How had the system of inequality begun? Where had ideal images of women such as those identified by Friedan come from? What had women been doing throughout history? Why had women's activities and accomplishments been denigrated or forgotten?

Such simple questions led first Lerner and then hundreds of women historians to research and describe women's past, to study the origins of their subordination, and to hypothesize about how it could have continued into the present. Without even making a clear declaration it became understood and then articulated by more theoretical historians like Joan Kelly that all of this study of the past had a profound connection to the present and the future. This unequal relationship between the sexes, feminist historians insisted, was clearly wrong. They reasoned that by analyzing the mechanisms of oppression in the past they could understand it in the present and have some sense of a new future in which neither sex was subordinated, in which each was valued and powerful.[27]

Between 1969 and 1981, Gerda Lerner wrote articles and a survey of United States women's history and edited two collections of documents that gave the first overall picture of white and black women's lives in the United States. These, with the pamphlet she wrote for the American Historical Association, *Teaching Women's History* (1981), gave cogent reasons for "a shift from male-oriented to female-oriented consciousness," to distinguish women's history from traditional history in general, and from social and minority history in particular. She also offered an explanation for women's exclusion from previous descriptions of the past, analyzed the state of women's history as it was evolving, and hypothesized about the new approaches that might make possible a universal history of both women and men.[28]

Because of their breadth of concerns and the clarity of their arguments, Lerner's first articles have a special significance in United States historiography. They were in the best senses of the word, provocative. In "The Lady and the Mill Girl: Changes in the Status of Women in the Age of Jackson" published in *American Studies* in the spring of 1969, Lerner explained why men's history did not describe women's experiences. Using the Jacksonian era as her example, she acknowledged that this had been an empowering time for men, but proved that it had the reverse effect for women, leaving them with fewer rights in comparison to men than they had exercised in earlier periods. This contradiction between democratic ideology and hierarchical reality, she believed, had caused a few educated and privileged women to formulate the 1848 Seneca Falls Declaration and to initiate a women's rights movement. "New Approaches to the Study of Women in American History," also published in 1969, emphasized the uniqueness of women's past in another way. Lerner insisted that not only was women's experience unlike men's but also unlike the newly "discovered" history of other groups, for example, the history of minority women and men.[29]

As Lerner continued to research and write, her tone became more strident, her statements bolder and more far-reaching in their challenges to the old definitions of history. In her articles of the 1970s she argued for the significance of women's history and the need to rethink the basic premises of the discipline. "Women are not a marginal 'minority,' and women's history is not a collection of 'missing facts and views' to be incorporated into traditional categories." As she explained in "Placing Women in History" (1975), "The next step is to face, once and for all and with all its complete consequences, that women are the majority of humankind and essential to the making of history."[30]

It was clear to Lerner, as it had been to her mentor, Mary Beard, that previous histories had "presented . . . a world in which men act and women are largely invisible." Earlier efforts to include women had proved inadequate. Past historians had merely "applied questions from traditional history to women and tried to fit women's past into the empty spaces of historical scholarship." In such works men "created, defended and advanced" civilization "while women had babies and serviced families and . . . occasionally and in a marginal way, 'contributed'."[31]

Lerner found women's exclusion more remarkable because even when men of formerly forgotten or denigrated groups acquired their chroniclers women continued to be ignored. As she would explain in her 1986 study of women's oppression, *The Origins of Patriarchy*, "The point is that men and women have suffered exclusion and discrimination because of their class. No man has been excluded from the historical record because of his sex, yet all women are."[32] Lerner blamed this unintentional, but no less effective, series of choices on "the androcentric bias of all academic studies and of the general culture." Western culture had traditionally assumed "that man is the measure of all that is significant and that the activities pursued by women are subordinate in importance." Thus women's lives and contributions had been omitted because what they had done was devalued, made inconsequential in a world described by those seeking to narrate only the actions of the politically and economically powerful male elite. This devaluation, she believed, even more than women's absence from past hierarchies, had caused their loss of history.[33]

Lerner also analyzed women's own contributions to and complicity with this denigrating process. Women had, she believed, internalized the oppressive ideology that decreed value and valuelessness, and learned "to distrust their own experience for the basis of verification and interpretation." Women became, in fact, participants in the perpetuation of their own subordination and the subordination of their daughters. "Women," she affirmed, "have always made history as much as men have . . . only they did not know what they had made and had no tools to interpret their own experience." It was this phenomenon that explained why "the subordination of women is of longer duration and more profoundly damaging in effect than that experienced by any other subordinate group."[34]

Realization of this internalization, of this contradiction between women's past reality and the recorded memory, she later described as "the dialectic of women's history." Those moments when women suddenly saw both their significance and their exclusion—the "clicks" as feminists called them—created a "dialectical force moving them into action to change their condition and to enter a new relationship to male-dominated society." This was the process that had motivated her as it had Mary Beard to value women's past. It also brought Lerner to a new perspective on her entire discipline. "All history as we know it," she asserted, "is, for women, merely prehistory."[35]

For Lerner believed that even the few histories of women that had been written up to the 1970s had been lacking. "Compensatory history" told of exceptional women, the president's wives, the queens, and mothers of kings, who exercised male power. "Contribution history" gave the stories of "lady" reformers who had in one way or another affected men's history. In both kinds of narrative the conceptual framework and the criteria of selection and inclusion reflected the male, not the female, world. As she explained in "Placing Women in History," "The true history of women is the history of their ongoing functioning in that male-defined world *on their own terms*."[36]

So the historian of women's first task was "to reconstruct the missing half—the female experience," to discover what that world "*on their own terms*" had been like. This reconstruction Lerner insisted would be different from men's history in another way. It would not be a monolithic past subsuming all women under the rubric of elite history; differences in race and class would be central to the new narrative.[37] This history from a female not a male perspective she called "transitional history." It required historians to formulate new analytical categories, new ways to determine that which was and was not significant. Words and concepts such as "roles and functions," "marriage," "reproduction," "sexuality," "images and realities," assumed new importance when women's lives were made the primary focus of the historian's research and analysis.[38] Lerner explained, "The central question raised by women's history is: what would history be like if it were seen through the eyes of women and ordered by values they define?" Using Simone de Beauvoir's terminology she asked, "What would the past be like if men were regarded as woman's 'other?'"[39]

It is this fundamental alteration of perspective that best exemplifies feminism's early impact on history and best explains why the reconstruction of women's past was potentially revolutionary. For it was by definition "a radical critique of traditional history" and a call for the "formulation" of a new "synthesis," "a history based on the recognition that women have always been essential to the making of history and that *men and women* [sic] are the measure of significance."[40]

Just as Lerner had combined writing and activism when she worked in the civil rights movement, so she combined them once she had committed herself to the advancement of women and the creation of a new women's history. As a member of the faculty at Sarah Lawrence in the spring of 1971 she suggested to the Committee on Restructuring the College that they authorize both a master's program in women's history and an undergraduate interdisciplinary major in women's studies. In September she sent letters to her women colleagues asking them to consider how they might develop "feminist courses" for these programs.[41]

Joan Kelly (1928–82), a Renaissance historian known for her work on the humanist Leon Battista Alberti, remembered how feminism had already affected her: "The women's movement was forcing new insights upon us, raising queries about what we thought we knew so well, and disturbing us with a sense of ignorance and inadequacy about our past."[42] However, she wrote a lukewarm response to Lerner's request. She mentioned a commitment to her course in Italian Renaissance culture and acknowledged that "it is possible for me to include some reading matter on the position of women in the Renaissance. . . . This probably could be done for only one session out of the 30 [sic] or so scheduled for the year, however, because of the paucity of material available in English.''[43] When Lerner persisted Kelly agreed to go out to lunch. She remembered that Lerner "talked for well over four hours on the almost infinite possibilities that lay ahead of me in women's history." In the end, Kelly "promised that for the coming weekend, I would think of my field and what I knew in relation to women."

As she later described it, the time that weekend "turned out to be the most exciting intellectual adventure" of her life, calling into question all that she had studied and learned. Kelly explained how it altered her view of her own specialty. "I knew now that the entire picture I had held of the Renaissance was partial, distorted, limited, and deeply flawed by those limitations.''[44] Like other feminists she later acknowledged the universal quality of her experience and thus her ties with her predecessors. She thought of Christine de Pizan, the early Renaissance writer and courtier, who had also once questioned European culture's denigrating image of women. "To this day every feminist who has followed Christine de Pisan [sic] has had to pass through the particular crisis of consciousness she described with as much self-awareness as Petrarch." She now understood de Pizan's self-appointed task "to oppose what seemed, and still seems to be, the overwhelming authority of the learned about women's inferiority.''[45]

Kelly began her opposition by reassessing the traditional images of early modern European women, in particular the four or five pages on the "Renaissance Lady" in Jacob Burckhardt's classic *The Civilization of the Renaissance in Italy*. In the same way that Lerner had investigated the differences between women's and men's experiences in the Jacksonian era of United States history, Kelly asked of this period, "Did women have a Renaissance?" She answered with a clear "no." At a time when men gained increasing liberty, the reverse happened for women. For example, as Kelly later explained in the essay that resulted from her questioning, a phenomenon like courtly love that had been thought to give women increased stature and importance had done the opposite, reinforcing "existing institutions and power relationships." Given her discoveries about Renaissance women, she concluded that historians would have to find other ways of measuring "loss or gain with respect to the liberty of women," new "criteria . . . for determining the quality of their historical experience." She ended the essay by suggesting three categories for research and analysis: women's economic, political, and cultural roles; the regulation of their sexuality; and each era's ideology about women.[46]

From the investigation of her own specialty, she turned with excitement to other periods. "Suddenly, the entire world of learning was open to me."[47] She worked to relate the new insights from Renaissance women's history to the broader spectrum of history as it had been traditionally presented. Nothing, she realized, could be taken for granted. She used an example from her own period to illustrate this discovery. Commentators on sixteenth- and seventeenth-century writings about women had usually dismissed the obvious misogyny as "a literary pose," nothing more than "acquiescence to a popular vogue." Kelly countered this view by asking "what men would think if women turned out a corpus of literature expressing disgust for men and marriage for a couple of centuries, then modified it to a generalized expression of contempt for men for four centuries more. Would that be a 'merely literary' matter?" She doubted it.[48]

Reconsidering women's past, she argued, forced historians to ask new questions not only about women's experience but about men's experience and about human history in general. If what had been accepted as discreet historical periods and as inclusive categories of analysis worked for men but not for women, what, she asked in her essay "The Social Relations of the Sexes," did this say about the validity of all previous histories. With her new skepticism she wondered about past explanations of causation, of former analyses of why things happened as they did.[49] In fact, she concluded, standard histories with their false suggestion of universality had failed in fundamental ways to describe the human experience. Efforts to meet this criticism with additions as had been done with the history of minorities would not solve the problem. She agreed with Lerner who wrote: "Women are a minority in no sense. Women are a sex."[50]

Although Kelly did not argue with Lerner's ideal of a new universal history, she hypothesized a different consequence of this unique feminist perspective. In "The Social Relations of the Sexes" she acknowledged Lerner's point that not just women but all of history's participants would benefit from this reinterpretation. But the result for Kelly had to be more than a new historical synthesis. She believed that the ways in which women and men interacted in the family and in society, "the social relationships of the sexes," as she called them, were as significant as race and class. She wanted historians to discover each era's definition of "feminine" and "masculine," the rationale for separation of roles, the designation of opportunities, access to and use of wealth and all other kinds of power. Kelly quoted Natalie Zemon Davis, who in the 1970s became the most well-known theorist of this approach. Davis explained, "Our goal is to understand the significance of the *sexes*, of gender groups in the historical past." In this way, Kelly reasoned, gender, or "the social relationships of the sexes," would become "a fundamental category of historical thought."[51] By the late 1980s and 1990s it would be this approach, this effort to understand the effects of gender on society, on topics as familiar as medieval mysticism, the *ancien régime* in France, or the politics of the Progressive Era in the United States, that would force consideration of what feminist historians had been demanding from the beginning, the radical transformation of all historical interpretations, even the most traditional political narratives.

Unlike Christine de Pizan and the other early feminist theorists she wrote about, Kelly did not come to her conclusions alone in her study. At the City University of New York, at Sarah Lawrence where she and Lerner co-directed the master's program from 1972 to 1974, at formal and informal gatherings she talked, exchanged questions, and refined answers. The first interdisciplinary course at Sarah Lawrence, "Women: Myth and Reality," she described as "one of the most significant learning experiences I have had." She saw "utterly new 'truths,' new relations among social phenomena, new significance in our past." She "felt intellectually renewed" and found these kinds of cooperation "energizing, strengthening my sense of myself as a woman and a scholar, and strengthening my scholarly purpose as I moved into Woman's Studies and Woman's History."[52] As a colleague Kelly was known for her openness and her generosity. She willingly shared her ideas and was encouraging about those of others. She was a painstaking writer; colleagues read multiple drafts of her two theoretical essays and of her examination of early feminist authors before final submission and publication. Younger scholars appreciated her readiness to help them with their research and analysis, how she "paid so much attention" to them. Alice Kessler-Harris remembered that "she forced you to take your own ideas seriously at a time when no one took us seriously."[53]

These experiences were not unique. Across the United States in university and urban centers women academics sought each other out and worked to overcome differences across disciplines and specialties. Kelly believed the greatest benefit "for me personally" of the collaborative experience at Sarah Lawrence had been "the sense of a collective intellectual, pedagogical, and political (feminist) objective."[54] In the service of this joint endeavor, the women of these groups made the 1970s a remarkable decade of historical thinking and writing unprecedented for its variety and productivity. By the early 1980s, as a result of their efforts, bibliographies of the history of women filled pages instead of paragraphs, and Mary Beard had been proved correct. Discovering their history had changed women scholars' perception of themselves and motivated them to action.[55] Study of the past had created feminists committed to the reconstruction of their own and all people's "collective memory."

4.

FEMINIST PERSPECTIVES

THE FIRST FEMINIST DECADE

In the spring of 1973 the participants in the first Sarah Lawrence women's studies program wrote their course evaluations. The historian, Joan Kelly, applauded the collaboration with other scholars, the acquisition of skills and methods from other specialties, and the opportunities to explore new approaches to the study of history. "For the first time in a long time I found myself reading widely and excitedly in a variety of disciplines and re-reading certain literary and historical works from a new vantage-point." The benefits went far beyond the formulation of new scholarly perspectives. "I feel a sense of integration of my intellectual, professional, and personal life such as I have never known before."[1]

Many of Kelly's contemporaries remembered the 1970s and feminism's impact on all aspects of their experience in the same way. There was no conflict between activism and scholarship, rather both became part of the overall feminist strategies for change. At UCLA, feminists, both faculty and students, helped to organize a hospital workers union, lobbied for city-funded day care, and collaborated on the first university-sanctioned courses in women's history.[2] There was, in addition, the excitement, the comfort of a common enterprise, and the satisfaction as each new piece of research and analysis appeared. Anne Firor Scott, whose book on southern white women of the nineteenth century was one of the first to appear, marveled at the "sharing of resources," the "speed," and the

"immense energy and commitment," all uncommon for those engaged in scholarly endeavors.[3] Linda Gordon later spoke of the "strong sense of collective
process" she felt with her friends and colleagues in Boston. "When I look back
on it I'm shocked at how hard I worked. Partly I was young and didn't have a
child so I had lots of energy, but also I was carried away by the political necessity
of the historical research that I . . . [was] doing."[4]

Feminist historians soon discovered that given the sheer volume of information, "to uncover [women's] past history and to interpret it is a task as enormous
as has been that of writing all existing history."[5] Carol Ruth Berkin and Mary
Beth Norton imagined themselves like latter-day Columbuses whose explorations
would "eventually change [our] comprehension of the previously known world."
In retrospect the innocence and expectations seem justifiable. As Berkin and
Norton foresaw: "Once thought to have been unrecoverable because of a lack
of sources, the history of American (and European) women of all races and
ethnic backgrounds proves upon examination to have been there all along. Historians just had to know where, and how, to look."[6] By the early 1980s specialized
articles, monographs, biographies, topical and chronological studies, collected
lives, descriptions of archival sources, collections of documents, general surveys
and biographical dictionaries for women in the United States and Europe, the
beginnings of studies of women in other parts of the world, all had been completed
in one brief decade.

The research, writing, and publication came to follow a pattern. Throughout
the decade women's historians continued to do original projects that turned into
articles and monographs that appeared in increasing numbers each year. At the
same time they began to edit collections of their specialized studies and of
excerpted documents illustrative of women's past attitudes and experiences.
Three of these early compilations continue to be used in the 1990s: Miriam
Schnier's *Feminism: the Essential Writings* (1972), key documents in the history
of feminist ideology; Lois W. Banner and Mary Hartman's *Clio's Consciousness
Raised* (1974), a collection of papers on a wide range of topics from the first
Berkshire Conference on Women's History; and Berenice A. Carroll's *Liberating
Women's History: Theoretical and Critical Essays* (1976), historiography, theory, and monographic studies in women's experiences in many eras and regions,
from the colonial Americas to twentieth-century Algeria. The two article collections in particular read now like a Who's Who of women historians. By the late
1970s general surveys of United States and European women's history had been
joined by edited works on China, Africa, Latin America, and the Muslim world
compiled by scholars who would become the leaders in their fields, for example,
Margery Wolf, Nancy J. Hafkin, June Hahner, Lois Beck, and Nikki Keddi.[7]

With more facts recovered, the research and the publications became more varied. Women's historians turned from the broad chronological organization of material to topical and racial or ethnic divisions. Karen Petersen and J. J. Wilson's *Women Artists: Recognition and Reappraisal From the Early Middle Ages to the Twentieth Century* (1976) was one of the first books in women's history published for a general, as well as a textbook-reading audience. Like many other feminist historians, Linda Gordon, in addition to continuing research for her study of the birth-control movement in the United States, collaborated on a more general project. Gordon, Rosalyn Baxandall, and Susan Reverby edited the collection *America's Working Women: A Documentary History, 1600 to the Present* (1976). Louise Tilly and Joan W. Scott wrote a survey *Women, Work and Family* (1978) to cover the same kind of material for French and English women. By 1978 Sharon Harley's and Rosalyn Terborg-Penn's volume on *The Afro-American Woman: Struggles and Images* was already the second major collection on black women's experiences in the United States.[8]

Initially women's historians had most in common with those writing the new kinds of social history because of their "interdisciplinary perspectives," their altered focus from the public and political to more family oriented experience, and their concern for groups omitted from previous narratives. As social historians had done in the 1960s those in women's history turned to the research of sociologists and anthropologists like Tamara K. Hareven, Michelle Zimbalist Rosaldo, Gayle Rubin, and Sherry B. Ortner. Their works offered new questions and new approaches to understanding women's lives as opposed to men's.[9]

In this first decade of women's history, references to the social sciences also validated what otherwise would have been considered unorthodox methods and sources. In constructing women's experiences historians had to reevaluate traditional materials: legal and ecclesiastical records, treatises, diaries, letters, chronicles of institutions and organizations. They utilized the new quantitative compilations and family history techniques from the demographers' studies of small communities. They relied on new materials, for example, "domestic artifacts" such as everyday articles of clothing and household utensils. Even the designs for homes could shed light on the ways in which women lived and worked. A survey history like Sarah Pomeroy's *Goddesses, Whores, Wives, and Slaves: Women in Classical Antiquity* (1975) used information from archaeological sites and literary texts, as well as insights gleaned from demographic, anthropological, and psychological studies.[10]

These feminist historians of the 1970s with their articles and books had embarked on what Gerda Lerner called "transition history." They were constructing the "woman-centered" narrative that they believed would "reveal what women themselves were doing, saying, and thinking, the factors that affected their lives, and the motivations that lay behind their actions."[11] Feminist scholars noted the unique features of this reconstruction that made women's historical experiences inherently similar because they were so different from men's. Some described women's "culturally determined and psychologically internalized marginality"; others "the persisting power of women," their resourcefulness, their ability to create "meaning, purpose, beauty and dignity in their lives despite the limitations placed upon them by the larger society."[12] The commitment to explore this gendered commonality contrasted with an equally strong resolve to show the multiplicity of women's experiences, the differences occasioned by class, race, culture, and nationality, what Nancy Cott described as the "complex unity that is women's condition," for feminist historians saw themselves as revolutionary in yet another way. They wished to break not only with the male orientation of traditional histories but also with the underlying assumption that the lives of the elite represented everyone's past.[13]

With each additional narrative goal the requirements of their "transition history" became more complex and the consequences more far-reaching. Feminist scholars realized that countering the "androcentric" and elite biases went beyond simply "adding another factor to our interpretation and thus correcting an admittedly glaring oversight." They came to see that even their separate studies of women's past necessitated rethinking all of the basic premises of the discipline. As Carroll Smith-Rosenberg explained, women's history "forces us to reconsider our understanding of the most fundamental ordering of social relations, institutions, and power arrangements within the society we study."[14] This need to "re-vision" history was all the more critical because feminist historians soon found that the traditional organizing concepts and thematic patterns actually obscured rather than revealed women's lives. Developments touted as "progress" in elite men's history too often, as Joan Kelly had argued about the Renaissance, meant "regress" in the lives of wives, mothers, and daughters. In fact, with older histories "structured about turning points of limited significance for the female sex" and focused on "publicly recognized events," the communally oriented more private worlds of women's activities simply disappeared.[15]

If the analytical concepts of men's history distorted and masked women's experiences, how then should the changes in women's lives throughout time be highlighted? What would women's history be like? Gerda Lerner and Joan Kelly were among the first to formulate questions, criteria of selection, and analytical categories to tease out these new theoretical approaches. Kelly looked to factors she believed dictated "the quality of [women's] historical experiences such as regulations governing their sexuality" or their "access to property, political power" and education. Others suggested examining women's history from the perspective of the different roles they performed, or the variations in their status

within a society over time. Natalie Zemon Davis was particularly interested in
"the range in sex roles and in sexual symbolism . . . what meaning they had
and how they functioned to maintain the social order or to promote its change."[16]

Researching the answers to these questions and following these themes
brought new analytical sophistication to women's history. Work on nineteenth-
century feminism, for example, revealed divisions among the leaders over goals
and suggested that property law reform and the winning of suffrage had been of
less significance for women than they had been for men. Women's control of
their own fertility and the availability of cheap reliable contraception assumed
importance. Continuing research showed the interplay between women's dependent and subordinate status and their many responses to each era's constraints,
between the accepted societal images and the lived realities.[17] For example,
Kathryn Kish Sklar wrote a biography of Catharine Beecher, who found ways
to redefine and value "domesticity," the ideal held out to nineteenth-century
privileged women, and previously described as confining. Judith Walkowitz and
Ruth Rosen investigated prostitution as a part of poorer women's strategies for
survival.[18]

As the studies built one on another, they brought a fullness and richness to
historical writing about both women and men. As Linda Gordon explained, it
enabled all historians to understand "the whole culture much better."[19] There was
Elaine Pagels's work on early Christianity,"What Became of God the Mother?
Conflicting Images of God in Early Christianity" (1976); Olwen Hufton's analysis of women in European revolutions (1971); Angela Davis's "Reflections on
the Black Woman's Role in the Community of Slaves" (1972); Julie Roy Jeffrey's analysis of the frontier experience (1979), to name only a few of the
studies that offered new interpretations of familiar periods by providing the
female perspective, as well as the male.[20]

In that first decade feminism and women's history appeared to be essential
one to the other. To write about women's past meant a novel valuing of female
experience, a decision that it was worthy of scholarly study. The very fact of
this unorthodox research became interpreted as a political act. From the beginning
feminist historians had acknowledged that their desire to reassess and reconsider
had a political as well as a scholarly motive. Their historical inquiries came out
of the intersection of the new, radical approaches to history and "the appearance
of a renewed women's movement."[21] Undoubtedly, research into women's past
led many scholars to feminism, to identification with women in other times and
places, women who were subject to expectations and constraints familiar to them
in the present. For others, already part of the contemporary movement, their
feminism took them "back into the past" in a search for "the origins of sex-
role stereotyping and of crippling patriarchy," the two phenomena that they

decried in the present. Whatever the cause-and-effect relationship, as Smith-Rosenberg explained, "our first inspiration was political," for the "particular gender assumptions" imposed on women in previous centuries "had shaped our own lives."[22]

When criticized by writers of traditional histories for the avowedly political character of their work, feminist historians drew on precedents from within the profession: James Harvey Robinson in the Progressive Era, Charles A. Beard in the 1930s, and Staughton Lynd in the 1960s. Ellen DuBois asserted, "We believed—we still believe—that the connection to a political movement is the lifeblood of feminist scholarship, not its tragic flaw." Others called the books of political and economic history "masculinist," and ridiculed any claims to a neutral or objective perspective in historians' writings. A feminist perspective was, in fact, necessary and potentially liberating; it freed women to act. "As long as historical actors and historians were represented as 'he,' " explained Joan W. Scott, women would find it difficult "to put into effect the equality they believed was their due."[23]

This connection between studies of the past and what needed to be done to change the future colored many women historians' thinking. Renate Bridenthal and Claudia Koonz described themselves as "new women" and saw their collection of essays on European women's history as part of the broader search "for a new identity," of the effort "to create a new social matrix" that would allow "freer attitudes" toward all aspects of women's lives. Others imagined women's "new self-determination" strengthened, and with practical lessons in "what has succeeded, what has failed," they would better "understand how to change the world."[24]

THE NEW SYNTHESES

The immediate "world" that feminist historians wanted to change was their own discipline. Initially they had imagined that women scholars' "findings will soon force the rewriting of the standard accounts of our nation's past . . . . perhaps more dramatically than anyone can predict today." By the early 1980s with almost 10 years of the new research available they could claim separate, independent status for themselves and their work. Hilda Smith asserted with authority the distinction between "feminist" history and the histories of the past.[25] But the overall impact on their craft and its content was minimal. Their writings constituted a vigorous, ever expanding subfield of a more diverse but still largely conventional discipline. Writers of traditional and revisionist history, women as well as men, paid lip service to the need to include women's experiences but the

overwhelming majority continued their research as before. No feminist was
satisfied with this.

In 1973 when Berenice A. Carroll assembled the collection of essays for
Liberating Women's History she did so in part to address this separate and, in
fact, subordinate place assigned to women's history. She wanted the collection
of historiographic essays and case studies to describe where the research had
come to and where it might go, and to offer "theoretical questions or models"
that attested to the formalization and analytical sophistication of feminist historical writings. Other feminists believed that this enunciation of the theoretical
bases of women's history would bring acknowledgment of its legitimacy and
thus speed the incorporation of women's experiences and perspectives into the
historical narrative. They looked to a time when all historians would take questions about women's history as a matter of course, and know what to answer
when asked: "What do we learn from it that we did not know before? . . . How
does a better understanding of the history of women enhance our understanding
of other issues as well?"[26]

The more extensive and thus the more visible the history of women became,
the clearer the alternatives presented to the profession. This new women's history
could either challenge or confirm the traditional narrative: "challenge [this narra-
tive] because its typicality was no longer assured; confirm it because the different
stories were so different as to be inconsequential."[27] Clearly, by the end of the
1970s, the majority of the profession had chosen the second alternative. For,
as many feminists acknowledged, "mainstream history" had remained largely
immune to their influence, little more than de facto programs in men's studies.
A 1977 panel on "western civilization" courses at the American Historical
Association convention brought together leaders of the profession to reminisce
and offer wise counsel. Not one of them mentioned the inclusion of women. In
describing the situation women's historians used phrases like "little tangible
progress," a "male-centered curriculum," and saw their work criticized as
"unscholarly," their courses as a "fad," taught by "dykes" for other feminists.[28]

Writers of traditional histories who took a more positive view suggested that
women's past fell under the rubric of "social history." Social historians were
not unsympathetic to this view. They saw the ways in which the new research
enriched demographic studies of the family, histories of nineteenth-century religious observance, and twentieth-century social welfare policy, all topics of this
subfield of history.[29] But the process of transformation that feminist scholars
envisioned required more than just "putting women back, as if they somehow
slipped out." And to make matters worse, with social history not all of the
women fit back in. For example, there was no place for the political activists,

for the vast numbers of participants in economic processes, for the feminist theorists. In addition, the underlying premises of social history negated a true synthesis. However neatly social historians "integrated" women into their narrative, they would always be fitting female lives to structures created to define and represent men's experiences not women's.[30] The philosopher Elizabeth Minnich explained the problem. "You don't simply add the idea that the world is round to the idea that the world is flat. You go back and rethink the whole enterprise." In an effort to "rethink the whole enterprise," feminist historians have formulated three alternative approaches to the synthesis of the newly discovered women's history and the traditional male-oriented narratives: (1) through Marxist theories of history; (2) through the division of human experience into separate "private" and "public" spheres of female and male activity; and (3) through the study of "gender" and its effects on history.[31]

Training in social history, combined with the political radicalism and feminism of the late 1960s, led women historians, especially those working in labor history, to try to use Marx's theories of history as a framework for a new historical synthesis, a method for analyzing both women's and men's lives. Even before feminist initiatives, labor historians had paid some attention to working-class women's history. They had acknowledged women wage-earners, and women's exclusion from the labor movement. Now male colleagues encouraged the new research. They published feminist historians' articles in their journals, enlisted women for their editorial boards, and founded new periodicals together.[32] *Radical America* devoted its Summer 1971 issue to women's history. In 1981 a leading male labor historian explained that feminism had "been of central importance in getting me to think about what else is involved in class beyond the relations of production."[33]

As a theoretical model of oppression and exploitation, Marxism seemed a promising way to understand women's experiences. Frederick Engels believed he had found the origins of patriarchy and the subordination of women in the advent of private property. A variety of historians saw connections between women's denigrated status and the emergence of industrial capitalism in the nineteenth century. Mary Beard hypothesized that this accounted for the oppression of women as a group rather than a class. Contemporary feminist historians described how capitalism and industrialization had changed families from the relative strength of producers to the relative weakness of consumers. They credited Marxism with a number of theoretical concepts that have become commonplace in women's history, in particular, the "fundamental notion of differences between appearance and reality . . . a sense of dialectics and contradiction," and the belief that "all historical situations [are] driven by conflict."[34]

Feminist historians also found revisions of Marxist historical theories useful for their analyses. E. P. Thompson and Eric Hobsbawm had written about the process by which members of the English working class came to "awareness" of themselves as distinct and separate, of how working men joined unions and political parties and thus acted out of their own experiences, not just in reaction to economic forces and structures. Feminist scholars made use of this shift in emphasis. Women too were agents not victims. They also came to "awareness" of their distinct and separate experience. But whereas Thompson and Hobsbawm saw men's "awareness" leading to class consciousness, feminist historians discovered another sometimes conflicting response from working-class women, consciousness of their gender as well as their class.[35]

Contemporaneous with the work of the English feminists Juliet Mitchell (*Woman's Estate*, 1973) and Sheila Rowbotham (*Woman, Resistance, and Revolution: A History of Women and Revolution in the Modern World*, 1974), the influential interpretive articles and books by United States scholars used Marx's theories to explore women's experiences from many alternative perspectives: Renate Bridenthal, "The Dialectics of Production and Reproduction" (1976); Linda Gordon, "What Should Women's Historians Do: Politics, Theory, and Women's History" (1978); Nancy Hartsock, *Money, Sex and Power: Toward a Feminist Historical Materialism* (1983); the economist Heidi Hartman's "The Unhappy Marriage of Marxism and Feminism: Toward a More Progressive Union" (1979) reprinted in the collection edited by Lydia Sargent, *Women and Revolution* (1981); and the legal theorist, Catharine MacKinnon's "Feminism, Marxism, Method, and the State: An Agenda for Theory" (1982).[36]

Key to the Marxist analysis was the presumption that a person's ties to class and to a particular "mode of production"—industrial capitalism—had caused his or her oppression. From the earliest efforts at synthesis, this first premise of Marxism created problems when applied to women's history. In nineteenth-century industrial societies, men's class identification came through their employment, through their relationship to capital. The "mode of production" determined their role and place in society. This was not the case with women. Their sense of function and class came through their relationship to the men of their families rather than through their interactions with the industrial economy. For men, the family acted as a "potential unit of resistance," for women (white women in particular) it often was "the locus of [their] oppression." Also, women's and men's circumstances as waged workers in the nineteenth century were rarely the same. Patterns of job segregation limited women to certain kinds of tasks, usually the least skilled, lowest paid, and most vulnerable to fluctuations in the economy.[37]

The more research feminist scholars completed, the more differences they discerned between women's and men's lives, the more additions and adaptations they had to make to keep even lower-class women within a Marxist framework. One of the principal theoretical additions by Marxist feminists concerned the effects of women's gender and sexuality, aspects never considered in the analyses of men's lives. These scholars broadened the usual analysis to include not only "modes of production," but also what they came to call "modes of reproduction," a concept implicit in Marx's writings but never emphasized. Initially, as defined by Juliet Mitchell and used by Joan Kelly in her essay on the "Doubled Vision of Feminist Theory," "reproduction" meant the control of women's bodies. Subsequent Marxist feminists used it to signify not only women's biological reproductive function, but also their cultural and social role as nurturers and educators, literally the reproducers, of the next generation of "workers." Kelly believed that this female function perpetuated not only capitalism, but also patriarchy. She explained that "in the poor family [women's waged labor] sustains the working population . . ." and "at the same time, this unwaged and unacknowledged work of women in the home, keeps women dependent on men and bound to a subordinate, servicing role."[38] An orthodox Marxist would insist that neither these systems nor women's condition could change until the modes of production had altered, in short, until the end of the class system.[39]

Although some feminist historians continued to try to fit women's experiences into a Marxist framework, others concluded that Marxism alone could not explain women's experience and therefore did not offer the synthesis they were seeking. In the end, and most damaging to the universal applicability of Marxist theories, women's historians could not justify the reliance on "class," and the end of the "class system," as the sole determining factors in the female experience. They doubted if industrialization was as significant for the mass of women as it was for men. They suggested that the number of a woman's children probably had more effect on the quality of her life. Finally, Marxism made no provision for the unwaged labor that also filled women's days. In this way many feminist scholars concluded that the premises and definitions of relevance of the Marxist systems of analysis were male in orientation. As in social history, women remained "secondary actors," "auxiliaries to the main event," " 'factors' to be integrated into predesignated categories."[40]

The Marxist-feminist historians who formulated and differentiated between the concepts of "modes of production" and "modes of reproduction," suggested the basis for the second approach to a synthesis of women's and men's history. In their writings they used "modes of production" to refer to the workplace and "modes of reproduction" to describe the more private areas of human experience, primarily, the household. This perceived distinction between "private" and "public" became a way for feminist historians to analyze what they called the "public and private spheres" of bourgeois life in the United States and Europe.

As with those who studied working-class women, these scholars began with the first questions asked by all feminist historians: What were the origins of women's subordination and why and how had it continued into the twentieth century? Like Marxist-feminists their work in United States history led them to the nineteenth century. In one of the earliest new articles in women's history, "The Cult of True Womanhood, 1820–1860" (1966), Barbara Welter wrote on the prescriptive literature popular in the nineteenth century that glorified the domestic image of the dutiful wife and mother. Welter suggested that this widely disseminated ideology could constrain women even more effectively than restrictive legal, political, and economic practices and institutions. In the next decade a number of feminist historians explored the apparent effects of this ideology and its interaction with the realities of privileged women's lives. The idea of women's relegation to the "private" world of the household and men's access to the "public" arena of power found easy acceptance as an analytical distinction even in traditional histories for it had echoes in the avowed ideals of contemporary culture. In some senses Betty Friedan's *Feminine Mystique* had been a response to these ideals as played out in women's experiences of the 1950s.[41]

At first seen as a negative, with more study of nineteenth-century women's letters and diaries, this apparent separation of women from the "public sphere" came to be lauded as a positive aspect of their lives. Carroll Smith-Rosenberg described how her research into the correspondence between two close women friends, Mary Hallock Foote and Helena DeKay Gilder, "radically transformed my approach to women's history." Smith-Rosenberg suddenly understood that up until this point she had been using "traditional male historical sources," and that this meant that she saw "women, not as they had experienced themselves, but as men depicted them."[42] In the resulting article, "The Female World of Love and Ritual: Relations between Women in Nineteenth-Century America" (1975), she used women's own writings and described the comforts and strengths they derived from their intimate friendships. Other historians believed that in these separate spaces women gained autonomy; that the creation of women's "private sphere" was an essential nascent mechanism for the beginnings of the women's movement. Estelle Freedman argued that United States women gained their political rights as a direct result of what she called "female institution building."[43]

Women's historians have agreed on the value of this analysis as a way of understanding the distinct experiences of a specific group of privileged women. It has not, however, proved to be useful as a way of synthesizing women's and men's experiences. In fact, some have argued that its emphasis on women's autonomy, on descriptions of women's "private sphere" diminished rather than increased the opportunities to study the relationships between the two sexes.

Other feminist historians have also emphasized that the distinction could be misleading, that this division "did not describe the society in which it arose so much as reflect it ideologically." Linda K. Kerber explained, there was a "self-contained quality" to the analysis that obscured rather than revealed women's interactions within their culture.[44] In particular, the more historians learned about the lives of nineteenth-century women, the more they saw the "spheres" overlapping. Kelly described waged women's circumstances: "Women's place is to do women's work—at home and in the labor force. And it is to experience sexual hierarchy—in work relations and personal ones, in our public and our private lives." Others wrote of the ways in which privileged women took the prevailing rhetoric of "domesticity" and used it to justify an overtly political, and thus public, involvement.[45]

Although Carroll Smith-Rosenberg was clear in her article that she was writing about only a limited group of women, subsequent readers extrapolated from her sample and imagined that they could describe a universal female experience. These glorifications of a separate "women's culture" and evocations of what came to be interpreted as an "essential" female way of life drew criticisms from scholars because they appeared to gloss over the differences between women and the differences in women's experiences. Nancy Hewitt, for example, discovered conflicts among as well as distinctions between women. "A closer examination now reveals that no such universal sisterhood existed, and in fact that the development of a sense of community among various classes of women served as a barrier to an all-embracing bond of womanhood." She explained that in the nineteenth century the idea of "separate spheres" became yet another mechanism by which one socially dominant group controlled another. In this case privileged women imposed their definitions of the family and the household on lower-class women.[46]

Even this emphasis on women's interactions with others in their society, however, did not alter the central problem of the concept of "separate spheres" when used to synthesize women's and men's history. This set of premises still led most easily to marginalization and exclusion, to a distinct investigation of the female past, not to an inclusive exploration of the interaction between women's and men's lives. Where a Marxist approach focused on the male experience, this focused on the female. Neither created what Kerber called "the bridge" from one history to the other. Nor had they facilitated women's historians' underlying goal. Neither of these approaches had convinced other practitioners that they must take the findings of women's history into account when writing their own narratives.[47]

Feminist scholars in general, and social and cultural historians, in particular, have been more hopeful about the possibilities of the third approach to synthesis that emerged from the first years of women's history. Conceived initially by Joan Kelly and Natalie Zemon Davis, the concept of ''gender'' from as early as 1980 was being advanced even in the pamphlets of the American Historical Association as a category of historical analysis as essential as religion, race, ethnicity, and class. As Davis explained, ''Study of the sexes should help promote a rethinking of some of the central issues faced by historians—power, social structure, property, symbols, and periodization.'' The most optimistic feminist historians have seen it as the way ''to demolish entirely the 'ghettoization' of women's history'' and the way to break down the barriers that enshrined the exclusively male orientation of traditional historical topics.[48]

Arguing the significance of ''gender'' as an analytical category applicable to all of human experience has not been difficult. Most historians agree that ''gender'' is by definition inclusive, a ''factor of all other relations.'' It covers everyone's history and rescues them from the ''sex-blindness of traditional historiography.'' Nothing is ''gender neutral.'' An analysis of the effects of gender takes all historians away from the histories of ''man'' as the universal. Instead they must describe ''men as men'' and women as women. Thus scholars avoid the particularity of women's history as well.[49] In addition, all who have begun to think about history in this way see nothing fixed, or essential in the manifestations of gender; rather each age, each set of historical circumstances, has produced its own definitions of feminine and masculine. The analytical possibilities seem infinite as historians turn to the study of ''gender systems in all their variety.''[50]

Joan W. Scott in her 1986 essay, ''Gender: A Useful Category of Historical Analysis,'' gave the first systematic explanation of this new synthesis. She described gender as ''a constitutive element of social relationships based on perceived differences between the sexes,'' ''the knowledge that establishes meanings for bodily difference.'' It was not only about women and men, but also, she continued, society's ''primary way of signifying relationships of power.''[51] Scott and others who work with this concept draw on insights from anthropology, the theoretical works of French feminism, and literary criticism. From anthropology, historians came to appreciate even more than they had before, with their explanations of relativism and subjectivity, that the ''simplest cultural accounts are intentional creations,'' and that ''interpreters'' ''construct'' not only these accounts but also ''themselves through the others they study.'' The anthropologist Michelle Zimbalist Rosaldo applied these insights to women's past and present experiences. ''It now appears to me that women's place in human social life is not in any direct sense a product of the things she does, but of the meaning her activities acquire through concrete social interaction.''[52]

From the heightened awareness of French feminist writers of the late 1960s and 1970s came a sense of the pervasiveness of gender in the meanings assigned to actions, in society's use of symbols, even of language. If, as anthropologists insisted, no interpretation could be fixed or separated from the "interpreter," then historians should abandon efforts to separate images and realities in women's lives and instead focus on the interrelationships between them. Adapting the techniques of literary criticism known as "deconstruction" to the process of historical analysis, they searched for what cultural historians have called the "mechanics of representation": how actions acquired significance, how symbols were created and used, how "words" not only "reflected social and political reality" but also "were instruments for transforming reality." In this way the historian learned not only about how changing concepts of gender functioned in a society, but also the obverse, how a society itself functioned by deciphering its use of gender.[53] Three books, though written by scholars in other disciplines, have become models of how this use of the concept of gender could be applied to history: Edward W. Said's *Orientalism* (1978), Mary Poovey's *Uneven Developments: The Ideological Work of Gender in Mid-Victorian England* (1988), and Denise Riley's *"Am I That Name?" Feminism and the Category of 'Women' in History* (1988).

Although some scholars have seen hazards in the deconstructionist emphasis on language rather than the "habits and practices" governing women's lives, and the potential disregard "for time or context," placing "gender" at the center of analysis has gained broad acceptance, especially among feminist historians. Advocates insist that this method "critically [confronted] the politics of existing histories" and even inaugurated "the rewriting of history" so important to women's historians. They have embraced it as the way "to relate our subject matter to the concerns of scholars throughout the subdisciplines of history."[54] They have used it for a wide variety of inquiries: studies of eighteenth- and nineteenth-century rural industry in a French village, of the evolution of the English middle class, and of industrial job segregation during World War II. They have demonstrated how the techniques of "deconstruction" can be applied to interpretations of the French Revolution, a staple of traditional histories. By including analyses of government policies towards women, for example, and of public, allegorical representations of the female, connections and comparisons with men's history inevitably arise. The differences between feminine and masculine imagery, between women's and men's experiences, study of the "winners" and the "losers," as one social historian called the approach, highlighted the state's use of power in new ways, and gave a richer analysis of the course of the Revolution as a whole.[55]

Sound as these techniques seem, ideas of "gender" did not transform the writing of history. The majority of practitioners continued to focus on men's activities and to marginalize, or exclude, even the obvious intersections with women's lives. In the 1980s feminist scholars, both women and men, found that they remained the principal proponents of synthesis. To have an impact it would not be enough to revitalize and transform women's history, to hypothesize new frameworks for describing women's and men's experiences. No matter how committed and how prolific they might be as scholars, other factors posed obstacles that frustrated their efforts to affect the way history was defined and interpreted. From the late 1960s on scholars in many disciplines came to understand the political relationship between the hierarchies of the academy and the valuing of research choices, between professional institutions and organizations and scholarly authority. To make pervasive and lasting change, women historians committed to feminism knew that they must not only challenge past scholarship but also the environment and circumstances in which it was produced.

III

THE
IMPACT OF
FEMINISM

For the 1980 International Congress of Historical Sciences, the American Historical Association sponsored a description of "Recent United States Scholarship on the History of Women." The 55-page pamphlet written by historians in both United States and European history documented a decade of unprecedented scholarly productivity: basic texts, essay collections, monographs, and articles, all touching on women's historical experience across class, race, and culture. These hundreds of new books and articles were the first impact of feminism. Feminist historians had literally created the modern field of women's history. For this field to survive and prosper, however, women historians and the history they had written had to become part of the established academic world and its canon. Only such acceptance would gain feminists their larger goals, the transformation of their discipline and an end to the professional marginality and exclusion that they and their history had always suffered.

From the beginning feminists knew that "the academy speaks . . . at least two languages: one the language of scholarship, the other [the] language of power."[1] With their writings women had shown their mastery of the language of scholarship. To gain more places for themselves within the academy, to make their research central and not peripheral to historical thinking and teaching, feminists also had to learn the language of power and how to use it for their own political and intellectual purposes.

Gerda Lerner understood the political aspects of the academic historian's world. In 1966 she set out the ways in which she hoped to influence the discipline and the profession: "by actual research and writing; by proving the existence of sources; by upgrading the status of women in the profession; by proving that there existed student demand in this subject and moving from there to design courses and graduate programs."[2] Lerner was thinking of the next 20 years of her life when she outlined these goals for herself. Other feminist scholars throughout the United States—for example, in West Virginia, Iowa, California, Illinois, Arizona, North Carolina, and Colorado—formulated many of the same strategies. Validation for their work and authority for themselves, they reasoned, would come with changes in circumstances: (1) when a significant number of women acquired tenured professorships; (2) when traditional graduate and under-graduate curricula included women's history and the feminist perspective; (3) when journals and university presses published articles and monographs by women scholars; and (4) when professional organizations accepted feminist historians as valued participants and elected officers.

5.

ACADEMIC TRAINING, EMPLOYMENT, AND PROMOTION

BEFORE THE FEMINIST MOVEMENT

In the late 1960s not only was history the study of a universal figure, "man," but the profession itself embodied the same gender-skewed definition. The French historian Fernand Braudel wrote with excitement of the Annales research center, "We have at our disposal, in nearly every discipline, young men who by training and ambition are entirely dedicated to research."[1] John Higham's standard work on the historical profession, *History: Professional Scholarship in America* (1969), gave the reader a pervasive sense of history as a masculine prerogative. The historian himself was understood to be a master of the discipline, a gentleman scholar able to mediate between his institution and the broader world, between the past and the present. Higham's epilogue on the 1960s and 1970s written for the revised edition in 1983, mentioned the burgeoning field of women's history only by implication. This was the "time of troubles" when "outgroups" demanded their own history. He did not list one of the new works by women historians.[2] In fact, only three women appear by name in the text: Elizabeth Donnan, the editor of an early collection of documents about the slave trade; Alice Felt Tyler, a social historian in the 1940s; and Caroline Robbins, author of *The Eighteenth Century Commonwealth* (1959), included not in her own right but because of her significance to the work of a male scholar. The professional collaboration between Mary and Charles A. Beard became authorship by the husband who completed his textbooks "with his wife's assistance."[3]

The masculine gendering of the historian began with the professionalization of the discipline in the 1880s. As with other fields, like law and medicine, each step in the process made it more difficult for a woman to gain access, first to graduate degrees and formalized training, then to employment, and finally to promotion. Historians have described the evolution of the profession from the late nineteenth century to the period after World War II. History acquired educational prerequisites and its practitioners, established credentials. It divided into distinct specialties and moved away from the public and the general reader to the shelter of the research university and narrow dialogues with other highly trained experts. In the popular mind the university became enshrined as a male preserve, and the professor of the 1950s appointed the "gatekeeper at the citadel of the elites."[4]

As if decreed by nature and traditional images of appropriate female and male roles in society, women scholars had no obvious place within this elite. Yet some very able and determined women did make their way into what Adrienne Rich has called the "man-centered university." Margaret Judson (1899–1991) remembered her days as a graduate student at Radcliffe. In the 1920s Widener Library was closed to women after 6:00 PM. "The authorities claimed that women students might be raped in these narrow, long, often deserted dark corridors." The resident Renaissance and Reformation scholar refused to teach women and closed the door in Judson's face when she came to speak with him. She took her orals in President Comstock's office. The occasion began with tea "and as a woman, of course, I was asked to pour."[5] The situation had not changed significantly by the end of the 1930s. Judson, researching a new project, gained only provisional permission to use the Harvard Law Library. She had to go in and out by "the *back* door" so that the head librarian would not see her.[6]

In 1949 women like Margaret Judson represented 20% of professional historians.[7] All but a select few, however, remained in the least prestigious academic institutions, and at the lowest ranks of the profession. Their training, the quality of their scholarship, the numbers of their published articles, did not vary significantly from those of their male peers. Simply, some young historians had made it and others had not, and women formed a disproportionate number of those who had not. Elizabeth Kimball graduated from Mt. Holyoke in 1921. "More or less by accident," as she explained it, she was asked back to be a "reader" by the chair of the history department, the medievalist Nellie Neilson. At the suggestion of Neilson and with a master's degree in hand, she went to England from 1925 to 1927 and returned to the United States with an Oxford B. Litt. A year teaching at Wells, another at Mt. Holyoke, but no offers of permanent employment, finally convinced her to complete a doctorate at Yale though, she said, "everybody knew I was just doing it to get a job." Even with the appropriate credentials, however, and her reputation as the editor of the records of England's fourteenth-century justices of the peace, the elusive tenured position never became available. "Yes," Kimball recalled, "I was always replacing someone."[8]

Margaret Judson had a full career as a historian, teacher, and administrator at Douglass College (known originally as the New Jersey College for Women). Even so, she remembered with some regret that in the course of her professional life "no offer of another position in history came to me," and that "none of my contemporaries among women professors in the east . . . ever left the women's college where first she was employed." As late as 1959 when she accepted a visiting professorship at the University of Michigan, Judson's expertise surprised one of her male colleagues who found it novel (despite the number of exceptional women scholars in the field) "that a woman historian wrote upon constitutional and political ideas and had done research in legal sources." One member of the history department explained to her why they had failed to appoint a scholar to the endowed chair for a woman historian she was filling temporarily: "The presence of a woman in department meetings would inhibit men from smoking or putting their feet up on chairs."[9]

Some women spoke out against the discrimination they saw as characteristic of the whole profession. Emily Hickman, a colleague of Judson's at Douglass, called for studies of jobs, ranks, and salaries in the 1930s. In 1956 Beatrice Hyslop of Hunter College, one of the most respected United States historians of eighteenth- and nineteenth-century France, wrote an open letter to the *American Historical Review*, the journal of the American Historical Association. Responding to an article describing the historical profession, she contrasted young women's and men's experiences. "Women historians," she explained, "ask for equality of opportunity." She posed the question that feminists would come to ask with more vehemence in the 1970s: "Is there something about history as compared with political science, languages, or natural sciences, that excludes competence on the basis of sex?"[10] But Hickman had a reputation for advocacy and unorthodoxy. Judson remembered that "she was a very powerful woman." Hyslop had a similar reputation among women historians as outspoken, "a live wire."[11]

More usually, this generation of women scholars remained apolitical. They valued a dignified, "professional" image and found quiet, less intrusive, ways to overcome or bypass the "institutionalized obstacles that effectively screen[ed] out large numbers of able women from full or partial engagement in higher education."[12] Some chose to ignore discriminatory practices. Judson explained that in an era of depression and war, "those of us in the early days . . . were darned lucky to have a job."[13] Some never married and thus avoided many of the inevitable conflicts altogether. A 1930s study of women Ph.D.s in all academic fields explained that 75% had remained single because "standards of domestic perfection" become "obstacles to professional advancement."[14] Others explained away prejudicial actions as single instances rather than a general pattern of discrimination. Many of the most successful, like Judson, taught in women's colleges, environments in which they could both advance the cause of women and establish reputations as exacting, innovative scholars. Among them were Lucy Maynard Salmon (1853–1927) at Vassar, an early member of the American Historical Association; Louise Fargo Brown, the winner of the 1911 Herbert Baxter Adams prize in European history; and Nellie Neilson (1873–1947) at Mt. Holyoke, the first woman to be elected President of the AHA.[15]

Others followed a different strategy. They achieved their reputations in tangential fields: like Mary Barnes (1850–98) in history education at Stanford, or like Louise Phelps Kellogg (1862–1942) of the State Historical Society of Wisconsin in public history. Helen Sumner Woodbury (1876–1933), an acknowledged expert in United States labor history, went into government service when her mentor at the University of Wisconsin told her that he could not offer her a permanent position on the history faculty.[16]

As in many categories of women's employment, World War II neither changed attitudes, nor diminished the obstacles. The number of women historians actually declined in the 1950s and 1960s, to only 12% of the profession by 1965.[17] In 1970 Willie Lee Rose headed an American Historical Association committee charged to investigate the status of women in the profession. From a survey of 30 institutions including the leading research universities, the major women's colleges, and a selection of liberal arts coeducational colleges, the Rose Report revealed the extent of the discrimination against women. In the period from 1959 to 1969 only three had advanced to the rank of full professor in the university departments of history at the University of California at Berkeley, the University of Michigan, and Yale. Women's colleges had offered more opportunity, but numbers of women full professors had fallen in the period from 13 to 10 out of 32 with that rank by 1969–70. The attrition had been even worse at the coeducational colleges like Carleton, Middlebury, Oberlin, Reed, Swarthmore, and William and Mary. Although women had represented 16% of the full professors in 1959–60 (4 of 25), only one woman remained in 1968–69, and she retired in 1970.[18]

The impetus for the Rose Committee's study came from feminist scholars within the American Historical Association. Beginning in the mid 1960s a significant number of women historians began to recognize that neither the excellence of their scholarship nor their willingness to accommodate traditional prejudices had opened the institutional hierarchy or changed the basic attitudes about women in the profession. When in the 1960s Blanche Wiesen Cook received her doctorate with highest honors at Johns Hopkins University, the principal readers of her dissertation took her to the faculty club to celebrate. As they walked in, one put his arm around her shoulders in a fatherly way and asked, "Well, Blanche, when are you going to stop all this nonsense and have babies." Sandi E. Cooper remembered her male professor's answer when she asked him what she might do once she had her Ph.D. "You'll probably get a job at a place like Long Island University as an adjunct," he replied.[19] In 1970 Jane S. DeHart could not find any job. She came to North Carolina with a prize-winning dissertation published by Princeton University Press, four years of teaching experience at Douglass, and an offer of tenure at Rutgers. Nepotism rules kept her from one position, the fact that they "already had a woman" from another. She finally was hired as an adjunct to teach an American Studies course in an English program, but only for one year. The chairman explained that she was too qualified to be "in the pool of non-tenured women."[20]

Marilyn B. Young's situation and feelings mirrored those of other young married historians in the late 1960s. At the age of 30 she had chosen not to teach and write, but to be a faculty wife and to care full-time for their children. She wrote in her journal: "How ineffective. I shall live out the rest of my life as if it weren't really happening and then die surprised. . . . I have no proper work, and for me that is hard. And I grow lazier, mentally, by the hour." She joined a women's group. Together they found comfort in shared frustrations.[21] Just as it had for other women, identification with the feminist movement gave a renewed sense of direction and purpose. Other members of this 1960s generation of feminists came to awareness, to their moment of "historical self-consciousness," through their work in the civil rights and peace movements. Initially, these women had identified with their male companions. Gradually, however, they realized that the same elitism and hierarchy that characterized the academy and society at large existed within their reform groups. Here as elsewhere in their lives, the old stereotypes of "female" and "male" survived. The time-honored assumptions about appropriate functions for women prevailed. Men led and designated only secondary roles for their female counterparts. Activist women could not help but hear and see the contradictions between the rhetoric of equality and the reality of men's discriminatory actions.[22]

Whether as members of these political groups, as part of the "consciousness-raising" support networks that sprang up all over the United States, or just as individuals, women scholars began to act on their own behalf, first on university campuses, then in their own organizations, and finally in those traditionally controlled by men. The 1970 Rose Report to the American Historical Association was but one of the consequences of their newly discovered feminism.

The careers of Anne Firor Scott and Natalie Zemon Davis illustrated the first impact of this renewed feminism on the historical profession. Both Scott and Davis combined marriage, children, research, writing, and teaching. Both published articles praised for their depth and originality and rose to named professorships at distinguished research universities. In the 1980s Scott and Davis were elected to the presidencies of the two major professional organizations for historians, the Organization of American Historians and the American Historical Association, respectively. They were transitional figures, trained in one era and advanced in another. Feminism created the favorable circumstances that made their advancement and their success within the academy possible.

From her days as a doctoral candidate Anne Firor Scott researched and wrote about women's history, but more or less by accident. At Harvard she wanted to study the Progressive movement in the South. Women's names and activities kept coming up as leaders of voluntary organizations, missionary societies, and the WCTU (Women's Christian Temperance Union), as members of clubs, as lobbyists, and suffragists. In the end it became a women's topic rather than a men's. Her advisor at Harvard encouraged her. Julia Spruill, one of the few historians of women in the era after World War II, "was like a retired athlete urging a younger runner around the track," Scott later remembered. "The 'New Woman' in the New South," Scott's first essay, appeared in the autumn 1962 issue of *South Atlantic Quarterly*, long before most historians considered women's contributions to the Progressive Era significant. Her book, *The Southern Lady: From Pedestal to Politics, 1830–1930*, came out in 1970, one of the first in the wave of publications about women's history in that decade.[23]

Scott's approach to her career was characteristic of others who advanced in the historical profession in the era of women's liberation. She, like Gerda Lerner, combined scholarship, family responsibilities, and activism. Before graduate school and marriage she worked in politics (including an internship with a California congressman) and with the League of Women Voters. Duke University hired her at the beginning of the 1960s when she was in her early forties.

She continued to use her talents not only to complete her own work, but also to advance the interests of all women. In 1963 she headed the North Carolina Commission on the Status of Women and edited the final report. She stayed on at Duke, wrote more articles and two more books, and became a full professor. The Organization of American Historians (OAH) chose her to chair its Committee on the Status of Women in 1970. She taught her first course in United States women's social history in the summer of 1971. In 1984 she was elected president of the OAH, the same year that she headed her department at Duke.

Natalie Zemon Davis succeeded without the same public feminist advocacy as Scott. The holder of a named history chair at Princeton University and president of the American Historical Association in 1987, she answered "no" when asked by an interviewer in 1981 if she had been "particularly conscious of professional problems related to being a woman."[24] She had eloped in 1948 in her junior year at Smith, even though it was against college policy. She explained in this same interview for *Radical History Review* that at the time of her marriage, she simply knew that she "was just going to be a professor or, at least, a historian," but had consciously rejected what she called "the Bryn-Mawr model of the 1920s." It never occurred to her not to marry and have children. In retrospect she prided herself on taking her general doctoral examinations in the seventh month of her first pregnancy. While teaching at the University of Toronto she helped circulate a questionnaire to graduate students trying to combine scholarship and family. The university had no accommodations for those who married and made no provisions for those with children. The administration ignored the report they submitted.

Even so, Davis felt no regret about the "slow down in my production" occasioned by the time taken to raise their children. "I liked the contrast between the conscious shaping of my life that went into my historical work and the effortlessness of my pregnancies." Though committed to "equality of careers," her husband's political radicalism and the persecution he experienced determined much of their life together and at times made her feel isolated professionally. "We automatically put the husband's interests first." She remembered that when he could he cared for the children on weekends; that was her time to go to the library. "I just plunged along," she explained in 1981, "and somehow it worked." Feminist scholars recall the excitement they felt reading the results of her early research. Drafts of some of the essays later published in *Society and Culture in Early Modern France* (1975) circulated widely and challenged all historians to rethink previous definitions of and approaches to social and cultural history. This collection, numerous other articles, two books, and participation in the making of a movie, "The Return of Martin Guerre" (1982), attested to her unique and original perceptions as a historian of sixteenth- and seventeenth-century Europe.

CHANGES, CONTINUITIES, AND DIVISIONS

In an era of expanding educational institutions, activist women historians of the late 1960s had believed that more doctorates coupled with the protection of government civil rights legislation would mean more women employed, and equitable numbers of women advanced to positions like Scott's and Davis's. Feminism would then have had its desired impact; it would have effectively countered gender discrimination in the historical profession. A 33-year-old married graduate student spoke in 1984 in much these terms. She described herself as living in a "post-feminist era where we take these things for granted."[25]

Women scholars have contested overt discrimination from the late 1960s to the present. Unquestionably, federal affirmative action policies, lengthy but successful suits against discriminatory administrations, and women's coalitions on university campuses and within professional groups had their effect, but the assumptions of the early activists proved premature. Little could be taken "for granted." The "institutionalized obstacles" remained more resistant than most had imagined. By the early 1990s more women had been admitted to graduate programs. A young scholar, especially if she were white and had outside funding, could assume that she would complete her Ph.D. in history. More women would find a first job. After that, however, their professional lives would be different from those of their male contemporaries. The inequities in employment and promotion continued; there were gains for women but they were not proportionate to their increased numbers. A young male historian had a better chance of acquiring tenure, would become a full professor sooner, and could command a higher salary. It would not matter that they had taken the same amount of time to gain the degree, had published the same number of works, had married or remained single.[26]

Studies made by the Committee on Women Historians (CWH) of the American Historical Association from the 1970s and 1980s gave a quantitative picture of the changes and continuities in women's professional opportunities. The CWH statistics documented the recalcitrant nature of the historical profession and the academy.[27] In the period 1970–74 women represented 15.8% of those receiving doctorates in history. By the early 1980s only one in eight of them had been made a full professor, whereas one in three of their male peers had risen to that rank. The 1980 CWH update of the Rose Report described the disparate employment situations. Women were "disproportionately clustered in insecure or deadend jobs; they receive tenure proportionately less than their male counterparts; and they continue to earn less than their male colleagues in all but the very lowest ranks." Of the women 39.9% made less than $18,000, whereas 49.4% of the men made more than $24,000. In addition, an overwhelming number of women taught only one or two courses, causing a virtual "feminization of part time [teaching]."[28]

The overall pattern had not changed by the end of the 1980s. The numbers of women Ph.D.s in history had continued to rise. Women represented 33% of those receiving doctorates from 1982 to 1988. A fair proportion gained tenure-track positions. After that, the spirit and the letter of the civil-rights legislation as it applied to the academy had been nullified. Only 2.9% had risen to full professor by 1988. The comparable figure for men in the same Ph.D. group (called a "cohort") was 12.1%. Of the women in the cohort, 8.9% remained adjuncts (part-time replacement staff), whereas only .6% of the men had to contend with such uncertain employment. According to the CWH by the end of the 1980s, women and men earned the same salaries at the lowest-ranking levels. Inequalities appeared as both groups rose in their departments with the greatest differences at the upper level of the profession. Overall in four-year colleges and universities women historians earned 80.6% of men's salaries.[29]

In summary, the CWH concluded that there had been improvement, but not enough. Women had gained access to the academy but were then stopped or slowed in their careers. In 1987 they represented 16% of all employed history Ph.D.s (granted between 1944 and 1986). Yet, just over half of them held tenured positions. A comparison of the original thirty colleges and universities of the Rose Report for 1968–69 and 1985–86 showed the ways in which women's situation within the academy remained inequitable (see Table 5.1).

Many have suggested reasons for the continuing disparities and inequities. Studies of women in the professions in the 1970s and 1980s described universities as particularly resistant to change. Some commentators have argued that in order to succeed women academics still had to rely on strategies once used by their predecessors in the 1920s and 1930s: they had to be "superperformers, subordinates, career innovators, or separatists." In terms of history in the 1970s and

TABLE 5.1: *Departments of History* [30]

	1968–69 All Ranks			1985–86 All Ranks		
	f	m	%f	f	m	%f
Research Universities	7	494	1.3%	52	378	12.1%
Coed. Liberal Arts	5	86	5.5%	20	87	18.7%
Women's Colleges	24	52	31.6%	24	50	32.4%
	1968–69 Full Professor			1985–86 Full Professor		
	f	m	%f	f	m	%f
Research Universities	2	272	0.7%	15	280	5.1%
Coed. Liberal Arts	1	36	2.7%	8	48	14.3%
Women's Colleges	10	19	34.5%	10	29	25.6%

1980s this would mean that a woman had to write the exceptional work, collaborate with the "great man," carve out a new field of expertise, or function in a separate women's studies program.[31]

According to the CWH's *Survival Manual for Women (and Other) Historians*, first issued in 1975, a woman's problems began before she even had her Ph.D. In the *Manual* the CWH described the discriminatory practices of the historical profession, what it called the "unwritten rules" of the academy.[32] For example, in the 1970s and 1980s women graduate students might find themselves isolated. Linda Gordon remembered her years at Yale: "I was just left alone."[33] The *Survival Manual* cautioned graduate students to learn "to take yourself seriously" because the faculty might not. "The politics and personalities in [your] department may continually undermine [your] efforts." Choice of a supervisor and a dissertation topic could be fraught with potential difficulties. Male advisors might "give poor guidance because they are convinced, consciously or unconsciously, that women have no creativity and will not do justice to a significant topic or that women will not finish their dissertations." A decision to do a topic in women's history might have other consequences. Hilda Smith "had trouble getting anyone to advise her at the University of Chicago when she wanted to research seventeenth-century English feminism."[34]

Other hazards could interfere with a woman's professional success either as a student or a faculty member. The 1991 edition of the *Survival Manual* warned that "sexual innuendo and harassment . . . happens more often than one might think." Formal grievance policies, many not delineated until the late 1970s or early 1980s, remained "restricted and lax." Only some universities had established procedures, all required extensive documentation, and in the end, the *Survival Manual* reported, "relatively few sexual harassers are actually prosecuted."[35]

Often the sexism would be so subtle as to go unnoticed: letters of recommendation describing appearance and demeanor rather than intellectual and scholarly accomplishments; "barbed comments at a job interview and questions for candidates about whether they plan to marry or to have children or how they manage to balance careers and families or whether their husbands approve of their careers." The 1975 edition of the *Manual* even cautioned women about their own attitudes—to avoid feminist rhetoric on the one hand, and "the girlishness trap" on the other, a misplaced responsiveness that fostered the image of the "abnormally sweet, smiling" woman scholar.[36]

Into the 1990s other discriminatory realities awaited women once they joined a department. They then encountered an "institutional culture," the "traditional masculine ways of thinking and doing" predicated on choices and circumstances better suited to a male than to a female model of the university historian.[37]

In particular, because women typically accepted primary responsibility for the household, the decision to marry and have children could become a negative factor in their efforts to advance within the profession. A young American Studies scholar described her dilemma: "If you are willing to play by the old men's rules and make your family a lower priority than your work, you may succeed. But if you try to find an area of compromise, you won't find allies."

Some women did not return to complete their degrees after marrying or having a child. Finding academic jobs for both wife and husband could turn one or the other into a commuter. Some could not relocate once children had started school. Others stopped working temporarily and then had the problem of explaining the "gaps" in their careers when applying for the next position. Given a limited number of years to publish, with publication a prerequisite to achieving tenured status, such a "gap," or time required for family responsibilities in addition to teaching, could delay or forestall promotion. Jane S. DeHart explained, "These presumably gender-neutral requirements, coinciding as they usually do with the years in which childbearing is safest, confront women with pressures and decisions that are hardly gender neutral in practice." In these circumstances women historians have felt torn between their professional and familial responsibilities. Often they described living two lives simultaneously.[38]

Linda Gordon could not afford to stay home when her child was a baby. The University of Massachusetts–Boston had no provision for birthing or maternity leave. What she remembered about those years of "the double day" was that "it definitely takes more energy for women." She explained, "If you are ambitious, either for recognition or to produce or both, and they usually go together, you are competing with men who almost never—even the most non-sexist of them—carry the domestic or other personal life burden of work that we have."

Gordon competed successfully and later became a professor at the University of Wisconsin–Madison, but while she was still a younger scholar teaching in Boston and writing her book *Woman's Body, Woman's Right: Birth Control in America* (1976), she experienced other constraints associated with her feminism and radical politics. Women students wanted a model, yet in front of her male colleagues she felt the need "to wear a mask," and to have "her guard up at all times." In a 1981 interview she explained that she decided to speak out and continued her political activities despite the risk. "You're just as likely to lose your job without having said or written anything useful."[39]

In 1991 the Committee on Women Historians bluntly attributed much of women's continuing disadvantaged status to the attitudes Gordon alluded to, "to sexism, to the unwillingness of male colleagues to recognize women's scholarly merit, and to the undervaluation of women's work in the academy as elsewhere."

Researching and writing women's history often exacerbated the situation. Some feminist scholars found "themselves isolated, ignored, or subjected to covert ridicule." Hired as specialists in women's history, they would be judged "incompetent" to work and teach in the more traditional geographical or chronological areas like "medieval and early modern" or German history. Successive editions of the committee's *Survival Manual* reminded readers that "prejudice against female scholars runs much deeper than it appears." The different editors made only one change in the phrasing; they kept adding more groups of women who might expect to be particularly disadvantaged. In 1991 the list included "feminists, mothers, lesbians, minority women, or commuters."[40]

By the mid 1980s the fact of some women academics' success created new kinds of problems that also affected feminists' ability to change the profession. The advancement of some created divisions and differences that eroded the former sense of community. The apparent contradictions to notions of "sisterhood" made it harder to continue protesting discrimination in unison. In the 1930s Virginia Woolf had cautioned women scholars to decide "on what terms we shall join the procession." More recently other feminists warned that women succeeding within hierarchical structures could become "amateur males."[41]

Women historians at the end of the 1980s acknowledged that acceptance within the academy could make even a feminist a party to the system and thus to the old discriminatory practices. When some of the first and second generation of women historians became very visible by their success, others felt a "sense of grievance" heightened by persistent ideological differences. Some pointed to friendships that seemed to lead to favors unequally distributed. Critics accused those gaining promotions of replicating the old system, of creating their own exclusive community. They called these new tenured professors "careerists," "more dependent upon approval from the academic establishment than from other feminist historians." They chided their colleagues for "avoiding difficult questions about the sexual dynamics of power" within the societies they studied. The harshest critics accused the successful of turning apolitical, of dissociating themselves from the struggles over status as they sought "to carve out" a place "for themselves which was both scholarly and safe." Some dismissed protestations of feminism without visible forms of activism as nothing more than "pedantry and moral abdication."[42]

By the mid 1970s generational tensions had also emerged. Even though senior faculty like Anne Firor Scott and Natalie Zemon Davis were well known for their support of younger historians, women scholars at a variety of academic institutions complained of lack of mentoring, of support not given, of encouragement withheld when they chose traditional male topics, or conversely, if they were feminists.[43] In addition, the inequitable pattern of women historians' employment created intense competition between women of different ages for lower and entry-level jobs. Twice as many women as men were applying for non-tenure track jobs; 15 times as many women as men for adjunct or part-time positions.[44] Already by the late 1970s lesbian feminists accused their female heterosexual colleagues of discrimination. "Compulsory heterosexuality," they explained, had not only denied lesbians their history but, as exemplified by the prejudices of colleagues, remained a central factor in "perpetuating male domination" of all women.[45]

Most divisive of the challenges to unity among women historians and thus to their collective feminist impact on the academy were the different circumstances and experiences of women of color and white women. Despite strong commitments to advance the interests of all women throughout the 1960s, 1970s and 1980s, African-American women, Native American women, Latina, and Asian women remained multiply disadvantaged, limited by economic resources, race, and gender.[46] The 1988 Committee on Women Historians' study to establish new hiring and promotion guidelines showed that significant numbers had not yet even gained access to Ph.D. training, let alone had the opportunity to rise within the profession. Between 1975 and 1988, 27.4% of the Ph.D.s granted to minorities went to women, roughly the same percentage as those granted to white women. The actual numbers, however, had a harsher sound. The 27.4% was in reality only 101 black women, 8 Native American, 41 Latina, and 42 Asian women, a total of fewer than 200 new doctorates in 13 years. In 1988 minority historians both female and male earned 39 doctorates. The total of 15 women in that cohort represented only 2% of all history Ph.D.s granted.[47] In 1978 Deborah Gray White attended one of the early conferences on black women's history, met other African-American women scholars, and discussed projects and research strategies. "For the first time," she later explained, "I felt like I had company."[48]

The election of Mary Frances Berry to the presidency of the Organization of American Historians in 1990 underlined how much more of a "superperformer" a successful minority woman might have to be. Both a historian and a lawyer, Berry excelled as a scholar, a high-ranking administrator at two different universities, and as an activist. She had, for example, in the course of her career been director of Afro-American studies and chancellor at the University of Colorado at Boulder, assistant secretary for education at HEW, and a commissioner on the United States Commission on Civil Rights. In 1987 she was appointed to a named chair in American Social Thought at the University of Pennsylvania.[49]

The pattern has been the same for all minority women. Deena González explained at the Committee on Women Historians panel organized for the 1990 AHA Convention that "we can count the numbers of Chicana historians on two hands—ten.'' González described the other kinds of prejudice they encountered, once having completed their training. When hired they felt isolated, were criticized if they taught other than ''their'' history, and had difficulty finding the formal support mechanisms they needed if they were to succeed according to traditional academic criteria.[50] Darlene Clark Hine described the African-American women scholars' situation: ''For the most part, [they] remain recent and still-powerless immigrants in the academy. They still have to work twice as hard and be three times better just to be perceived as average and win tenure and promotion.'' On the one hand, Hine continued, the university and local community pushed the black woman historian forward as a role model, as ''the representative of a minority, a woman, or a black.'' On the other, there was her isolation in a largely male, traditional, ethnocentric university. Even her scholarship was held in question for ''there still persists the slightly raised brow about the legitimacy of black women's history.''[51]

The harshest critics, while cognizant of continuing male and especially white, male authority within the academy, have blamed those who achieved success, especially the white women, for not contesting discriminatory patterns and practices vigorously enough. They see the feminist movement's original ideals of egalitarianism and diversity given way to ''elitism, ethnocentrism, and a disregard for diversity.'' In fact, many women of color perceived the ''feminist impact'' on the academy as the advancement of the already privileged. Rosalyn Terborg-Penn has raised the issue of race at women's history conferences and professional gatherings, for example, at the Wingspread Conference on Graduate Education in American Women's History in 1988 and at the Conference on Women's History and Public Policy at Sarah Lawrence in 1989. When she spoke at the Sarah Lawrence meetings she felt she was challenging ''the old guard'' and that ''most, but not all, of the white women were not listening to us.''[52] In particular, women of color charge that the very definition of ''feminism'' has become different for the two groups. Deborah K. King described ''the necessity of addressing all oppressions'' not just gender discrimination as ''one of the hallmarks of black feminist thought.'' Only such an approach, she argued, would bring the ''liberation of all peoples.''[53]

A 1986 study of the two leading interdisciplinary feminist journals, *Signs* and *Feminist Studies* described other ways in which minority disadvantages had been compounded by some women's success. The article described the editors of these journals as ''gate-keepers'' (the term originally applied to academic men). In this role, they included too few minority women on their editorial boards and among their authors. By denying participation to significant numbers of minority women, the editors gave an ''erroneous notion of universal womanhood'' and made it easier for others to discriminate against them as well.[54]

The philosopher Elizabeth V. Spelman has suggested how this could happen, how despite leading feminists' efforts to be inclusive they could foster a sense of exclusion, how an awareness and valuing of difference by one group could be experienced as discrimination and inequality by another. From the first days of the feminist movement women activists in general, and many white women historians in particular, while acknowledging differences of race and class, at the same time extolled the similarities among all women. As Elsa Barkley Brown has explained, these similarities, this "essential experience" as women was usually defined from their white, middle-class perspective. While distinguishing between being a woman and being black, white women could not see to make the same distinction for themselves. Rarely did they write about being white and being a woman. Thus their accounts of the past usually indicated when the participants were NOT white, rather than when they were NOT black. By declaring who and what was different in this way, and then by calling for the inclusion of others, the white female members of the profession unintentionally created and then maintained a dominant, apparently exclusive position. As Spelman explained, "Welcoming someone into one's own home doesn't represent an attempt to undermine privilege; it expresses it."[55]

Women of color have responded to their multiply disadvantaged situation and their feelings of secondary status with proven feminist strategies. Minority women historians like Berry have gone ahead to write their own definitions of feminism, their own history, and to build their own careers. By the late 1980s bibliographic articles had been published in leading women's scholarly journals. They constructed images of the past with "no necessary contradictions between public and domestic . . .; the community and the family; male and female; race and sex." Their research portrayed "intersections and interdependence" in black women's lives and "reflected the complicated dialectic of being integrally part of the larger American story, while also being quite distinguishable and apart from it."[56] Critical of minority men in the profession who set other equally exclusionary priorities, women of color established their own women's history archives, created their own networks, and conducted their own teaching panels and institutes.[57] Their scholarship and activism has brought change. For example, Hine has held a named professorship at Michigan State University since 1986. In 1991 Terborg-Penn became the chair of the American Historical Association Committee on Women Historians.

The work of all feminists contributed to these changes. The article about "gate-keeping" and the essays on black feminist theory appeared in *Signs*, one of the very journals being criticized. Feminist historians of all backgrounds organized and found sponsors for meetings like the conferences at Wingspread and at Sarah Lawrence at which the issues of diversity and white ethnocentrism could be raised. In retrospect, it seems inevitable. The contradictions were inherent in the desire for a feminist common cause despite the heterogeneity of the protagonists. Competition and implied hierarchy have become the natural corollaries of difference in many groups, not just among women historians. None of this can be made to disappear. Rather these consequences must be acknowledged. In 1984 four feminists offered a prescription for a renewed sense of unity: "We don't have to be the same to have a movement, but we *do* have to admit our fear and pain and be accountable for our ignorance. In the end finally, we must refuse to give up on each other."[58]

6.

COURSES, GRADUATE PROGRAMS, AND PUBLICATIONS

WOMEN'S HISTORY AND WOMEN'S STUDIES

The inherent tensions and disunity that women scholars have tried to explain and dispel in the 1990s seemed less significant in the first years of what historians have called the "second wave of feminism." With so much to change, the simplicity of the issues in the late 1960s and early 1970s made unanimity among feminist academics possible and practical. The denigration and disadvantage they all shared made the general fight for recognition and status both for themselves and for their newly discovered women's perspective their first priority.

And there was so much to do. In those early days feminists in the academy realized that their battles would be played out in many arenas, not just in department meetings and tenure hearings, but also in their seminar rooms and lecture halls. They learned quickly that there was a reciprocal relationship between professional success and the acceptance of their newly formulated specialty. As the scholastic community accepted women's history as a viable subject for teaching and research, so its practitioners gained validation and authority as historians. Their articles and monographs found journals and publishers. Publications added lines to vitas and justified tenure and advancement. As women historians rose within the professional hierarchies, so their history rose in prestige and gained a place in university and college course offerings.[1]

The same kind of reciprocal relationship existed between women's history and women's studies, the interdisciplinary study of women's experiences. The women's movement, women's studies, and women's history developed together. A feminist historian did not usually act alone. Collaboration and success in one area meant collaboration and success in another. In addition, just as writing women's history had political implications, so did teaching and the formulation of new programs from a feminist perspective. Florence Howe, an early advocate and creator of women's studies, explained: "In the broadest context of that work, teaching is a political act: some person is choosing, for whatever reasons, to teach a set of values, ideas, assumptions, and pieces of information, and in so doing, to omit other values, ideas, assumptions, and pieces of information. If all those choices form a pattern excluding half the human race, that is a political act one can hardly help noticing. To omit women entirely makes one kind of political statement; to include women as a target for humor makes another." She continued, "To include women with seriousness and vision," was "simply another kind of political act." The implications were far-reaching. Linda Gordon explained, "By its very existence, women's studies constitutes a critique of the university and the body of knowledge it imparts."[2]

Feminists like Gordon and Howe saw the old scholarship and the processes of academic inquiry "trapped by male supremacy," and formulated in ways that "subtly subsidized" women's oppression. This was particularly true of history with its "universal man," its traditional formulations of the past with "historical actors and historians . . . [all] represented as men."[3] These feminist scholars reasoned that transforming the teaching of history, transforming the syllabuses of this and other disciplines would ultimately change society. In 1975 Gordon described her sense of mission: "It seems to me that we ought to see ourselves forthrightly and unpretentiously as the academic wing of the women's liberation movement."

From the beginning feminist historians committed themselves to all women's "liberation" and an end to exclusionary practices in the broadest sense. Marilyn J. Boxer in writing about the founding of the National Women's Studies Association (NWSA) in 1977 remembered that they attacked "deeply held, often sacred beliefs," "vested interests," and the "institutional hierarchy." They opposed not only "sexism but all bias—racism, class-bias, ageism, heterosexual bias."[4]

The curricula these scholars designed in history, literature, and social science reflected these attitudes. They worked to find examples from all women's lives and to present to their college and university classes representative descriptions of all women's experiences. When Temma Kaplan taught the first women's history course at UCLA in 1971 she called it "Women and Capitalism" and had students read not only the classic works in English women's labor history by Alice Clark and Ivy Pinchbeck but also the chapter on black women in Mary White Ovington's *Half A Man: The Status of the Negro in New York* (1911).[5]

These first courses, called "undergraduate specials" at Stanford, often came from women's informal meetings outside the academy. They might be held in someone's living room, in a newly founded women's bookstore, or in a trailer parked on the campus, like the one at Sonoma State College in northern California that served as the "Women's center" for a variety of feminist groups. They had the model of the "free university movement" that many had participated in to generate support for civil rights and opposition to the Vietnam war. In their caucuses and teach-ins they passed mimeographed bibliographies, syllabuses, and draft articles from group to group for comments and encouragement. At the University of Toronto, Natalie Zemon Davis and Jill Conway compiled one of the first book lists for European women's history; precious copies circulated at feminist scholars' gatherings across North America. Beginning in 1970 Berenice A. Carroll initiated regular listings of courses and "Research in Progress" with the first newsletters of the Coordinating Committee on Women in the Historical Profession (the feminist caucus within the American Historical Association, founded in 1969). Programs in women's history sprang up all over the country in every kind of academic circumstance, at the New Orleans Free School, Portland State University in Oregon, and the University of Chicago. Nancy Cott and Susan Groag Bell created and taught courses while they were still graduate students. These young scholars had realized Mary Beard's ideal of "a woman's university-without-walls."[6]

Anne Firor Scott at Duke in North Carolina described the early 1970s as an "exhilarating" time. Even her daughter Rebecca was writing about "Women in Stuart England" for her college history class. Some likened it to a "Feminist Enlightenment." Much was similar to that era in eighteenth-century Europe. Women historians felt the same sense of isolation from and antagonism to traditional institutions. They saw themselves as the vanguard of a new intellectual flowering. "Dismissed as political or ignored completely by many colleagues, we responded by forming a community of scholars that cut across genders, ideologies, race, and class. Sharing ideas, sources, and material, instinctively seeking safety in numbers, we did the one thing that could develop a new field quickly. We learned from each other with an elan which is rarely seen in academic life."[7]

They felt collaborators in a grand cooperative endeavor. One work of theory was to be superseded by another; one monograph to become part of a larger

project. The editor introduced a collection of articles arising out of a symposium
on "conceptual frameworks" for ancient, modern European, and United States
women's history "not as finished work, but as part of a process. We hope
they will stimulate thought, clarify ideas, and help us all to a higher level of
understanding."[8]

History courses usually formed a key component of the multi-disciplinary
women's studies programs that developed in the same spontaneous and unorthodox ways. As women's studies grew in significance, so did women's history.
San Diego State College in California (now a university) offered the first officially
sponsored women's studies program consisting of ten courses in 1970. Feminist
scholars created a six-course program at Cornell in 1970, and one at the University of Indiana in 1973. From then on the field of women's studies grew dramatically with 150 new programs by 1975 and another 150 by 1980, making the
total of individual courses taught from a feminist perspective in the thousands.
Organizations like the National Women Studies Association, newsletters, and
national conferences brought women scholars together, publicized their ideas
and efforts, and aided in the process of transformation. Already by 1980 studies
of the "impact of women's studies" were being completed, sponsored by groups
as prestigious as the National Institute of Education.[9]

By the late 1980s women's history as a core subject within the interdisciplinary field of women's studies had become institutionalized. In 1982, 25 universities granted graduate degrees in women's studies. The Universities of Southern
California, Rochester, Wisconsin, Brown, and Rutgers had endowed chairs for
their faculty.[10] Library reference sections had multiple volumes of bibliographies
on women, everything from recommended core collections to regional, chronological, and topical categories, to listings of dissertations. Patricia K. Ballou's
Bibliography of Bibliographies on Women had gone into its second edition by
1986 with seven pages of entries on history.[11]

By 1987, 57 multidisciplinary research institutes devoted to women's issues
(including women's history) had been created throughout the United States.
Many had been funded from outside sources. The Rockefeller Family Fund
supported SIROW (Southwest Institute for Research on Women) at the University
of Arizona; the Mellon Foundation funded the Wellesley College Center for
Research on Women; the Ford Foundation gave to establish Centers for Research
on Women at the University of Washington–Seattle, Duke, the University of
North Carolina–Chapel Hill, Spelman College, Memphis State University, and
Stanford. The United Nations Women's Decade Conferences in Copenhagen in
1980 and in Nairobi in 1985 saw the creation of an international women's studies
network. By 1987 there were almost 500 programs in the United States. Of all
colleges and universities, 49% offered concentrations in women's studies includ-

ing a range of public and private institutions such as Ohio State, the University of Maryland, University of Colorado, the Universities of California at Berkeley and Los Angeles, Harvard, Princeton, and Yale.[12] Some institutions, funding agencies, and philanthropic organizations took a particular interest in women's history. They played a significant role in its establishment as an accepted academic field. Special collections at Radcliffe, Wellesley, and Smith gave reality to Mary Beard's dream of women's history archives. Radcliffe's Bunting Institute (founded in 1960) in cooperation with the Schlesinger Library on the History of Women offered research funding to historians and to other women scholars. In the 1980s the Pembroke Center for Teaching and Research on Women at Brown University and the Women's Studies Research Center at the University of Wisconsin–Madison both embarked on projects with a strong history component, "the cultural constructions of the female" and "motherhood."[13] Specific historical projects and individual scholars received funds from the Carnegie Endowment, the Rockefeller, Mellon, and Russell Sage Foundations. For example, the National Endowment for the Humanities supported Andrea Hinding's *Women's History Sources: A Guide to Archives and Manuscript Collections in the United States* (1979), and Joan Kelly's work on the history of feminist thought.

As it had in employment and promotion, success gave room for argument and division among feminist academics. The acceptance and institutionalization of women's programs highlighted inherent contradictions and posed new political and intellectual challenges. Effectiveness in the first years had been predicated on unity. Feminist historians and academics in general looked to the "essential" qualities of being female, aspects shared rather than the particular differences experienced because of class, ethnicity, race, or sexual orientation. Despite protestations and actions to the contrary, the voices speaking of commonalities appeared to hide or devalue the obvious diversities. Even more significant, the voices most often heard within the academic establishment still seemed to be those of the white, relatively privileged, heterosexual majority.

African-American women historians' perspective was representative of that of women academics who felt that women's history (and women's studies) had developed "without consideration of [their] experiences." As early as the mid-1970s Rosalyn Terborg-Penn saw racism within women's history groups and sexism within the black studies movement, conflicts that Deborah Gray White later identified as between black and white feminism on the one hand and black feminism and black nationalism, on the other. Terborg-Penn explained, "For every two steps we take, we seem to be pushed back at least one." Most important, black feminist scholars came to believe that for them there could be no separation of the "women's struggle from the race struggle."[14]

Terborg-Penn and other activists had a solution. "This will continue until we take control of our own destiny.'' Just as women together had made their own field, so now black women historians created their own organizations, funded conferences, wrote articles, monographs, and bibliographies. The Association of Black Women Historians held its first annual meeting in 1979. The members produced a survey of black women scholars and their research, ran workshops on teaching, applied for and received NEH (National Endowment for the Humanities) funding for a conference in 1983 at Howard University on ''Women in the African Diaspora'' (also published as a book in 1987), and in just over a decade created an extensive list of articles, monographs, topical and survey histories, about black women in the United States.[15]

With black women's history as with women's history in general, the success of the new specialty gave it strength and ensured its survival within the academy. But survival was not the only goal. All feminist historians, like their counterparts in other disciplines, envisioned not just the creation and validation of studies from women's perspectives but the transformation of all perspectives. They wanted the study of women incorporated into every aspect of history teaching and research. They feared that like regional, ethnic, and racial studies established in the 1960s women teaching about women would mean only separate courses, separate institutes, and thus marginalization and increased vulnerability. Their fears proved correct. In 1976 a group of women faculty members at Princeton completed a study of the impact of feminism on traditional courses. They received 355 syllabuses from 172 departments. Despite the acknowledged success of women's studies, they could find little if any change in the required and standard courses offered by separate departments. At best a few women ''luminaries'' appeared in a history or literature course. Otherwise there had been no significant integration of women's and men's perspectives in the regular curriculum.[16]

As a result, feminist historians began to seek money for a different task. To transform traditional history programs at all educational levels they needed to prepare and disseminate a vast array of resources. They went from what one scholar described as ''resurrecting and reassessing the lost women of history'' to ''recovering source materials and making them accessible.''[17] Not only primary sources, but lists of readings, surveys of work to date, ways to organize courses, all became available in the late 1970s and early 1980s. They wrote the first bibliographic articles for feminist and other specialist journals during this period. The Conference Group on Women's History, part of the feminist historians' caucus within the American Historical Association, from 1975 published bibliographies annually in its newsletter.

These were the beginnings. Women spoke at professional meetings, organized panels on teaching, wrote articles for journals like *The History Teacher* on how to incorporate women's materials into standard courses. At the same time, textbook and trade publishers brought out basic texts and collections of essays in both United States and European women's history. By the late 1980s a wonderful range of essays, pamphlets, bibliographic guides, sample syllabus collections, and curriculum packages had been published to aid in the integration of women's history into traditional courses.[18] In 1990 United States scholars participated in the founding of the International Federation of Societies for Research in Women's History, thus affirming feminist historians' commitment to the multiplicity of women's experience in the past and their unity of purpose in the present.

From the beginning Federal funding had been significant in women historians' efforts at integration. The NEH supported institutes at Sarah Lawrence, Stanford, and Princeton to introduce materials to high school and college faculty. NEH funded Gerda Lerner's pamphlet on teaching United States women's history for the American Historical Association. Published in 1980 it gave a comprehensive picture of the underlying "concepts and strategies," of the topics used by many instructors, and extensive bibliographic notes for each section. Lerner paid special attention to sources for teaching about women in minority groups. FIPSE (Fund for the Improvement of Postsecondary Education) gave money for curriculum integration. By 1983, under the sponsorship of the Organization of American Historians, D'Ann Campbell of Indiana University and Elizabeth Fox-Genovese at the University of Rochester had supervised the creation and publication of two volumes of materials for teaching, one for United States history courses, and one for courses in "Western Civilization." A third volume for women in Africa, East Asia, Latin America, the Caribbean, and Southwest Asia appeared in 1988. WEEA (Women's Educational Equity Act) made money available for those working to change history and social studies in primary and secondary schools.[19]

When Lerner's teaching guide was published in 1980 she had already spent almost 10 years building the master's program in women's history at Sarah Lawrence. She and Joan Kelly had applied for and received a $150,000 grant from the Rockefeller Foundation for this and two other academic programs, women's studies for the undergraduates and a course to develop organizational skills for women community leaders at the School of Continuing Education. The master's program began in the fall of 1972 with six students ranging in age from 22 to 53. The three-year grant made collaboration possible among an impressive array of women scholars with specialties in many different periods and regions. For example, Alice Kessler-Harris, Mari Jo Buhle, Barbara Engel, Ann Lane, Kathleen Casey, and Marylin Arthur taught with Lerner in the course of the 1970s. By the end of the 1970s this master's program remained relatively unique. Although in 1978 there were 26 graduate programs in women's studies, there were only three in women's history: for the MA at Sarah Lawrence and the University of Maryland–College Park; for the Ph.D. at the State University of New York–Binghamton.[20]

While integration has remained the preference of many individual historians, the 1980s saw dramatic institutional recognition of women's history as a field in its own right. Those seeking to quantify the feminist impact on history have pointed to this different, but nonetheless significant, change. In 1988 the National Endowment for the Humanities sponsored a conference on graduate training in United States women's history. Almost all of the participants had risen to the top of the academic hierarchy. Acknowledged specialists, they came from 63 public and private institutions, all of which granted graduate degrees in women's history. Even more indicative of feminism's impact on the discipline was the fact that 14% of the scholars in attendance had received their training in this new field, not in a traditional historical specialty. Although Rosalyn Terborg-Penn was critical of the white cast to this women's history, no one disagreed with Linda K. Kerber's closing remarks. She commented with pride on the emergence of this second generation of women historians who had been schooled in their own, and not men's history. In the decades since Gerda Lerner's 1969 article appeared calling for "New Approaches to American Women's History," feminist historians despite setbacks and differences had proved that an audience existed, had created a range of materials for teaching, and had legitimated women's experiences as subjects for scholarly inquiry.[21]

PUBLICATIONS: BOOKS FOR SCHOLARS AND TRADE PUBLISHERS

Persistence, political acumen, and the hard work of scholarship explained feminist historians' impact on the academy. By the early 1990s whether a woman historian was pleased with the progress or disheartened by the continuing institutional inequities and potential marginalization, change could be measured in numbers of graduate degrees awarded, academic appointments and promotions made, numbers of courses and programs established. All acknowledged the exponential growth in the numbers of publications by feminist historians and from women's historical perspective.

Publication of materials in women's history served many functions for feminist historians. It gave women their own past, their own heroines, and thus the pride and motivation of "historical self-consciousness." It made readings and materials available for courses and specialized knowledge accessible to other scholars. Finally, feminist historians knew that publication was a key prerequisite in their fight for equity within the academy, because publication, more than any other criteria determined authority and status among historians, female or male, of color or white.

The same kinds of obstacles that impeded women's access to graduate programs and the higher ranks of history departments affected their access to publishing. Traditional ways of thinking dominated the field. Only "significant" work by "important" scholars merited inclusion in the best known, most respected journals like the *American Historical Review* (AHR, published by the American Historical Association). When in 1970 Temma Kaplan submitted her article on "Spanish Anarchism and Women's Liberation" to the AHR the editor told her that when he first read the title page "he thought that his secretary was playing a joke on him." He did read the piece but rejected it because the research was "too narrow for the AHR."[22] The same prejudicial criteria governed decisions by university and trade publishers, who counted on the recommendations of established historians when considering a manuscript. Rarely would a woman historian's work, even on traditional subjects, be deemed "original" enough, rarely would her reputation with the male leaders of the profession designate her as "important."[23]

Other characteristics of the "institutional culture" of the academic world compounded a woman historian's difficulties in preparing research for publication, especially if she were among the first females to be hired in previously all-male departments. Academic historians usually produced their work in time taken from their regular teaching and professional responsibilities; the more senior in the hierarchy, the fewer teaching and administrative responsibilities, and thus, the more time allowed for research and writing. In addition, the most successful historians had leaves, fellowships, and grants from outside sources, to give them the additional time and money for travel to archives, research assistance, and the unbroken months needed to complete an article or monograph.

Yet, women historians in the lowest ranks of their departments had none of these advantages, and in some instances even less time and access to funding than male colleagues at the same level. As a junior department member, a woman, and a feminist, these would be years of heavier teaching and committee responsibilities. Active in the feminist community in the 1970s, a woman historian would take time to lobby with other women for courses and services. She would be called on to counsel the women students, and often was the only female available to "represent" women for her department in university forums.[24] Given these increased professional obligations, access to leaves and to outside funding became even more significant for women scholars. Yet these academic awards were distributed by the same individuals who made tenure and promotion decisions with their traditional perspectives about the discipline, about what constituted valid subjects for research and about women's appropriate functions in society.

Surveys done of outside funding in the 1970s and 1980s showed an appallingly low percentage of women receiving grants from foundations. A 1981–82 study conducted by the American Historical Association of another source of money, departmental research support, indicated the average, or mean, for women to be $2,984; for men, $18,933. The survey showed the greater disadvantages for minority women. Their average support was $1.22. The equivalent figure for minority men was $565. In addition, when budgets had to be cut in the 1980s, the ways in which research priorities had been set made it that much harder for funders to imagine giving their money to a woman scholar.[25]

Just the fact of being female might make a difference in publishing decisions. A study of the process of article selection for journals in six academic fields showed that pieces received a lower rating when they were known to be written by a woman than when the author's sex was not revealed. The same sexism in all likelihood affected the process of selection for grants and leaves. A woman's professional record might look different from a man's. She might not have advanced as quickly, or had as many publications. There might be "gaps" in training or employment, time taken to fulfill family and household responsibilities. She might appear to be researching an unacceptable topic, or presenting it in an unacceptable way. In 1977, for example, the National Endowment for the Humanities denied a woman historian's application for a conference grant (conferences gave scholars opportunities to present their research, almost equivalent to publication) on "Women, Revolution, and War," as "excessively feminist, too weighted with woman participants," and in general, "not balanced."[26] All of these considerations created a convenient rationale for those within the academic hierarchy who wanted to ignore, or disapproved of, women and feminism. They were simply guarding and preserving "standards." These unorthodox projects did not merit grants or leaves. With fewer publications, advancement would have to be denied. Remaining at a lower rank meant less time and money, and so on. There was no prejudice; there were no villains, no martyrs. The denigrating attitudes and systematic exclusion could be perpetuated without apparent agency, masked in the rhetoric of traditional scholarship.

In 1948 Mary Beard attended a dinner with four professors from Johns Hopkins. She wrote to a friend of the men's reaction to her mention of women's history. "They spur me to work on, for there is no use merely bemoaning their naivete and its attendant bigotry. We've got to feed out so much work that they will be drowned in the flood."[27] Her words seem prophetic in retrospect, as if feminist scholars had taken up the challenge. Already by 1975 they would report that "a massive effort to reconstruct women's historical experience is underway.''[28] By their energy and intelligence feminist historians broke the pattern. They made time, they found support, they researched, they wrote, and they published.

The *Cumulative Book Index* for 1969 (an early version of the guide to *Books in Print*) listed six collective biographies of women and four books on women's history topics: one by Beard, one by a male historian, William O'Neill, on nineteenth-century feminism, M. J. Hughes's classic on medieval women healers, and Julia Spruill's work on southern colonial women. In 20 years everything about book publishing had changed. The 1989–90 edition of *Books in Print* had three close-printed pages of women's history, four pages of women's biographies, and hundreds of listings throughout the volumes under more specific categories like the Women's Christian Temperance Union (WCTU), Muslim religious doctrine, and scores of references to books on individual women, everything from heads of state to explorers. Women historians appeared throughout the guide.

To have a vivid sense of the dramatic change imagine the book exhibit at the 1969 American Historical Association (AHA) annual convention. Perhaps O'Neill's book on the women's movement was prominently displayed because of its novelty. Perhaps works by a few select women scholars could be found among the many books by men. Walking the aisles of the 1990 AHA publishers exhibits would be a completely different experience. Women authors and women's topics were commonplace. Both trade and university press catalogues listed their wares including many books by and about women. The publishing houses cited survey histories and textbooks with women contributors and about women's history, biographies of women from every region of the world, biographies of men by women, monographs about every epoch, from every kind of topical or analytical perspective, both feminist and traditional, all by women scholars. The Free Press prominently advertised the paperback edition of Sara M. Evans's *Born for Liberty: A History of Women in America*. Oxford University Press did the same for Jane S. DeHart's *Sex, Gender, and the Politics of ERA*. HarperCollins's featured display was for Marilyn B. Young's newest book, *The Vietnam Wars*. Houghton Mifflin and D. C. Heath had textbooks and collections of readings in European and United States women's history. Heath's catalogue noted that the eighth edition of Bailey's *The American Pageant* had been expanded to include ''new material on the family, women, blacks, Hispanics, and native Americans.'' Trade publishers like Routledge, Beacon, Penguin, The Free Press, and HarperCollins had special supplements or separate sections for their women's history titles. Others offered regional or topical series about women, like G. K. Hall/Twayne's set on twentieth-century United States women, Garland's on women and religion, and Zed's on women of the Third World. Carlson publishers proudly announced a projected 16-volume collection on United States black women, edited by Darlene Clark Hine.

Yale was the first university to establish its own imprint in 1908. Since that time university presses have functioned in a special capacity in the academic world. They have been willing to publish works that could only command a limited scholarly and research library market. Their selection of a manuscript has often established the professional credentials of its author. Some university presses have played a significant role in the validation of women's history and, by offering access to publication, in the accreditation of women scholars. At the 1990 AHA convention the presses at Columbia, the universities of Nebraska, Chicago, and Pennsylvania advertised their special series in women's history and feminist theory. Others, like Yale, Harvard, Rutgers, Michigan, Johns Hopkins, and Minnesota particularly promoted their titles by and about women. The University of California Press described itself in its convention catalogue as "one of the premier publishers of women's history."

Neither university nor trade publishers had initially rushed to fill their lists with works in women's history. They did not seek out women scholars. In fact, The Feminist Press, founded in 1970 by Florence Howe and Paul Lauter, was the first to issue and to commission works on women in history and in a variety of other disciplines. (By 1990, even women's presses had proliferated dramatically. Women book publishers filled a guide of their own with over 250 entries.) The tremendous growth in the field came because of simple demand. In particular, trade publishers discovered that women's history sold and made profits.

Hugh Van Dusen, an editor of Harper Torchbooks in 1969, described how they came to publish their first women's history/women's studies title, *Not in God's Image: Women in History from the Greeks to the Victorians*. Julia O'Faolain and Lauro Martines (at UCLA) contacted him with their idea for a document collection in European women's history. They explained that they could do any necessary translations and assured him that given the popularity of women's studies on west coast campuses that their book would be well worth publishing.[29] Van Dusen remembered that the paperback division had a number of younger editors—some feminists, some peace activists—but that they had only investigated reprints of books on women's topics. He negotiated a contract and the O'Faolain and Martines collection appeared all by itself in the 1973 catalogue as the company's first "Women's Studies" listing. Harper and Row's second major title, *Women Artists: Recognition and Reappraisal From the Early Middle Ages to the Twentieth Century* evolved out of a course at Sonoma State College that Van Dusen heard about from his west coast publishing scout. He went to northern California, took Karen Petersen and J. J. Wilson to what they knew to be one of the best French restaurants in Sonoma County, and encouraged them to turn their lectures and slide collection into a book.

With titles such as these, by the mid-1970s women's history (and women's studies) had become "the biggest growth area in the whole paperback division" of Harper's. Van Dusen remembered, "Every book worked." In 1990 Petersen and Wilson's *Women Artists* was still in print with cumulative sales of over 36,000 copies. Harper and Row's two-volume survey history of European women, *A History of Their Own: Women in Europe from Prehistory to the Present* by Bonnie S. Anderson and Judith P. Zinsser, issued in hardcover in 1988, in paperback in 1989, with book club and foreign contracts, sold over 60,000 copies in its first two years. As Van Dusen explained in 1990, women's titles overall made up almost 10% of the company's total sales, over $10 million a year, and remained "one of the most reliable categories we have."

Given this publishing success, by the 1990s scholars wishing to familiarize themselves with the field of women's history consulted not just footnotes and specialized book lists in the last pages of monographs, but reference guides, dictionaries of individuals and institutions, handbooks, and bibliographies of bibliographies. A glance at the reference section of a research library today reveals everything from Susan Mosher Stuard's *Women in Medieval History and Historiography* (1987) to Sally Shreir's listing of contemporary women's movements around the world. There are dictionaries of women artists, of black women composers, and a *Handbook of American Women's History* (1990). To begin, a scholar might consult *Women: A Bibliography of Bibliographies* (1986) that refers to 30 guides and essays specifically in women's history, with others cited in the topical and regional listings.[30] For primary research materials a historian would go to the two-volume *Women's History Sources: A Guide to Archives and Manuscript Collections in the United States* (1979) with over 20,000 entries.

PUBLICATIONS: ARTICLES AND CONFERENCE PRESENTATIONS

Over the decades patterns have evolved by which historians conceive of and complete their new works of scholarship. A guide to women's archival materials was so important to feminists because their historical investigations began with primary records of events: diaries, letters, pictures, the images and words of past contemporaries. Analyzing sources like these led to interpretations of events and to tentative hypotheses. It has become customary within the profession for these drafts, these potential chapters of a book to be submitted to conference organizers or to the editors of a select group of journals. Male historians have counted on this progression in the making of their books and their careers; women historians, however, could make no such assumptions. Gaining access to conference rostrums and the pages of the most prestigious academic publications posed the same obstacles for feminist historians as had the other institutions of the profession. Journal editors and conference program chairmen entertained the old discriminatory, sexist attitudes: skepticism about women's scholarly competence and dismissal of the chosen topics of inquiry as too political or of little significance.

The 1968–69 compendia listing historians' articles barely noticed the category of "women." *America: History and Life* (for journals in the United States and Canada, publishing articles on North American history) had one-fourth of a column, a total of 46 entries arranged by state. *Historical Abstracts* (for the history of Africa, Asia, Europe and Latin America from journals all over the world) used countries as the organizing principle for its 27 listings. The two guides had more entries on the Australian Air Force and the War of 1812 than on women. To make matters worse, what had been included reflected traditional historical categories and stereotypical views of women's roles in the past. A number of European journals published articles on the suffrage movements because of their political nature. Drawing on ancient prejudices and images, a piece in a United States journal implied that a woman had been instrumental in George Washington's defeat at the battle of Long Island; another, on pioneer life in Nebraska, was entitled "Sunbonnet and Calico."

As in book publishing, all of this had changed by the end of the 1980s. One historian called it a "virtual explosion of new scholarship on women."[31] The 1989–90 edition of *America: History and Life* had over four pages of listings under the heading "women" with numerous cross references and detailed breakdowns and subheadings by era, country, and topic. The articles cited covered a wide range of North American women's experiences: Iroquois women of sixteenth-century New York; California taxi dancers; M. Carey Thomas's presidency of the women's college Bryn Mawr; nineteenth-century Catholic women's orders; modern black dramatists; Japanese-American immigrants' lives; the Women's Trade Union League. For the history of women in other parts of the world, the listings in *Historical Abstracts*, though not so dramatic in the increased numbers of citations, showed the same range and variety of categories with cross-referencing and detailed subheadings. There were articles on well-known women such as St. Teresa of Avila and Mary Wollstonecraft, and also women traditionally ignored or forgotten. Entries included pieces on Japanese anarchists at the turn of the century, eighteenth- and nineteenth-century Irish linen workers,

Augsburg prostitutes, the Romanian women's movement, the effects of Brazilian labor law from 1880 to 1920, Egyptian peasant women in the nineteenth and twentieth centuries, and women's political participation in Malaysia since World War II.

What explained the change, the decisions to publish what would formerly have been rejected? With no significant profits from the sale of scholarly journals (most continue to be subsidized by universities), access to this branch of publishing did not come from popular demand. Studies of the late 1960s and 1970s show the reluctance of the older, best known journals, and some acceptance from new interdisciplinary and radical history publications. But as in so many other aspects of the feminist impact on history, real validation and legitimacy came through women's independent initiatives, the creation of their own journals.

Ellen DuBois and her colleagues did a study of professional journals for the years 1966–80. They asked in particular about the appearance of scholarship about women. Given the numbers of women scholars working in women's topics, their answers gave an indication of women authors' access to publication as well. Of the five disciplines surveyed, history and philosophy were the least receptive. In 1969 only 1.3% of the articles in ten selected history journals concerned women's experience. As feminist historians began to complete their first research, the figures for the 1970s rose to between 4% and 6%. In 1980 women's history pieces constituted 6.45% of the articles published.[32] As DuBois and her co-authors predicted, most receptive to women's writings in the 1970s were the journals reflecting the new approaches to social and cultural history, and those with avowedly "New Left" editorial policies. In addition to individual articles by feminist historians, between 1973 and 1975 the journals of *Marriage and the Family*, *Interdisciplinary History*, and *Urban History* published whole issues on women's past experiences.[33]

The 1988–90 statistics for the three leading history journals of the earlier surveys showed the mixed impact of feminism. Articles in women's history constituted 33% of those published in the *Journal of Social History* for 1988–89 and roughly the same number, or 31% for the *Journal of American History* in the next year 1989–90. The percentage for the most traditionally oriented of the non-specialist journals, the *American Historical Review*, varied from 6%–27%. In 1990, 27% of the articles were either by women historians or about women's history. This reflected, however, a special issue on "gender," an analytical approach of particular interest to women scholars. Only three other articles by women historians appeared in that year and these were on topics without a feminist or women's history component.[34] To gain regular access to publication, feminists had to create their own journals.

With the appearance of *Feminist Studies* and *Women's Studies* in 1972,

academic feminists inaugurated a rich and enduring tradition of women's scholarly publications. Each of the founding editorial boards of these journals made
a strong commitment to feminist topics, to the newest methods of inquiry, and
to the eventual transformation of society. In most cases the impetus for these
publishing initiatives arose out of the same feminist collectives and support
groups that produced the first courses and interdisciplinary programs. *Women's
Studies* began at Queens College in New York City ready to "chronicle changing
consciousness." The members of the "editorial collective" of *Frontiers*
(founded 1975) at the University of Colorado saw themselves as a forum for
dialogue and a means to raise awareness. Ann Calderwood, the first editor of
Feminist Studies, began distributing women scholars' work out of her apartment
in the late 1960s. With formal publication in the summer of 1972, she explained
their overall goal: to present "responses to feminist issues and analyses that open
new areas of feminist research and critique." The editors in the first issue of
Signs: Journal of Women in Culture and Society (founded 1975) published by
Barnard College (now out of the University of Chicago), described the journal
as part of "The New Feminism," in the vanguard of the new scholarship,
committed to using "concepts, tools, and techniques of modern study . . . to
compensate for old intellectual evasions and errors, to amass fresh data, and to
generate new concepts, tools, and techniques." Each journal wanted to have an
impact for the future. Their editors believed that "disciplined research illuminated by a feminist perspective . . . can contribute to effective social change."[35]
These were but the first. The number of journals grew so dramatically that
beginning in 1980 libraries subscribed to *Feminist Periodicals*, a quarterly listing
of the varied and increasingly specialized women's publications.[36]

    In each instance historians made significant contributions both as editors and
authors to the interdisciplinary feminist journals and newsletters that proliferated
in the 1970s and early 1980s. The first issue of *Signs*, for example, included
three history articles, one on Queen Elizabeth I, one on women in China, and
the piece that initiated the positive evaluations of privileged women's experiences, Carroll Smith-Rosenberg's "The Female World of Love and Ritual: Relations between Women in Nineteenth-Century America." It was not, however,
until 1989 that a separate journal exclusively devoted to history appeared. The
editors gave the reasons for the *Journal of Women's History* in their "Statement
of Purpose." They explained that the existing feminist journals were receptive
but simply could not "accommodate the geometric increase in research and
writing in women's history." The "traditional history publications" remained
slow in accepting research about women. They noted that these older journals still
devoted 90% of their pages to articles with no mention of women's experiences.
Women had become a "separate group," to be studied in isolation, diverted to

the margins of the historical record, or lost amidst discussions of "gender." They saw "the vast theoretical and analytical work of feminist history" neither in need of separation nor integration, but rather as an "alternative," a third form of history that could become the "vehicle for . . . transformation" of the whole discipline.[37]

In the same ways that the editors of traditional journals had dismissed women's scholarship, so too had the leaders of the established professional conferences. In 1970 the program chairman for the American Historical Association accepted three panels in women's history: "Feminism—Past, Present, and Future," "Wage-Earning Women in Industrial America," and "Women's Experience in History: A Teaching Problem." When, however, Berenice A. Carroll of the newly organized women's caucus presented a fourth proposal, he chose to refuse it on the grounds that women's history was "not intellectually interesting."[38] To feminist historians it could seem an impossible situation. Such refusals presaged a familiar rationale that perpetuated discriminatory attitudes and practices. With their subject demeaned, how could they gain a hearing or change attitudes? Without dialogue they could not acquire scholarly validation for themselves and their analyses. In this context a separate conference of their own offered a way to begin the process of rewriting the definition of what constituted history and of achieving status within the profession.

Mary Hartman remembered when she approached Louise Dalby, a professor in French history and president of the Berkshire Conference of Women Historians, at the organization's spring meeting.[39] Every year this group of women scholars breakfasted together at the December AHA conventions and met annually on their own to discuss research and to enjoy weekend walks in the countryside. To assistant professors like Hartman and Lois Banner, Dalby and the other senior scholars seemed exclusive and imposing; the ways in which decisions were made mysterious. Hartman and Banner spoke nonetheless. They mentioned the work being done in women's history and suggested that even though this was not the primary interest of most members (who had made their reputations in more traditional histories), that perhaps the Berkshire Conference could "do something in this area." Dalby gave them $50 and told them they could be the program chairs.

A year later in March of 1973 with a $500 foundation grant, friends co-opted to a program committee, and endless volunteer hours, the First Berkshire Conference on the History of Women convened at Douglass College to discuss "Historical Perspectives on Women." Dalby remembered worrying about the bills, imagining that 75 would come and then having to "turn people away." Estimates of attendance at this first conference vary from 500 to 1000 to hear two days of panels, the papers of 40–50 women scholars, all in women's history.

Even the co-chairs were surprised by the response. The conference was convened again in 1974 and became a regular event on feminist historians' calendars. By 1978, the "Big Berks," as it came to be called to distinguish it from the informal spring gatherings, had the highest attendance of any historical meeting short of the American Historical Association annual convention. With over 2,000 attending on average, the Berkshire Conference on the History of Women repeatedly demonstrated the vitality of women's scholarship and the interest in women's past.[40] The conference became yet another way to give a quantitative measure to the feminist impact on history.

This separatist feminist strategy of establishing women's publishing houses and feminist journals, and of organizing separate conferences to present their own history, had historical precedents. The Fall 1979 issue of *Feminist Studies* included Estelle Freedman's article on the successes of nineteenth-century women activists in the United States. She argued that working from their segregated "private sphere" they had advanced the cause of feminism, not impeded it, as previously interpreted. Freedman saw the creation of a separate set of cultural circumstances, of these women's institutions and organizations, as part of "the process of redefining womanhood by the extension, rather than by the rejection, of the female sphere." Strengthened by their association and their common pride these women braved the male political and economic leaders of their day and forced social change. Freedman believed that this strategy would work in the twentieth century as well.[41] The success of feminist historians in the expansion of curricula and the proliferation of all kinds of materials in women's history attested to the prescience of her analysis. By using their own networks, by creating their own courses, journals, and conferences, feminists had an impact on the institutions of scholarship as a whole.

Success fostered success. As feminist historians brought changes in one aspect of the academic world they found change in another facilitated. Women historians' own professional organization, the Berkshire Conference, had made possible the first women's history conference. The "Little Berks" played a key role in another aspect of the feminist efforts to alter the historical profession. At its meetings women scholars not only presented their work and enjoyed time with friends, but in the 1970s created coalitions that first criticized and then brought reform to what initially appeared to be the most closed and traditional of all male historians' preserves, the American Historical Association.

7.

PROFESSIONAL ORGANIZATIONS

Once a year in the last week of December anywhere from three to four thousand historians gather in some big hotel in a major city in the United States for the convention of the American Historical Association.[1] Although many view the specialized regional and topical scholarly meetings that take place during the rest of the year as of more significance, there is still a certain aura to the annual meeting of this oldest of the historians' professional organizations. Founded in 1884 as the first step in the "professionalization" of the study of history, for many decades the American Historical Association performed the role of "protector," embodying in its members and its leadership an elite, traditional image of the historian and his history. Events and decisions of the last two decades have democratized and altered this image. Yet, many of the acknowledged greats of the profession, the holders of the named chairs from the most prestigious research universities still like to be on the program and to make their presence known at the AHA, as it is called within the discipline.

The elegant pale-blue-covered program for the 1969 convention gives a picture of the way it used to be. The typeface is neat and fine-lined, printed on thin, shiny paper that feels like old magazines when you touch it now. Publishers in their advertisements told of new history texts and monographs on familiar topics, organized according to familiar periodization. "Berkshire" then called to mind not the Conference in Women's History but a series for survey courses with paperbacks on the Crusades, the Renaissance, and the Age of Louis XIV. Holt, Rinehart, and Winston could publish a title like *Man in Western Civilization* without thinking twice.

C. Vann Woodward, a historian of the southern United States, presided over the association as the gentlemen, teacher-scholars met in Washington, D.C. to discuss their work, to initiate, to mend, or to maintain political and social ties. The sense of a network of established male historians paying their $15 membership dues and congregating once a year for drinks and discussion pervaded the listings of the panels. This was the world of traditional history told in the traditional manner: "City Aristocracies in the Renaissance"; "The Enlightenment and Society"; "The Comparative Study of Revolutions"; "The Diplomacy of 1848"; "The Merchant and Society in Early Modern England"; "American Agricultural Policy in the Twentieth Century."

Nothing in the 1969 program would suggest that this was the convention at which a new generation of feminist historians spoke out on behalf of women and women's history. Instead women hardly appeared at all. William O'Neill's history of the suffrage movement and feminism in the United States, *Everyone Was Brave* (1969), was the single work in women's history advertised in the program. Fourteen women historians gave papers out of a total of 380 session participants. They spoke most often on traditional topics, a few from the perspective of the new social and cultural history: "Spanish Towns in the Golden Age"; "Morality and Taxation in the Thirteenth and Fourteenth Centuries"; and on Beatrice and Sidney Webb as intellectuals in politics. Two of the women came, in fact, from other fields. A sociologist presented her work on "Student Activism in Chile," and a literary critic spoke on Van Wyck Brooks, both for a panel in United States cultural history. There were only two sessions on women's history. A female commentator presided over "Women in the United States in the Nineteenth Century," but all of the papers were presented by men. In contrast, two women scholars presented their research for a panel on Reformation women.[2]

A comparison of this 1969 program with that of the 1990 meeting in New York City demonstrates the impact of feminism on this aspect of the profession. In 1990, of the 140 panels, 38 (27%) specifically addressed issues of women's experience and explored history from the perspective of gender. The 268 women who chaired sessions, read papers, and gave comments made up 37% of the total participants.[3] They spoke on topics as varied as "Women and the Law in Renaissance Italy," "Women in Trades in Early Philadelphia," "The Paradoxes of Women's Citizenship," "Saints, Abbesses and Wives in Northern Europe from 700–1200," "Female Adolescence in the Early Twentieth Century," and "Contextualizing Feminism in France, Britain, and Latin America." In fact, women historians participated in sessions in every category of history, for example, on Lewis Mumford, Early English Colonization, the Deconstruction of the Nation State, Alliance Diplomacy of the French General Staff, the Construction of Jazz Memories, and the Renaissance Papacy.

Overall the program gives a clear sense of the AHA's efforts to become "the umbrella organization for all historians," an organization consciously more diverse and less elitist.[4] The 1990 AHA convention no longer seemed a conclave of white, male, ivy-league university professors. The listings of women officers and committee members reflected this more inclusive character of the AHA. In 1969 women constituted 4.5% of the Association hierarchy (5 of 112). No women served as elected members, or as delegates to other scholarly groups; rather all five were on the 17 appointed committees of the Association, including those that distributed prizes for exceptional works of scholarship. The hierarchy looked very different two decades later. In 1989–90 women held 42% of the elected offices (including three of the eleven seats on the governing council), 41% of the seats on standing committees, 45% on ad hoc and joint committees (including seven of twelve seats on the Program Committee for 1990). Women sat on all but four of the book-prize committees.[5] By their presence on the program, by the positions that they held within the AHA, women had proved themselves as professionals and gained parity within the organization. In addition, the many panels and papers devoted to women's topics and a gender perspective indicated the viability and significance of women's experiences to the study of history.

These changes, these accomplishments on behalf of women and women's history, did not evolve naturally or easily. Not all women historians agreed on goals and priorities. Change in one aspect of the Association's procedures, activities, or priorities, might create conflict in another. Yet, feminist historians, both women and men, argued and pressured continuously for the organization's transformation. Within the American Historical Association a pattern of advocacy and a successful strategy emerged throughout the decades from 1969 to 1990. First, feminists proved that exclusionary and inequitable practices existed. This led to the first efforts at remediation. Women historians were elected and appointed to offices and committees. Having gained a voice within the organization, they used their authority to highlight the institutional obstacles that they perceived throughout the profession in general and within the academy in particular. With statistics, with testimony from interviews, with carefully written reports, they built a case for an official policy statement by one or another AHA division. In this way the governing council of the AHA came to acknowledge and to work for the end of discriminatory practices within the profession. The organization sponsored ongoing studies of the status of women and their circumstances, issued professional guidelines on admission to graduate school as well as on hiring and promotion, published manuals and booklets addressed to women historians' needs and to further the teaching of women's history, and gave support to public policies such as passage of the Equal Rights Amendment.

FIRST CHALLENGES

In 1969 the historical profession had its own "institutional culture," its own "politics," a whole panoply of unspoken presumptions and attitudes that underlay and appeared to justify the exclusion or relegation to secondary status of all but a selected, homogeneous male elite. Even in 1990 some established writers of traditional histories continued to write with respect of these factors. They saw them as the way in which the American Historical Association had in its early decades transformed "a scholarly avocation," a hobby, "into a discipline, a source of authority in American intellectual life."[6]

Although the nineteenth- and early twentieth-century leaders of the AHA granted admission to women, especially those with multiple university degrees like Nellie Neilson of Mt. Holyoke and Lucy Maynard Salmon of Vassar, none of them imagined women participating in the same way as their male colleagues. In 1905 the men planned meetings in "smokers" while the women were expected to go to the tea organized by the Colonial Dames for the wives of members. Elizabeth Kimball attended the university "smokers" in the 1930s, but she went with another woman, not alone. Few women held executive or administrative positions before the 1960s. Though 19% of the members in 1920, women constituted only 5% of those in leadership roles. By 1933, only five women had sat on the executive council out of a total of 96 possible appointments. Although historians like Salmon, Emily Hickman of Douglass (then known as the New Jersey College for Women), and Mary W. Williams of Goucher insisted that women be treated equally with men in the profession, asked for statistical studies of jobs, ranks, and salaries, and put forward candidates for the presidency and other offices of the AHA, the membership at large remained indifferent.[7]

When in 1940 Nellie Neilson was elected second vice-president and thus placed in line for the presidency (in 1943) it was perhaps more a measure of the unorthodoxy of the year than of any change in the usual deprecating attitude towards women scholars. By the time of her nomination Neilson had achieved "elder statesman" status within the Association. An accomplished medievalist, she had studied at Bryn Mawr and with noted scholars in England. She had served on the AHA Council, on the editorial board of the *American Historical Review* (AHR), and been active in numerous British professional organizations.

By 1940, however, she had finally retired from Mt. Holyoke and was so fragile physically that she collapsed in the middle of her presidential address.[8]

In the 1930s and 1940s when Hickman, Williams, and other women scholars protested in AHA committee and business meetings, and nominated their colleagues for offices, they spoke not only as representatives of their institutions but also as members of the Berkshire Conference of Women Historians. Dorothy Ganfield Fowler commented proudly on Neilson's election, "We did get a president of the AHA."[9] This women's professional organization had been the idea of a few women scholars coming home on the train from the December 1929 AHA annual convention in North Carolina. On returning to their campuses they sent letters off to 67 women historians in the northeast and convened the first meeting for the following spring, in 1930.

Although the women scholars on that train must have felt the subtle and overt prejudices of their male peers, their initial reason for founding their own historians' group was not political. Calling themselves the Berkshire Conference of Women Historians, they described their organizing aim differently. They sought to create a "greater sense of comradeship in our craft," remembered Louise R. Loomis, one of the early members.[10] This was their first priority in the early years when 20 to 25 historians gathered for a country weekend at the end of the university and college term in May. By tradition, they chose a small inn with good food and resisted efforts to follow any kind of formal program. Instead the women scholars exchanged ideas on courses, programs, and research. Kimball explained, "Well, we walked and we talked . . . and we learned to know each other."[11]

In the early decades the members of the Berkshire Conference came from similar backgrounds, from families who believed in college and graduate degrees for their daughters. Most had been trained at one or another of the women's colleges founded after the Civil War. They held academic appointments at these same institutions, for example, Vassar, Wells, Bryn Mawr, Wellesley, Smith, Wheaton, and Hunter. Many even shared the same specialty, early British legal and economic history.[12] Participants like Viola Barnes of Mt. Holyoke scrupulously protected the groups' intellectual reputation by restricting the invitations for membership. Others, Hickman and Margaret Judson of Douglass, for example, worked to broaden the group. Hickman's membership, in fact, "gained the entrance of New Jersey which," Judson explained, "was always a controversial question." After World War II thinned the attendance, Judson, president from 1948 to 1950, broke with accepted procedure and invited Caroline Robbins of Bryn Mawr "without asking official approval."[13] Subsequently, just as Hickman had introduced her as a junior Douglass faculty member so Judson brought a

number of young colleagues in the late 1950s and 1960s, including Emiliana
Noether, Sandi E. Cooper, Mary Hartman, and Jane S. DeHart, all of whom
would play important roles in the more political future of the organization.[14]

The Berkshire Conference fulfilled its early purpose, creating a network of
women historians who could support each other in a variety of ways, both
intellectually and professionally. All valued the "regular informal contacts with
each other." Noether remembered why the meetings were significant for her:
"So that when I go to the annual AHA I see some faces I know and I'm not lost
in a sea of men who all look alike." In 1971 Noether brought Mary Beth Norton,
a young Harvard Ph.D. The only woman graduate student in her field by the end
of her first year (one dropped out and one transferred to another program), Norton
found the first dinner a kind of revelation. She noticed feeling "something
different," but "couldn't quite figure out why." Then she realized, "It was the
first time I had been in a group of professional women." In that moment, what
feminists identify as a coming to "historical self-consciousness," Norton saw
that "my entire environment had been male."[15]

Realization like Norton's of the overwhelming maleness of the historical
profession coupled with the political momentum of the women's movement at
the end of the 1960s caused the younger members of the Berkshire Conference
and the new generation of women historians throughout the United States to
become dissatisfied with the old customs and privileges, the prejudiced attitudes
of organizations like the American Historical Association. Many had already
identified themselves as feminists on their own campuses, or in their departments.
They used the occasion of the AHA annual meeting in 1969 to challenge the
established hierarchy and to protest what they saw as overt discrimination within
the organization. Many in the profession remember the 1969 convention as
the time when radical and leftist historians nominated Staughton Lynd for the
presidency of the Association, loudly argued politics at the business meeting, and
pressed for resolutions against the war in Southeast Asia. In fact, the feminists'
actions—Berenice A. Carroll's petition to the AHA Council and the founding
meetings of the new caucus of feminist historians, the Coordinating Committee
for Women in the Historical Profession—had the greater significance in the long
term.[16]

Berenice A. Carroll, a member of the political science department at the
University of Illinois–Urbana, initiated the challenge and the protest in September 1969. As Carroll remembered it, her decision to speak out was part of her
general peace and anti-war activism at the time; she had been the New Jersey
representative to the national board of SANE (Committee for a Sane Nuclear
Policy). Trained as an historian she had left Douglass when the head of the
department told her that "they wanted to hire a man." There were already so

many women in the department, she was told, and anyway she "would be likely to leave them to follow [her] husband elsewhere."[17] Carroll's gender and the strict application of nepotism rules kept her from being given a permanent position by the history department at the University of Illinois. Instead she accepted an appointment, later tenured, in the political science department.

It was because of this set of circumstances that Carroll came to be at the fall 1969 convention of the American Political Science Association (APSA) when feminists, including members of the Chicago Women's Liberation Union, protested discriminatory practices within that organization. Carroll joined the first executive committee of the women's caucus they and like-minded colleagues established. She remembered deciding without hesitation to pose similar challenges to the members of the historical profession. All that year, in fact, she kept "finding that wherever I went when I raised these issues a lot of people responded."

Carroll was also secretary-treasurer of the Conference on Peace Research in History. While in New York for one of its meetings she consulted Carl Schorske, a well-known historian of Europe who was president of the Conference and also an AHA council member. He suggested that she petition the Association. Using the APSA resolutions as a guide, she circulated a draft to friends and colleagues and to other women activists whom she hoped would join her in establishing "an independent women's caucus." The result was a petition of women's grievances and plans for a meeting of women historians at the convention in December.[18]

The AHA Council considered Carroll's petition in October and using her wording voted to establish an ad hoc committee to investigate the charges of discrimination, to determine the status of women within the profession, and to "publish and circulate widely the results" of its findings. They subsequently asked Willie Lee Rose, a prize-winning historian of U.S. Reconstruction, to chair the group.[19] Meanwhile at the Convention in December, Carroll gathered with 17 women historians to organize what would come to be called the "CCWHP", the Coordinating Committee on Women in the Historical Profession. At their first public meeting 100 people endorsed her petition with only one amendment, on the significance of women's history.[20]

This amended petition was forwarded immediately and became the basis for the first resolutions of the CCWHP to the newly constituted Rose Committee. Speaking both "the language of power and the language of scholarship," it became in many ways the feminist blueprint for the American Historical Association for the next 20 years. It asked the AHA to condemn all forms of discrimination against women at every stage of their careers. A formal grievance procedure was to be instituted. The petition called for acknowledgment that combining "career and family responsibilities" affected women differently than men. It urged the AHA to endorse "a flexible attitude" toward part-time study, reconsideration of nepotism rules forbidding the employment of wives and husbands, university-supported day-care, and federal legislation allowing child-care as a business deduction. Given the need for ongoing advocacy the resolutions called for time and facilities at AHA conventions for meetings of feminist groups, space in AHA publications for their reports, and the opportunity for women to participate at all levels of the organization. The petition also looked to the future and called on the AHA to "actively support the recruitment of women into the historical profession" and "to stimulate scholarship, research and discussion" of the neglected field of women's history.[21]

With the CCWHP resolutions in hand, and a formal AHA mandate to evaluate the status of women historians (including individual accusations of discrimination) and to formulate recommendations for the Council, the Rose Committee had its first meeting in April of 1970. For the next eight months the six members gathered data. They sent questionnaires to 30 representative colleges and universities; they visited campuses and interviewed students and faculty. Their investigations clearly documented prejudice against women and disproved claims that secondary status came from women's own lack of commitment. Instead the Committee found that women historians not only desired employment, but showed evidence of high productivity. Contrary to popular misconceptions, women were more productive when married, not less. In the words of the Report, the members concluded that the findings "leave us no doubt that prompt action on the part of the AHA is required."[22]

The recommendations of the Rose Committee went from general statements of policy to specific suggestions on action. Echoing the amended version of Carroll's petition, the members called for "formal disapproval of discrimination" against women in admission to graduate programs, hiring, and promotion, and condemnation of the adverse "conditions of employment" under which so many worked. With this acknowledgment of the existence of sexism and the pledge to eliminate discriminatory practices, the AHA was "to work actively" toward encouraging more women to join the profession by "enhancing the opportunities available to them."

To realize these policies the Rose Committee recommended the creation of a permanent committee on women historians. Only in this way, the Report argued, could the "sustained attention and pressure indispensable to an advance in the status of women" be achieved. This "continuing surveillance of institutional policy" would mean yearly studies of ranks and salaries with model departments applauded and publicized. Those discriminated against would, through the new committee, have access to advice and remedies. Encouraged by the committee, the AHA was to support history departments in their efforts to alleviate the kinds of problems occasioned by women's different circumstances—restrictions on part-time degree candidates, inflexible policies on transfers of credits, nepotism, and implicit and explicit penalties for birthing and maternity leaves. The Report also urged the participation of more women in all aspects of the AHA and cooperation with women's advocacy groups in other professional organizations. As the Rose Committee explained, the consequences of these policies would be positive and far-reaching: "To increase the opportunities open to women in the field of history is to advance the quality of the profession itself."[23] The AHA Council endorsed the Report in its entirety and recommended its provisions to the annual December business meeting, thus making the goals of the Rose Committee the official goals of the American Historical Association.

Not all women historians agreed with the action Carroll and the other feminists had taken. Some scholars within the AHA were openly hostile, even members of the Berkshire Conference who in earlier years had taken the lead in pressing for women's professional recognition and participation. Carroll recalled an officer of the Berkshire Conference in 1969 "looking at us very askance." Though ready to speak about discrimination against women scholars, they preferred to work more quietly to bring about change. Berkshire Conference members were not alone in fearing that the young feminists were "too abrasive" and "too demanding." Older women historians found the language of petitions and lists of grievances "too strident." They saw women's scholarly legitimacy which they had worked so hard to establish endangered by the direct phrases and militant stance of the feminist historians. "Radicalism," caucuses, and resolutions to the business meeting looked "political" in a world that they continued to believe was above politics.[24]

By 1978, however, many of those in the Berkshire Conference who had been skeptical and disapproving spoke with pride of the feminists' accomplishments within the AHA. At the Fiftieth Anniversary meeting of the Conference Louise Dalby recalled a subsequent achievement: seven women nominated by petition, and one who "came within ten votes of winning." "We took a lot of flak," the elder scholar remembered, but now feminist candidates were regularly on the ballot. "I realized," Dalby concluded, "that women could be good historians and political activists at the same time."[25]

THE FEMINIST COALITION

Throughout its history the Committee on Women Historians (CWH) has continued to define its primary role in the terms of Carroll's 1969 petition and the original 1970 mandate from the American Historical Association to the Rose

Committee. In 1981 the CWH advocated the advancement of the status of women through "surveillance of institutional politics and practice" and the development of "the sustained attention and pressure" needed to remove the implicit and explicit institutional obstacles to women's equitable advancement. The strategies to combat discrimination have remained the same through the years. Periodic collection of data from representative colleges and universities (with a 75% response rate in 1983, for example) gives "a current picture of the standing of women in the historical profession." In each instance, the statistics have proved women's continuing relative disadvantage to men.[26] From the data, graduate admissions and hiring and promotion guidelines have been formulated, first in 1981, then in 1984, and 1990. Formal endorsement by the AHA Council followed, making the guidelines official Association policy; then came publication and widespread dissemination by the AHA. Repeatedly the Committee emphasized not only the lack of equity demonstrated by "the presence of systematic discrimination against women" depriving them "of their rightful place in the profession," but also the effects on the profession as a whole with the loss "of the full benefit of the talents of an increasing portion of its members."[27]

In addition to establishing admissions and employment guidelines, from its first meetings, the Committee addressed the immediate grievances of women historians. The Rose Report had in part been based on complaints from individuals, accounts that had convinced the members that "the problems appearing in our letters are general."[28] Initially the Committee sent federal HEW guidelines to department chairs and dealt directly with specific grievances. In the early years of the Committee the administration of the AHA was wary of playing what it considered to be a direct "political" role in such matters. In 1974 the Council refused the Committee's request to "act as amicus curiae," though it did not discount the possibility in specific cases.[29]

From 1974 on the Committee accepted that primary responsibility for complaints should go to the Professional Division of the Association but found other ways to support and encourage women scholars. As explained in one of its 1980 publications, "integrating previously excluded groups into a white male collectivity is not easily or automatically accomplished."[30] Until the early 1980s members gave advice to individual complainants anonymously. They wrote pamphlets on the practical realities of being a woman in the profession. The first one, entitled *Survival Manual for Women (and Other) Historians*, was ready for sale at the 1975 AHA convention. The editors, Eleanor Straub and Suzanne Lebsock, described the purpose of the *Manual*: "The history profession operates for the most part by unwritten rules and historians who have had no coaching in these folkways often come to grief." By committing the "rules" to paper and making them public women could begin to understand how to act in their own best interests.[31] Succeeding editions of the *Manual* have attempted to alert women to all of the potential hazards by covering more topics: how to choose and apply to graduate school; how to survive a course, select a supervisor, or apply for grants; how to make a case for tenure, deal with sexual harassment, or deal with unemployment.

Given the documented sexism within the profession, as early as 1972 members of the Committee in collaboration with the women historians' caucus, the CCWHP, collected sample complaint forms and model class action suits, and sponsored affirmative-action workshops and panels at regional and national professional meetings. The situation had not changed significantly by the 1990s. The 1991 *Survival Manual* described shifting jurisdictions and confusing or unwritten procedures. Each of the three editions of the *Manual* assumed that women would need to know how to initiate such a suit. In addition, the authors encouraged readers to seek out senior women scholars on their own campuses and at professional meetings, and to join or organize their own women's group. "The female survival rate," they explained, "rises dramatically when caucuses go to work." Should a woman wish to make formal charges of discriminatory practices such a group would be essential.[32]

To answer department chairs who claimed that they "wanted to hire a woman, but could not find one qualified for the position," the CWH sponsored publication of three editions of a Directory of Women Historians (1975, 1981, 1988). The Directory, originally a suggestion from the Rose Committee, began as a card file in 1971, became a computerized list by 1973, and then a book in 1975 with names arranged by regional specialty, by period of expertise, by topics, and by current occupation. The 1988 edition listed 1,300 women historians in all fields and periods, from every part of the United States.

In its early years the Committee used a variety of tactics to focus members' attention on all aspects of gender discrimination. At the behest of the Committee, the Association sponsored mailings of the hiring guidelines to history departments across the country and publication of CWH recommendations and reports. (The Committee has had its own featured column in the newsletter called "Roses and Thorns.") By the early 1980s the Committee had established that it should have two slots on the annual convention program, often co-sponsored with the CCWHP and its Conference Group on Women's History (CGWH). Traditionally one investigates some aspect of the status of women in the profession, the other presents new research in women's history.[33] In 1972 a panel presented suggestions on "Life Styles for Women Historians." Mary Frances Berry spoke in 1973 on the ways in which the government interacted with universities to improve women's status. A 1976 panel addressed the problems of women in part-time employment. The status of minority women formed the basis of the panel in

1981. More recently the time was used to take stock, to assess the effectiveness of feminists' efforts and initiatives within the profession and the Association.

Historians have traditionally been evaluated for hiring, tenure, and promotion on the basis of their research. Research became known through presentations at professional meetings and through publication. Often one led to the other, participation in a panel gave importance to a work and access to a journal for the scholar. The CWH came to realize that certain unspoken traditions and openly prejudicial decisions kept women from equitable participation in this process. Inequities in convention participation became obstacles to publication of their work, to the awarding of prizes, and thus to the recognition needed either for initial employment or advancement. The Committee looked for ways to end the discriminatory practices.

The AHA annual convention was a professional meeting that the Committee believed it could influence. It followed its usual strategy of establishing the fact of discrimination through statistical studies, then pressuring the organization for redress. In part as a result of its efforts, the number of women participants increased from 3.9% in 1969 to 16.2% in 1979.[34] The percentage continued to rise in the 1980s, and in 1990 more than adequately represented the percentage of women in the Association overall. As a significant number of women spoke on women or gender, the increased number not only indicated the broader acceptance of women historians, but also of women's history and the gender perspective as viable subjects of historical inquiry and analysis.

This acceptance of women's participation and of women's topics led to a different but no less familiar consequence, the potential marginalization of women scholars. For although women historians and their research appeared more often on the program, they were segregated, separate from panels perceived to be "mainstream history," being analyzed by "regular" historians. In 1983, for example, 47% of the panels had no female participants.[35] Beginning in 1982 the Committee took up the question of this unspoken, subtly discriminatory practice. Although individual chairs of the Program Committee expressed their sympathy with the problem and informally encouraged the principle of "gender balancing," it was not until 1987 that the Council accepted the addition of an explicit proviso to the program guidelines. In 1990 the program committee requested (but did not require) changes in all proposals composed of exclusively female or male participants. Of 140 panels presented, seven failed to meet the new guidelines: two had only women, five had only male participants.[36]

As another way of giving women historians access to publication, and thus validation as scholars, the CWH challenged the policies of *The American Historical Review* (AHR), the official journal of the AHA. The prestige of the journal assured recognition to those who appeared in its pages. Yet, both the authors chosen and the book reviewers assigned were overwhelmingly male historians. The CWH reasoned that the disproportionate number of male authors and reviewers in the AHR indicated that women historians had been competing for inclusion in its pages at a disadvantage. In the late 1970s and 1980s the Committee followed its strategy of meticulous counting to establish a case and then advocacy for a specific policy change. Members of the Committee monitored the AHR and forwarded their findings and the concerns of the CWH to the editors. Changes in editorial policies came as advocates of more traditional histories retired. The percentage of women reviewers steadily increased in the 1980s to between 18 and 20% by 1990 (18% in 1990). The numbers of female authors remained more variable, from highs of 27% in 1984 and 33% in 1990, in years with special issues on women's history and gender, to a low of 6%. The average of approximately 15% included scholars writing on all kinds of historical topics, not just from the new perspectives.[37]

In the two decades of the Committee's existence there has been a clear increase in the numbers of AHA book prizes going to women historians, especially since 1980. From 1980 to 1990, 20 women (representing 12% of the recipients) have won prizes in 17 possible categories. These prestigious awards reflect both the increased number in the profession and their acceptance as scholars, not only in women's history but in all areas of historical inquiry. The establishment in 1983 of the Joan Kelly Prize gave particular recognition to scholars working in the fields of women's history and feminist theory. To date, women have won all of the awards in this category.[38]

At the 1990 AHA Convention the participants in the CWH panel applauded the Committee's achievements, the principles established, the practical gains realized. At the same time they admitted the continuing resistance within the profession and the entrenched nature of sexist prejudices in some institutions. The 1990 Annual Report and the 1990 Guidelines indicated what had and had not been accomplished by the Committee in its 20 years of feminist advocacy. Its 1990 periodic survey of women historians' status showed that one major goal had been realized: more women had entered the profession, completed their training, and acquired a first job, often one leading to consideration for tenure. Still, inequities persisted. Joan Jensen, chair of the Committee in 1990, spoke of "indirect discrimination." Statistics continued to show veiled but no less effective opposition to women's promotions within departments and to women's salary levels being made equal to those of their male peers.[39] The situation of minority women, whether African American, Latina, Asian or Native American, remained even more inequitable. In 1988 these women represented 2% of all history Ph.D.s, as compared with 8.3%, the number receiving doctorates in all fields. Only a serious commitment on the part of the AHA and separate initiatives on behalf of these women (and men) would make a difference. The establishment of a Committee on Minority Historians in 1990 demonstrated the priority to be given to their situation in the future.[40]

Over the course of the 20 years of its existence the CWH discovered that some problems originally identified in the CCWHP resolutions and the Rose Report had intensified, not ameliorated, with the increased numbers of women in the profession. For example, the 1990 Guidelines called on departments to establish "flexible and creative responses to the needs of two-career couples," especially when one or the other spouse was offered employment by a college or university outside of a major urban area. The Guidelines protested a new aspect of salary discrimination. As women and men had come to retire, past inequities in salaries affected their pensions. Women with the same years of service, at the same level of advancement, received less. The Committee recommended "lump sum adjustments" to assure women benefits equal to men's at the same rank. Lastly, the 1990 Committee drew attention to the new ways in which universities and colleges still avoided equitable hiring practices in their job searches. Some history departments failed to advertise, some tailored the description to a specific individual, or when applicants applied altered the criteria so as to disqualify those who had already submitted their documents. In addition, the most well-endowed institutions created new categories of employment that were off the salary scale and tailored to the interests and experience of a particular scholar. Negotiations remained private. Public competition, in fact, served no purpose; for only one person, usually a man, qualified.[41]

The relevance in 1990 of the 1969 resolutions of the Coordinating Committee on Women in the Historical Profession was but one way in which the CCWHP continued to be of significance in the work of the AHA Committee on Women Historians. From the first letter sent out by Berenice A. Carroll in the fall of 1969 describing her wish to create "an independent Women's Caucus . . . to thrash out all that needs to be done and keep the pressure on, information flowing, etc.," the CCWHP performed a variety of collaborative functions. In the early years, the CCWHP played the radical role in this feminist coalition. Sandi E. Cooper, "national chairwoman" from 1972 to 1974, expressed the group's prevailing view in their newsletter: "We must request the more extreme and the more 'exorbitant' if we are to get anywhere."[42] Cooper, who had only been prevented from participation in the 1969 founding meetings because she was giving birth to her daughter, came to her feminism while in Europe doing research for her dissertation. As she described it, she "slowly slid into things," from a new perspective on the Vietnam War to efforts "to create space in the history profession for peace studies," to energetic advocacy for women. On one of her characteristic pale purple dittos sent to the CCWHP Steering Committee, she defined her goal for the organization: "being prickly and nettly and thorny and never being satisfied."[43]

In this radical role the CCWHP pressured the AHA in ways the formal committee could not, especially in the early years when, as one member described it, the CWH had "a sense of being under siege."[44] The mid to late 1970s when Joan Kelly, Jane S. DeHart, and Joan W. Scott chaired the AHA Committee, and Cooper, Joan Hoff-Wilson, and Catherine Prelinger led the CCWHP, were years of particularly fruitful collaboration. The CCWHP contributed ideas, energy, and lobbying skills. For example, in 1972 and 1973, the CCWHP presented resolutions at AHA annual meetings and lobbied with the AHA Council for continued commitment to women's concerns. It protested when budgetary cuts, politics, and different priorities threatened to undermine the effectiveness of the CWH. The approval in April of 1973 of a "two-year full-time appointment of an Assistant Executive Secretary" with responsibility for women's questions, and subsequent formal recognition of the Committee itself in the reorganization of the AHA structure, ensured the CWH's survival as an effective advocacy group.[45] In addition, many important CWH policies originated with the CCWHP or came to completion only with its assistance: employment guidelines and grievance procedures; women's increased participation at AHA conventions and provisions for child-care during the sessions; workshops, a pamphlet, and two NEH-funded summer institutes on the teaching of women's history (in 1976 at Sarah Lawrence, in 1978 at Stanford); the establishment of the Joan Kelly Prize.[46]

Finally, the CCWHP was always "a source of talent." To contribute names of candidates and to advance women within the AHA fit with other early goals of the group. From its inception the leaders saw the CCWHP "democratizing . . . professional organizations and . . . creating a supportive feminist environment within them." It took an active part in efforts to make the AHA more broadly representative of historians from diverse backgrounds and in differing professional circumstances.[47] The first priority in 1972–73 was election of feminists to AHA offices. Cooper submitted a list to the chair of the nominating committee, candidates "who are best known for their commitment to the advancement of women." When the 1972 choices became public and Cooper discovered that women had been nominated but not those suggested by the CCWHP, she tried a different tactic. She sent letters to the nominees asking their views on key topics and planned to publish their answers in the CCWHP newsletter.[48]

Beginning in 1974 Cooper's idea of questionnaires to all candidates for AHA offices and publication of their answers became a regular feature of the Coordinating Committee's newsletter. In 1980 a CCWHP letter to the chair of the AHA nominating committee even queried the names submitted by others for the presidency, men known to be "insensitive to women's and minority concerns." Such a choice, the CCWHP explained, "reflects disdain for the concerns of the majority."[49] In the end, however, it was feminist representation on the nominating committee itself and not suggestions from outside groups that made the difference. From 1974 on, one-third to one-half of the members were women.[50] Natalie Zemon Davis's election as president in 1985 was considered a victory for the feminist coalition. (She served as vice-president in 1986 and president in 1987.)

While working to diversify the AHA, the CCWHP actively sought to broaden its own membership. Leaders encouraged women at every stage of their career to join. An undergraduate and a graduate student were among the volunteers who served on the original steering committee. The CCWHP sought to foster similar groups across the United States, and through a process of affiliation created a powerful feminist network. In 1989 there were 14 affiliates representing every section of the country and many major urban areas. All helped to organize exchange of research among members; some also dealt with issues of employment and women's status within the profession.[51]

In the 1970s the CCWHP and the CWH tested this network in their efforts to help women historians. When universities and colleges began to hire fewer faculty and to allow positions to lapse, when funders gave less money for innovative research, the CCWHP supported a variety of remedial initiatives and pressured the AHA to give its endorsement as well. Women historians became particularly vulnerable to what Cooper called "the growing, gnawing backlash at NEH." Resistance to women's concerns increased within the AHA. For example, opponents within the organization labelled resolutions for equitable hiring practices as "quota systems." This was reverse discrimination that would deprive qualified (white) men, lower standards, and interfere with "academic freedom." In a 1973 AHA-sponsored panel on employment, an established male historian at Princeton suggested that the profession ignore the employment crisis. He explained that "a kind of normal 'social darwinism,' will eventually solve the problem."[52]

As advocates for women historians and as part of its commitment to research in women's history, the CCWHP decided on a more active role. It facilitated study groups for discussion of new work and endorsed organizations like the Institute for Research in History in New York City, which sponsored grant applications for members and found funding for members' projects, including specialized conferences, documentary films, museum exhibits, and a monograph series in women's history. The CCWHP policy of support for "unaffiliated scholars" became a CWH recommendation to the AHA Council. The group's letter to university presidents and department chairs on offering institutional affiliation and thus library access to "independent scholars" became the model for a similar AHA mailing. By February of 1981 the CCWHP could report that 26 academic institutions had granted affiliated status to scholars.[53]

Also in the 1970s cooperation with the CCWHP took the CWH into feminist issues of significance outside the academy. At their initiative, and as a result of the pressure they mobilized, the AHA broke with its long-standing effort to appear apolitical on national women's issues. By the fall of 1977 a number of professional organizations had voted to boycott those states that had not yet passed the Equal Rights Amendment to the constitution by refusing to hold their annual conventions in their cities. D'Ann Campbell, chair of the Organization of American Historians' Committee on the Status of Women, had already introduced motions in her organization; she encouraged those in the AHA to do the same.[54] In cooperation with the CCWHP, the CWH voted a resolution calling for a boycott. Presented with the resolution, the AHA Executive Council chose to submit the issue to the members by mail. When to its surprise the motion passed, the Council claimed procedural irregularities, tabled the resolution, and postponed discussion until the next annual meeting in December of 1978. Feminists at the August Berkshire Conference on the History of Women organized a petition to resurrect the motion. The Annual Report of the CWH, published in November, was filled with discussion of the issue. Joan W. Scott and Joan Hoff-Wilson, chairs of the CWH and CCWHP, used their networks to gather signatures of AHA members favoring the resolution. The CCWHP used its network to encourage AHA members to withhold their annual dues from the Association (placing them in an escrow fund). Scott and Hoff-Wilson lobbied the Professional Division of the AHA to pressure the Council. The feminist coalition prepared for a public battle at the business meeting of the Convention. Then just at the last minute the Council voted the resolution through. Scott announced the triumph at the CWH annual breakfast meeting.[55]

Historians interpret the AHA's endorsement of the ERA and its boycott as but one of the ways in which the Association had been changed not only for women but for all historians who for one reason or another did not fit the traditional image of the university scholar. Alice Kessler-Harris, a former chair of the CWH, believed that the Committee in particular had forced the organization "to confront issues that it would have preferred to ignore," everything from its nominating practices to the significance of an after dinner alumni gathering.[56] Committees, studies, guidelines, networks, directories, manuals, all guaranteed new voices and new participants. These accomplishments could be quantified.

Feminists also pointed to less tangible, but no less significant changes. Cooper felt that historians like herself had challenged the "lock step of the academic career," "transforming some of the human relations of the profession" along the way. Just as the stereotype of the male historian had been questioned, so had that of the isolated female scholar. Kessler-Harris went even further in her positive analysis of change. "Women," she explained, had become by 1990 "part of the clock-work," "part of the mechanism," fully integral to the functioning of the organization.[57] Despite its exclusionary origins, of all of the areas of the professional historian's world, the AHA had proved the most responsive to feminist challenges and had been most affected by feminism.

8.

MEN'S HISTORY REVISITED

UNIVERSITY SCHOLARS
AND SCHOLARSHIP

Over 20 years ago Gerda Lerner called for "New Approaches to American Women's History," and Berenice A. Carroll and other feminists petitioned the American Historical Association to investigate the status of women historians. In surveying the impact of all that was initiated in those years, feminist scholars have been both encouraged and discouraged by what has changed and by what has remained the same. For feminist historians it appears to be a question of "a glass half full or a glass half empty."

Some cannot believe that so much has happened in so short a time. Historians usually think in terms of many decades, even centuries, as the measure for altering relationships between groups, especially for relationships as ancient and as ingrained as those governed by gender in Western culture. They perceive a clear feminist impact on history both as a discipline and as a profession. Alice Kessler-Harris had called the creation of the new field of women's history a "great intellectual leap." The vast numbers and varieties of course offerings and publications attest to its significance and its continuing vitality as an area of historical inquiry. Since the late 1960s scholarship has moved from descriptions of what men said and did to women, to narratives of what women themselves accomplished and of how they viewed their own lives. A third generation of feminist scholars trained in women's, not men's, history now defines new perspectives and priorities. Increasingly varied and sophisticated analyses of the hows and whys of women's experiences across time, place, class, and race appear with each new trade and academic publisher's listing. Without question, as one feminist has phrased it, "women's history has arrived."[1]

Acknowledgment of women's history and of women scholars' accomplishments has come from the profession at large. Between 1981 and 1990 four women won the prestigious Bancroft prize in United States history: Mary P. Ryan, *Cradle of the Middle Class: the Family in Oneida County, New York, 1780–1865* (1981); Suzanne Lebsock, *The Free Women of Petersburg: Status and Culture in a Southern Town, 1784–1860* (1984); Jacqueline Jones, *Labor of Love, Labor of Sorrow: Black Women, Work, and the Family from Slavery to the Present* (1985); and Laurel Ulrich Thatcher, *The Midwife's Tale: The Life of Martha Ballard Based on Her Diary, 1785–1812* (1990). Women hold research professorships and named chairs in universities across the country. Even though inequities persist, women have become a significant presence in every kind of academic institution and professional meeting.

As Ellen DuBois has pointed out, however, to be honored as colleagues was but one of the ways in which feminists wanted to have an impact on the discipline and the profession. To have the study of women included does not necessarily mean that there has been any alteration of the ways in which all history is conceived and written. DuBois asked in 1985 "to what degree has the study of women become part of the general scholarly inquiry," to what degree is it seen as relevant even to research previously focused exclusively on men? Has it caused the adoption of analytical syntheses encompassing all people's experience? In short, have feminists changed the basic framework of historical study?[2]

For some male historians the new feminist scholarship has had this effect. As early as 1981, Carl Degler believed that women's history had caused "historians to devise fresh methods for analyzing the past" and had required them "to rethink some of their old formulations . . . [and] explanations for events and developments." Women scholars have shown the value of interdisciplinary approaches, of new research materials and techniques, of "personal sources" like oral testimony, diaries, letters, and the everyday artifacts of ordinary lives. As Degler explained, historians saw a new history "because new evidence has been discovered, and also because we now have new eyes, that is a new sensitivity, with which to examine the past."[3]

Women historians and their research have enriched the writing and increased the analytical sophistication of social and cultural histories. This, in turn, has enhanced the stature of these two approaches within the discipline. For example, historians like Linda K. Kerber, Darline Gay Levy, Harriet Branson Applewhite, and Lynn Hunt have explained how different eras conceptualized and used "gender." They have demarcated the changing meanings of "feminine" and "masculine," and thus broadened our understanding of the ideologies of the early republic of the United States and the first years of France's 1789 revolution. Historians now write of the "gendering" of the state and of citizenship. They describe how women responded. In the United States, for example, they became "the mothers of the republic," the custodians of the family and of "civic morality."[4]

Family historians have acknowledged the ways in which social pressures and historians' constructions have altered the reality and the concept of "family" over time. They now describe women's roles and experiences as distinct from men's, and thus have moved their analyses beyond the statistical impersonality of the first studies to rich, multifaceted, interpretive narratives. In work like Linda Gordon's on nineteenth- and twentieth-century social welfare recipients in Boston, and Elaine Tyler May's on suburban families of the 1950s, historians have come to appreciate the complexity not only of relations between the culture, the state, and the family, but also within the family itself.[5]

Suzanne Lebsock believes that this ability to see diversity and difference is "the hallmark of much of the best of women's historical writing in the 1980s." She was thinking of the "conscious exploration of divisions among women along the lines of race and class," but attention to the intricacy and variety of human experience characterizes all of the most original scholarship in women's history.[6] Some feminists suggest that their decision to document and interpret these diverse memories of the past has helped to force other historians, even those working from traditional perspectives and in traditional men's history categories like politics and economics, to new thinking. Male analysts of the discipline see an actual "fragmentation" of historical studies, a "proliferation of historical knowledge," that "wonderfully broadens and deepens our appreciation of human experience." James Kloppenberg has applauded feminist and minority historians for bringing a "self-consciousness" about the ways in which societies have constructed their past. He foresaw all historians acknowledging the political nature of their own writings, the "subjective" choices they have made when deciding which of the many possible recreations they will record. Such awareness Kloppenberg hoped would "at last doom the simple-minded objectivist myth." Mary Hartman has been even more optimistic. She believes that historians are in "the process of changing all the ways of seeing history." They are embarked on a radical "re-visioning" of the past, nothing less than "dismantling the notion that there is a real history out there" and accepting the idea that there are many historical "truths" and not just one.[7]

Other feminist scholars take a more pessimistic view of their impact on the discipline and the profession. They agree that women's history is now accepted as more than a politically inspired "fad," but see its effects as "still modest" compared to all that should have changed. They use words like "appropriation," "containment," "marginalization," "ghettoization" to describe what they think has happened. Women's history has become part of regular course offerings, women's studies has achieved permanent status as a separate interdisciplinary specialty often with its own faculty and institutes. There are journals of women's history, prizes, and conferences. Overt discrimination against women professionals and against study of women's past is over. As Judith Bennett has explained, however, more subtle kinds of resistance and denigration still have their effect. For example, scholars have sometimes substituted "gender" for "women" as more neutral and more acceptable, and with a resulting loss of feminist perspective. Even worse the institutionalization of studies of women has "too often [been] at the cost of isolation and segregation." For many it is as Gay Gullickson described it: "From my perspective, women's historians are like unexpected and uninvited guests. We have arrived, but we have been left to fend for ourselves, unfeted and unwelcomed."[8]

A whole host of assumptions still accompanies the hiring of a woman historian whether or not she specialized in women's history or some other field. The very presence of a woman can be seen as a threat to "traditional values," the admission of someone who will foster "the interests of marginal people." Appointing a woman may still be associated with a change in, and by implication a lowering of, "standards." It has remained convenient to identify women scholars by their gender first. Departments proudly point to the female member of staff and suggest that her hiring fulfills not only the need for "gender balance" in personnel but also in course offerings. They presume that all women can teach women's history and conversely that anyone trained in this field cannot teach anything else.[9]

Whereas in the 1930s and 1940s a successful woman historian was perceived in one way and evaluated by fixed criteria, however inapplicable, so now with the same persistence, there is another image and another means of devaluation, equally inappropriate for its uniformity. Formerly a woman historian was supposed to "think and act like a man"; now she is assumed to think and act like a feminist. The suggestion that feminist scholars and their research, especially if it is on women's topics, are "essentially second-rate" lingers, even if unspoken. For too many in the profession, according to Berenice A. Carroll, "the fundamental attitude towards women and particularly the assessment of women's intellectual work has not changed."[10] In history, "original" scholarship remains the property of men. As a result, although hiring guidelines have been established and hiring practices made public, women seldom receive the most lucrative and prestigious appointments. Into the 1990s the "exceptional" historian was likely to be male, and the "senior woman faculty member" "a rare creature."[11]

Those who are dissatisfied with the progress of the last 20 years also have a negative view of their colleagues' responses to feminists' efforts to reformulate analytical frameworks, to find ways to write about both women's and men's experiences. In the late 1970s and 1980s social historians often expressed their commitment to the "integration" of women's and men's histories. Even so, in the early 1980s few of the radical male scholars read feminist works or viewed their authors "as part of the community of radicals."[12] Recent studies of immigration and labor history showed that many of the techniques and insights of women's research had been accepted, but that in their writing, the major scholars continued to subsume women's experiences under the rubric of "the family."

Immigration historians ascribed no significance to women's unique role in creating the networks and communities essential for survival, and showed no understanding of the ways in which women facilitated the process of acculturation for their men and their children. For example, historians wrote on Irish immigration and described men's problems and triumphs, but without ever indicating that the majority of immigrants from that country were women. Stories of factories and "no Irish need apply" emphasized the effects of industrialization on men's lives. These accounts left no place for analysis of women's separate success at finding employment in domestic service and their adjustments to urbanization, the aspect of American social change of consequence to their lives. Hispanic women have had similar treatment in histories of the United States frontier; they were rarely mentioned, and then only in relation to the men of their families. Few studies of Asian immigrants have noted the different experiences of the small number of women allowed entry in the overwhelmingly male populations, or analyzed the effects such gender-skewed ratios had on the development of Asian-American institutions.[13]

Despite the new research on women and labor and the enthusiastic endorsement given to the methods and analytical insights devised to bring out women's experiences, "working-class history has remained a preserve of male workers." For the majority of labor historians, men were workers and only secondarily members of families. Men did skilled, waged labor and organized unions. In contrast, women were primarily wives, mothers, and daughters who did not unionize and only occasionally entered the labor force to do unskilled work.

Fixed images such as these masked the significance of gender and ignored the ways in which it "decisively shaped" the realities and the histories of waged labor, of work, and unionization. For example, gender affected definitions of skilled and unskilled; many women's skilled jobs in factories and service industries have been devalued in relation to men's. All people's work and family lives intersect and interact. Men, as well as women, have gone in and out of the labor force. The concepts of workers' "resistance" and "consent" await new analysis from a gender perspective. Unions discouraged women's participation or excluded them altogether, yet women found alternative ways to protest unfair employer practices and poor working conditions. Feminist labor historians argue that there has been neither an "essential" female worker, nor an "essential" male worker, no simple duality of difference, of subordination and domination. Rather, all lives demonstrate "the coexistence of multiple gender meanings" across time, place, and circumstance.[14]

In the late 1980s traditional stereotypes and old ways of perceiving women persisted even in the work of leading social historians known for their studies of the interrelationships between women and men. In a review of two books by women scholars, Lawrence Stone listed what he called his "ten commandments" to "govern the writing of women's history at any time and in any place." Some "commandments" all feminist scholars would agree with; others jar. He insisted that historians cannot consider women "a distinct caste," nor write about them "except in relation to men and children." The vast majority of scholars make no equivalent proviso for men, as if males could be described outside of their gender, as if men's experience had a neutral universality that women's history could never hope to attain. Joan W. Scott has explained this reluctance and resistance to viewing women and men in the same ways. "What is at stake," she believes, "is a refusal to recognize the particularity and the specificity of men." When feminists suggest that there has been a "masculinist" as well as a "feminist" history, critics raise the old-fashioned cry of "subjectivity." Even Stone included as one of his commandments a warning that feminists "shalt not" allow their ideology to color their analyses.[15]

The "accusations of partisanship and the fears of politicization," as Alice Kessler-Harris characterized it, continue to be powerful critical devices despite the widespread acceptance within the profession of the ways in which all historians can be influenced by the attitudes and circumstances of their times.[16] Feminist scholars remember the reviews of Linda Gordon's 1976 history of the United States birth-control movement: the *Journal of Social History* claimed she was "getting the goods on chauvinists"; the *American Historical Review* described her as "enslaved to politics." The *Journal of American History* stated it most succinctly: "This is not history."[17] Scholarly journals continue to give such criticism a hearing, particularly when it is directed at feminist historians. G. R. Elton, an eminent English constitutional historian, used this kind of accusation in his review for *The American Scholar* of Joan Kelly's book of essays, *Women, History, and Theory* (1984). Elton accepted that there had been omissions in the historical record, but wondered "whether women's history has grown up sufficiently to permit a voice to one who appreciates its aims but is not committed to its current results." He then proceeded to invalidate those results: women's history was not good history, and its practitioners were not good historians.

"Feminist historiography," he insisted, is nothing more than "history written by fanatics." For, "feminism is a religion, and feminist history constitutes an attempt to underpin dogmatics for that religion." Elaborating on the metaphor, Joan Kelly then became a "prophetess," whose death elevated her "to sainthood," for cancer is "a charismatic disease in such circles." Her essays naturally became "History according to Saint Joan." He briefly queried why male historians in the United States (and by implication not in Britain) had been swayed by these writings and receptive to these feminist criticisms. Only psychology explained these men's behavior; they "had long regarded women with a mixture of respect and apprehension." Elton saw this apprehension as justified. He explained that such women wrote these polemics with but one goal, "for the purpose of today substituting female dominance for male."[18]

All writers of traditional history, whether male or female, have not turned away with such vehemence, but they have turned away from women's history nonetheless. In the 1990s while acknowledging the "new" histories, these scholars remain wedded to the old valuations and priorities. They continue to believe that history can be written for its own sake; that neutral, self-evident choices can be made, with no consequences, with no other effect. Although a book of women's history might appear on their course syllabus or in their bibliography, they insist that the most appropriate topics for study are those associated with men's exercise of power in its most obvious political and economic forms. When questioned by feminists about the inevitable omissions, their answer remains straightforward. "Surely, you don't mean that men have not exercised power in history?" As one feminist explained, "New facts might document the existence of women in the past, but they did not necessarily change the importance (or lack of it) attributed to women's activities."[19]

Louise Tilly described the response of "a crusty old historian of the [French] Revolution" after hearing Joan W. Scott's speech on Olympe de Gouges, author of the Declaration of the Rights of Woman and victim of the Terror. He asked "in his own eastern twang, 'Now that I know that women were participants in the Revolution, *what difference does it make*?' " Tilly did not record Scott's response. Perhaps she reminded the elderly scholar of points from her presentation addressed to this very question, the insights that the history of this early feminist gave about revolutionary definitions of citizenship, concepts of liberty, and the uses of power.[20] But whatever Scott said, however persuasively she argued the usefulness of women's history and the efficacy of "gender" as a category of analysis, neither she, nor other feminist scholars, have altered the traditional frameworks of history and their axiomatic male perspective. Whatever feminist scholars have demonstrated through their research or explained in their theoretical works, they "have failed to convince historians of other subfields that one set of questions should be replaced with another."[21] For the majority of historians, whether identified with the more radical or the more traditional approaches to history, study of women's past in conjunction with men's is not a matter of course; it has not become part of the everyday analytical questions and answers across the discipline. And, most significantly, the burden of proof continues to lie with feminist historians, with those who wish to include and rethink, rather than with those who have excluded. As a result, for men like the "crusty" French Revolution scholar, comfortably protected by the old premises and traditional criteria, there may never be a convincing answer to his question. There may be no way to prove to him "what difference it makes."

TEXTBOOKS AND
SECONDARY EDUCATION

At the end of the 1980s Gisela Bock wrote that the time had come to replace men's with women's history as the "general" story of humanity.[22] Although she meant her suggestion to be provocative more than practical, feminist scholars can easily imagine its realization, new courses in "Western Civilization" with women's narratives as the basic reading and women's experiences as the core of the class lectures and discussions. Supplementary texts would be used to present selected facts of men's lives. But with the majority of scholars so reluctant to alter old ways of thinking and presenting history, the opposite alternative has been chosen for college and secondary-school classes. Textbooks of the 1990s tell men's history, divided into periods that reflect events of significance to them. Revisions to "integrate" women's experiences are discreet subsections or separate chapters. For example, the most recent editions of Bailey's *The American Pageant* (1991) and Palmer and Colton's *History of the Modern World* (1992) have many listings under "women" in their indexes and chapters devoted to reformers and empresses, but the perspective and the overall analysis and organization remain the same.

Textbooks authors, both women and men, who are more oriented toward the new emphases on social and cultural history made the same compromises. Like their more conservative colleagues they retained the standard divisions of men's history and interspersed their narratives with separate paragraphs or sections on women. Neither group attempted an integrated history; neither made "gender a category of analysis" as pervasive as class, race, or culture. All of these scholars left the "regular" text more or less intact because they assumed it could be "supplemented" by a wide range of readings specifically on women. This has meant, however, that any synthesis, especially any combining or gendering of women's and men's histories, would have to be done by the instructor in the lecture hall, or by the student after reading first in one book and then in another.

In theory, feminist textbook writers could have experimented with new emphases and new organization. Few have. Instead, even the texts dealing only with women's experiences follow the periodization and themes of men's history. Their authors have chosen not to use alternative divisions proposed by other historians or by feminist scholars in other disciplines, even though there is general agreement that these alternatives better reflect women's past. Undoubtedly, as feminist scholars and their publishers argue, the familiarity of categories and organizing principles made the books "fit" standard course syllabuses, but these characteristics did little to challenge the old frameworks, or to alter the traditional ways of assigning value and significance.[23]

The same minimal adjustments characterize efforts to alter primary and secondary social studies and history programs. Everyone acknowledges that the situation and the resources for teachers have improved. State and city boards of education have had the best of intentions. They write of the role educators must play in changing society's images of women and men, in breaking the old constraints for girls and boys.[24] Their staff-development materials and instructional pamphlets cite statistics about the classroom books from the 1960s and 1970s when 27 United States history texts, including one entitled *Man in America*, mentioned women on 137 out of a possible 29,000 pages. They invite today's teachers to examine their own approaches and the materials in their classrooms to identify lingering biases: how women are omitted, how women's history is distorted, how stereotypes are encouraged by unthinking use of old phrases and images.[25] Numerous local boards of education and three state education departments—Illinois, Louisiana, and Minnesota—have mandated that units on women must be included in the curriculum.

But it is as if the educators and the authors of the new texts were "uncertain what to do with all this new information." Writers and publishers have chosen the same solution for these students as they did for those in college: commitment to the "integration" of women into the old narrative, but their actual segregation in separate paragraphs and pages of texts and teaching guides. Complementary series exist as well, such as Susan Hill Gross and Marjorie Wall Bingham's *Women in World Area Studies*, but they also tend to follow the traditional themes and periods of men's history.

Studies of United States history textbooks showed the standard approaches. In most instances women came after all of the usual men's topics under a subheading like "family life" or "women's roles." Whether or not the authors intended all that came before to be about men, the division clearly suggested this. Individual women often appeared paired with a man who was active in a similar way. For example, William Lloyd Garrison and Sojourner Truth would be mentioned in the same paragraph on United States abolitionists. In these accounts no specificity was given to the woman's experience. Obscuring difference in this way perpetuated the assumption of a single universal experience—men's. Sojourner Truth was named. This was new and appropriate. But her bravery, her eccentricity, and her black perspective became part of a New England white man's crusade, a kind of "disappearing integration." Women's involvement in politics, their nineteenth-century reform organizations, their fight for the suffrage, and the 1960s liberation movement merited whole sections or chapters. Neatly separated, however, the women's experiences remained tangential to the other, more "significant" events in these time periods.[26]

These high-school and college textbooks and programs all claim to be a form of "integration." But as Elizabeth Minnich has explained, "Integration is inadequate if it means only including traditionally excluded groups in a dominant system of thinking."[27] Students from the 1950s would have no trouble finding their way through the table of contents of even the most recent classroom history books. There has been no synthesis, no transformation.

Worst of all, despite the public education initiatives and administrators' efforts to create "gender-balanced" curricula, the leading educational reformers, the academic experts on social studies and secondary-school history, have not set the inclusion of women's history as a priority in their evaluations of existing programs, nor in their suggestions for new sequences and narratives. Paul Gagnon's study for the United Federation of Teachers, *Democracy's Half-Told Story: What American History Textbooks Should Add* (1989), noted the need for more on military strategy, but made no special mention of women. The National Commission on Social Studies in the Schools in its "Charting a Course: Social Studies for the 21st Century" (1989) was willing to make statements about contemporary educational concerns. It emphasized the importance of "multicultural diversity" in the curriculum, and cautioned educators that "Religion is a sensitive issue." Yet women appeared only once in the many pages of detailed analysis and description of curricula—as "suffragists" in a long list that began with "Native Americans." A feminist historian would be particularly discouraged to see that as early as kindergarten and the first primary grades an exercise on historical time suggested that the children learn to mark generations by naming their "grandfathers."[28]

The Bradley Commission purposely enlisted the support of a wide range of historians from all levels of education and with many different specialties, including a secondary-school teacher who had co-authored a series of supplementary women's history texts. The report, *Building a History Curriculum: Guidelines for Teaching History in Schools* (1988), mentioned "the family," "gender structures and relations," and "the new prominence of women." But it would be hard to imagine how these concerns were to be addressed practically. There was no obvious explanation of what would have to change if women's experiences held equal place with men's or if gender became a significant analytical category. Quite the reverse in fact. For example, "Topic 3" in the section on world history advocated study of the "major landmarks in the human use of the environment from Paleolithic hunters to the latest technologies." The phrasing suggested a world reminiscent of "the ascent of man." Women as gatherers and inventors, as the sustainers of families across the millennia failed to appear in this male-oriented delineation.[29]

Those who have tried to explain the persistence of these sexist attitudes, who want to break through the discriminatory barriers that remain at all levels of education, fall into a circular system of justifications. Textbook editors and authors (many of whom are historians from colleges and research universities) bemoan the fact that they must curb their desire for change because conservative state or local boards of education control the choice of textbooks. Public education administrators portray recalcitrant teachers unwilling to give up their faded, yellowed notes and lesson plans. The best teachers explain that there is no money for new books and materials, and that even if there were, they must teach to old-fashioned qualifying tests and to external examinations that pay little or no attention to women.[30] No group within the system perceives itself as powerful enough to bring about the changes many officially favor.

The staff experts at Educational Testing Service (ETS), the organization that creates the achievement and advanced placement tests that high school juniors and seniors take in the United States, disavow any active role in determining what will and will not be taught and studied. They see themselves and the tests they create as neutral, merely reflections of what others, especially "the colleges," want. According to the College Board its first responsibility is to provide a "reliable" test that, in the words of the examiners, "works." To be reliable the test results must differentiate among the students, with some doing very well, others poorly, and the majority somewhere in between. Multiple-choice questions, a staple device of all their history examinations, have to "work" statistically. For example, questions with oddly skewed results for one type of student would be reassessed. Those that over 95% or less than 5% of the students answer correctly would be eliminated.[31] By implication, the inclusion of a diverse number of gendered or women's questions would either be too easy or too hard or favor some students over others.

Like state and local educational authorities the College Board has issued guidelines calling for "gender balance" in all its tests. The subjects for the history multiple-choice questions, however, and for the document-based questions and the essays of the advanced placement history examination are ultimately determined, according to ETS, by what already exists. Staff members solicit descriptions of college courses, they look at the popular textbooks, they study high-school curricula. The findings of this research become mitigating factors that take precedence over internal guidelines and over particular recommendations from those who compose and select questions. Thus, a senior examiner's sense that ETS remains "neutral." In the end only what was already emphasized by their constituency appeared in their tests.

ETS reports that their correspondence and their surveys indicate that "more" is being done about women. Their examinations showed this. In fact, questions reflected the pattern of introductory college courses. More women appeared than in previous years, but only in predictable eras and categories, or tangentially. In the advanced placement tests for 1989, 1990, and 1991, document questions often included a woman's writing among the selections, for example, Harriet Martineau on Jacksonian democracy in the 1990 United States test, Olympe de Gouges on enslavement in the French colony of Haiti for the 1991 European exam. When questions have been specifically concerned with women, the focus has been on the usual political events or social reform movements. The whole of the 1989 European document question asked students to compare arguments for and against women's suffrage. In most years an imaginative student taking the United States or the European test could turn an essay question in social or cultural history so as to focus it on women.

The 1985–86 Graduate Record Examination, a test now required by many universities for admission to graduate programs, showed how "integration" worked when the method of testing was multiple choice and students had to answer all the questions. In theory this examination could be more rigorous and more inclusive of other histories. The students would have completed college, perhaps as history majors, yet few questions even mentioned a woman's name. Out of the total of 190, eleven required knowledge of women's history. Predictably, six questions concerned suffrage and women's political rights, the other five were on men's topics, and the woman was the wrong answer.[32] Following ETS's rationale, these choices reflected not their thinking, but the priorities of graduate history programs across the United States.

Since the late 1970s all examinations have undergone what ETS calls a "sensitivity review." Staff go over the questions to ensure every kind of "balance'' and to look for inadvertent stereotyping or potentially discriminatory phrasing. This is an internal review. In addition, in every subject category a committee consisting of representatives from colleges and high schools oversees the entire test-writing and evaluation from beginning to end. The ''AP Test Development Committee'' for history, for example, consists of three high-school teachers who have taught advanced placement courses and served as ''readers'' of test answers and three faculty from AP accrediting institutions. At the meetings members ''reach a consensus'' on what can be fairly asked of precollegiate students.[33]

Those feminist scholars, both women and men, who have served on this committee see hard-won changes. They cite examples to demonstrate the ways in which women's perspectives and gender analysis have been made a part of the examination. Feminists critics see this as only a beginning. They argue that the present kinds of inclusion fall short of ETS's own guidelines and leave intact traditional periods, categories, and analytical approaches. Most important, these critics question the neutrality of the tests and of the process by which they are written and evaluated. As those who work with ETS are largely recruited through recommendations from past committee members, from the established professional organizations, and from those who have participated in the College Board's own conferences and activities, how, skeptical feminists ask, could radically different perspectives prevail? In fact, critics suggest, the entire process of external examinations by its ''neutrality'' inadvertently reinforces the old-fashioned frameworks and the male-oriented ways of describing the past.

Secondary-school teachers committed to a more inclusive history are left with impossible choices. Should they change their syllabus for a few multiple-choice questions and the chance that an essay can be interpreted from a gendered perspective? Should they replace a standard topic like the study of interwar diplomacy with a unit on twentieth-century women's work lives? Most high school faculty would answer no. The advanced placement and achievement tests partially determine their students' academic opportunities. School administrators and the most articulate national education reformers speak of test scores as a measure of teacher competency. The risk appears too great.

Listening to those who are party to this system, to the teachers, testing service examiners, and educators, college and university scholars would seem to have the most opportunity and authority to break the patterns of justification and resistance. In fact all activists in the academy agree on ''a continuing need for the feminist critique of the dominant tradition and all that was born within and of it,'' but they do not agree on how to make that ''critique'' most effectively, nor on how to make lasting, essential changes in the ways in which history is defined, researched, and made accessible. In the late 1960s and 1970s every act for women's history and women historians, whether in the classroom, a department meeting, or a professional conference, made a feminist statement. The context of the times gave each action, each piece of research and writing, a fresh, provocative quality and political implications. In the 1990s neither the battle lines nor the definitions of victory are so clearly drawn. To some, feminist visions of women's history and women's professional participation are seen as commonplace, to others their demands, however carefully phrased, are dismissed as cant or rhetoric. Even women scholars have sometimes questioned the efficacy of their academic work in improving women's circumstances: "In what sense do writing books and articles, giving lectures, and teaching classes change material conditions?"[34]

Many feminist historians, however, continue to assert that scholarship can transform the discipline and advance the cause of women. Some, particularly those with specialties in social and cultural topics, propose that the incorporation of "gender" as an analytical category for all historical analysis is the solution. Their research and writing have demonstrated how this approach can have an impact on the discipline. Others, like Judith Bennett, disagree. Bennett warned that joining these "reciprocal dialogues" about integration and synthesis may impoverish women's own history and turn all research once again to "male-centered and male-defined" investigations. True dialogues, she argued, will come only when those in traditional fields turn to women's questions. In the meantime, she advocated a more consciously political, feminist history, a return to studies of patriarchy and of what she saw as the most important historical question: "Why and how has the subordination of women endured for so long and in so many different historical settings?" She has revived ideas of the late 1960s and early 1970s when women scholars discovered that identifying the nature and causes of women's past oppression could "directly enhance feminist strategies for the present."[35]

Whichever theoretical approach they take, all feminists believe that they can expect more than just increased understanding of the past and identification of successful tactics from these scholarly endeavors, from this new "collective memory." Women's history not only challenged the old methods, perspectives, and professional traditions, but also sanctioned new attitudes and expanded opportunities. In this way history became both cause and effect, a device for bringing all women from "consciousness raising to social change," from pride in knowledge of the past to action in the present, to creation of a different future.[36]

9.

THE POPULAR FEMINIST INITIATIVE

LOCAL TACTICS TO NATIONAL STRATEGIES: THE PERSONAL IS THE POLITICAL

While women scholars have worked from within the academy, there have also been effective feminist initiatives outside of colleges and universities, in local and state government agencies, in factories and offices, at social and professional gatherings. The leaders of these groups publicize women's history as part of their overall strategy. They ignore theoretical questions of integration, transformation, and gender analysis. They simply want people thinking and talking about women's history, valuing women's accomplishments and contributions. The impact of such appreciation they see as twofold: women will act to bring about change; men will not oppose that change.

Most influential of these "grassroots" initiatives has been the National Women's History Project (NWHP), which from the late 1970s has dedicated its efforts to advancing multicultural women's history in virtually any place, shape, or form that seemed to catch people's attention. The women who conceived the NWHP began promoting women's history in their community, Santa Rosa, California at the local branch of the state college. They continued their efforts first as volunteers and then as paid staff members of the Sonoma County Commission on the Status of Women. Their first activities included presenting their own slide show about women notables, encouraging a group of high-school students to evaluate history textbooks and library resources, and requesting that area teachers celebrate international women's day in their classrooms. By 1990 their week-long Sonoma County celebration had become National Women's History Month, declared by congressional resolution and commemorated throughout the United States. The group of friends had become the National Women's History Project with a staff of seven, and a budget in the hundreds of thousands of dollars. Over 300,000 catalogues went to classroom teachers, leaders of non-profit organizations, public education administrators, state equal employment opportunity commissioners, and corporate affirmative-action officers, all of whom acknowledged the group's expertise and their particular vision of history as a means of raising awareness and countering discrimination against women.[1]

This idea of a public celebration of women's history evolved in the mid 1970s when Molly Murphy MacGregor was taking extension courses at Sonoma State College.[2] She worked with other feminists on plans to make an event out of International Women's Day, March 8. The establishment in 1975 of the Sonoma County Commission on the Status of Women "to eliminate discrimination and prejudice on the basis of sex" created the local institutional framework for taking the event out into the community. In October of 1977 MacGregor, Bette Morgan, and Evelyn Truman, all volunteers with the Commission's Task Force on Education, proposed that the local schools observe a Women's History Week. In their proposal to the Commission they acknowledged that it would be "impossible to cover Women's History in only one week," but they hoped that "this exposure will inspire students and teachers to question further and discover more of women's heritage."[3]

Their first week, March 6th through 10th, 1978 set the pattern for subsequent local commemorations and for the kinds of events that would ultimately be organized throughout the United States. The Task Force enlisted everyone's help. When school administrators seemed reluctant, they went straight to the teachers. They talked to local politicians, to federal and state equity officers, to leaders of women's organizations. They developed the idea of "Community Resource Women," women with all kinds of jobs and talents willing to go into classrooms and speak about their lives: artists, carpenters, dentists, a salmon fisher, needle-workers, all pleased to be asked and able to hold students' attention. MacGregor and other members of the Education Task Force took a slide show on women's history that had originally been done for a class at the state college and presented it for women's groups and school assemblies. In February they ran a one-day conference suggesting resources and activities with the motto, "A Woman's Place is in the Curriculum." When their week in March had arrived and passed, they could point to success across the county: approval from county officials, 90 elementary and 30 secondary schools participating, and support from the feminist community.[4]

By the next year's commemoration in March of 1979 Sonoma County and its rural communities had instituted a wide range of activities in connection with women's history, including teacher workshops sponsored by the Commission on the Status of Women and Sonoma State College, library displays and talks, and a printed guide for a week's worth of classroom activities. In 1979 they organized their first parade to Santa Rosa's Courthouse Square. The parade gave public officials, storeowners, and women's groups something practical to plan for, something specific to do. More than any other of their ideas the parade made women's history week into a community event that everyone participated in and around which all kinds of activities could be organized. Most important, the parade made the week other than a feminist statement by a few dedicated activists. The County Board of Supervisors, community leaders, and local educators could imagine it as an apolitical act and think of their support and participation as simply a way to honor women's experiences and contributions to United States history. One early organizer remembered how significant it seemed "that women could have a parade all their own."[5]

These practical choices and tactics differentiated MacGregor and the Commission from other local feminist initiatives and explained their early effectiveness and their subsequent impact. They had a single mission: to expand and sustain awareness of multicultural women's history. They believed that this new awareness would change attitudes, lives, and futures. Boys and men would come to understand that the majority of women for most of their lives have two jobs, their household and their waged work. They argued that historical omissions and distortions had robbed "our children, and all members of society . . . [of] the richness of women's heritage and often the inspiration to become active participants in society." They saw this new knowledge as a way to make all women "more self assured, more responsible for our deeds, and more optimistic about the power we have over our lives." As MacGregor explained at the press conference just after the California legislature's declaration of the state's first Women's History Week, "We're trying to make them understand that they are the makers of history, that it's their responsibility and if they sit back and let someone else make those decisions for them, they lose out on life, and we lose out on the kind of culture we want to live in."[6]

Their goal from the beginning was to find ways to spark this awareness and to inspire this sense of power, to identify clear, simple tasks, symbolic acts and words that turned a concept into something practical and tangible. In their hands a feminist scholar's commitment to alter the discipline of history became one month out of the year to celebrate women's past. They valued any positive response to their initiative. It might be a banner across a Santa Rosa shopping center parking lot, a women's history group meeting in a factory cafeteria, a community college art show, a slogan on a beige canvas tote bag, one working women's song in a school assembly, a display of women's writings in a bookstore window. Alice Kessler-Harris once said, "a token is better than none," and this was how MacGregor and her colleagues thought as well.[7] Their organization, the National Women's History Project, grew in turn to encourage and sustain the observance. Everything, as MacGregor explained, became a "vehicle" for implementing the overall goal, the understanding and acceptance of multicultural women's history. In this way the National Women's History Project offered what Gerda Lerner suggested the women's movement needed, "new structures and focus," that gave "continuity" to feminists' efforts to bring other women and men to "historical self-consciousness."[8]

In order to have the broadest possible support and participation, MacGregor and her colleagues avoided language or pronouncements that might turn away supporters. They knew they were feminists, but they felt no need to emphasize it when they went to give their slide presentations or wrote their fliers. MacGregor had, in fact, worried about the first parade and the ways in which massed groups of women might alienate the northern California rural community. Mary Ruthsdotter, a volunteer who became chair of the Commission on the Status of Women, rewrote the original curriculum guide to remove what might have been considered "leftist" rhetoric. When they stopped working with the Commission and formed their own organization, this sensitivity intensified. They changed their 1982 Women's History Week poster when they realized that green and white were the colors associated with the National Organization for Women and with the campaign for the Equal Rights Amendment. As one member of the group explained, the ultimate goal was for people to understand, "it's not political, it's just history."[9]

Their approach, MacGregor proudly announces to workshop participants, "by just about any standard you can name has been a success." They have made popular celebrations of women's history a national reality. The 1987 Congressional resolution turning National Women's History Week into a month-long commemoration justified passage with a series of clauses describing the role of "women of every race, class, and ethnic background," and the need to value and include their "critical" and "unique" contributions to the history of the United States.[10] By 1990 in cities and suburban and rural communities the month meant multiple activities on many days, some officially initiated by municipal, state, or federal authorities, others by voluntary and educational organizations and institutions, some spontaneously generated. State and city departments of education send display materials and sponsor workshops. The New York City Commission on the Status of Women publishes a calendar with different events for each day and distributes voluminous information and curriculum packets. Affirmative-action offices, like the one in Portland, Oregon, and human resource departments, in Bloomington, Indiana, for example, encourage activities. In 1990 the United States Patent Office organized an exhibit on women inventors, and the NASA Space Center in Houston sponsored a month-long program of events. The Hazelton, Pennsylvania, and Booneville, Idaho, historical societies used the occasion to initiate oral history projects.

Throughout the 1980s the range of nongovernmental organizations that used and promoted the month expanded exponentially; everything from the Iowa Inter-church Forum to the Cherokee Nation of Oklahoma, the American Association of Retired Persons, and Kirkland Air Force Base in New Mexico. Even industry became involved. There is a women's history club at Bell Labs in New Jersey, and a women's group at AT&T in Lisle, Illinois who wrote a newsletter and put posters up in the company cafeterias.

Cities and organizations have thought of innumerable ways to publicize women's accomplishments in the past and present. They exhibited art works, and sponsored plays. They brought in women speakers much like the original Sonoma County "Community Resource Women," with every kind of expertise: authors to read their work, like Molly Ivins of the Dallas Times Herald, the mystery writer Sara Paretsky, the novelist Sandra Cisneros, and memoirist Maya Angelou; politicians like Shirley Chisholm, Geraldine Ferraro, Chief Wilma Mankiller (leader of the Cherokee Nation), and Reita Rivers who had worked with Jeannette Rankin (the first woman to serve in Congress); the folksinger Gerri Gribi; and Bonnie Dunbar, the astronaut. Local and national groups sponsored writing contests and award banquets to honor local notables. The National Organization for Women offered $1,000 prizes to the winners of its essay contest. Other kinds of events encouraged broad participation in more active ways, like the women's history fair in Canton, Ohio, and the candlelight march in Moro Bay, California. Although it did not occasion as much publicity or involve as many people, Laura Hotchkiss Brown's banner showed the power and excitement that designation of this month has generated. A former Columbia student, Brown hung a 140-foot banner across the decorative facade at the top of the university library. Where Socrates, Aristotle, and the male intellectual elite had been named, now everyone on the campus saw proclaimed instead Christine de Pizan, Simone de Beauvoir, Virginia Woolf, and other feminists.[11]

The local initiative became a national phenomenon, the local tactics part of national feminist strategies, all because MacGregor read about a women's history institute for community leaders at Sarah Lawrence College. She sent off everything they had in the Commission office about what they had done in 1978 and planned for 1979, hoping that she would be chosen as a participant. (She was then Deputy Director of the Commission, a paid staff member, no longer a volunteer.) MacGregor and her colleagues thought of this institute as a special opportunity, "the chance to go national," the means to excite women in other parts of the country so that they would "go back and do it within their own organizations." The Californians imagined women's history week celebrations all over the United States. The story of the response from the Institute organizers is now part of the lore of the National Women's History Project. No word came, nothing for weeks until finally a very thin envelope arrived. Sure it was a rejection, MacGregor waited until she was alone to open it only to find a brief message from the co-sponsors of the institute, "Congratulations—you have won a sistership."[12]

Gerda Lerner, one of the organizers of the Institute, had from her 1971 presentation to Sarah Lawrence's Committee on Restructuring the College, spoken of education in women's history not only for students and scholars, but also for those outside the academy. A volunteer activist herself in the past, she particularly hoped to attract and involve women community leaders. Between 1972 and 1977 the college sponsored a fellowship program for such women, offered seminars for them in women's history, and enlisted their participation in a conference on "The Future of Housework, the Role of the Housewife, and Sharing Arrangements for Child Care."[13] In the late 1970s Lerner and Barbara Omolade of the Women's Action Alliance applied for a grant from the Lilly Foundation for a nineteen-day women's history institute for community organizers. With the $55,000 award, Amy Swerdlow, the director of Sarah Lawrence's women's history program, and Omolade enlisted faculty and selected participants. They chose 39 women from varied groups across the United States. In addition to MacGregor from the Sonoma County Commission on the Status of Women, representatives came from the Girl Scouts of America, Comisión Feminil Mexicana Nacional, the Lesbian–Gay Task Force, the National Council of Negro Women, the Leadership Conference of Women Religious, Rural American Women, National Abortion Rights Action League (NARAL), and Carolyn Reed's organization for Domestic Houseworkers.[14]

In addition to the lectures and discussions organized by the institute leaders, MacGregor wanted time for the participants to learn about each other's organizations. She needed such an opportunity to convince them to inaugurate their own women's history week celebrations. They were given one evening. MacGregor explained the idea of a women's history week and showed slides of the 1979 parade. Though not all of the participants would have described themselves as feminists, they all supported the goals of the women's movement and believed that knowledge of women's history would not only make their organizations work better but also benefit the cause in general. They saw the potential of the Sonoma County events at once. It seemed natural to use this institute as a means to publicize the idea of a national commemoration, a federally recognized national women's history week. Some of the participants and the graduate student teaching assistant, Pam Elam, reworded and expanded the 1978 Sonoma County Board of Supervisors' resolution. Gerda Lerner read it at the Smithsonian breakfast in Washington, D.C., that both honored notable American women and celebrated the end of the Institute. The participants's resolution called on Congress to establish a national women's history week. In this way the idea became part of the press releases for the Smithsonian event, and gained its first national hearing.

Elam, a feminist lawyer and former executive director of the Kentucky American Civil Liberties Union, took on the task of making the Institute resolution a reality. She and Peggy Pascoe, the other graduate student instructor, began the campaign with letters to mayors, to governors, and to members of congress. That autumn the staff of the women's congressional caucus—from the offices of Barbara Mikulski, Patricia Schroeder, and Elizabeth Holtzman—met with Elam and MacGregor and agreed to support a bill. Everything happened very quickly. *Ms.* published a short piece on the idea. Requests for information and materials came from all over the country, deluged the Sonoma County Commission office, but demonstrated the immediate popularity of the concept. The resolution was introduced 26 February 1980 but with too little time for passage before March and the week of the 8th, the time around international women's day designated for the celebration.

But the lobbying efforts had their effect. On the 28th MacGregor answered the telephone at the Commission. She put the operator on hold when she heard that it was the White House calling to speak with "Ms. MacGregor." After she picked up the receiver again, Carter's special assistant, Sarah Weddington, came on the line to tell her that the president had decided to issue a "Message" declaring National Women's History Week. This presidential support and Elam's and Pascoe's efforts led governors in 16 states (including California) to make similar proclamations. To gain passage of the congressional resolution a network of women politicians, community organizers, feminist activists, and women historians worked throughout 1980 and 1981. The Committee on Women Historians at the American Historical Association enlisted the executive director's support. When Gerda Lerner became president of the Organization of American Historians, she brought that group's endorsement as well.[15]

Mary Ruthsdotter remembered that the 1981 Congressional vote gave them "the legitimacy we'd been hoping for all along."[16] This success justified decisions already made. With the experience of the first parade, MacGregor, Morgan, and Ruthsdotter began to experiment with ideas for their own organization and with ways to raise funds outside of the Commission on the Status of Women. By 1981 they had separated in a variety of ways. MacGregor left the Commission in the spring of 1980, and with Morgan, Ruthsdotter, and two other supporters, Maria E. Cuevas and Paula Hammett (then a student at Sonoma State), the five women named themselves the National Women's History Project, an independent nonprofit organization.[17] They stopped doing all the work on shared typewriters in someone's kitchen or living room and moved to their own offices, patched-together space donated by Nell Codding, owner of the local regional shopping center. They painted, built shelves, and stored materials in the bathroom so that they could save the few rooms for work space. They acquired their logo, Kathleen Smith's design for the county group, Women of Color. (Smith is a Native American, a Pomo/Miwok.) With MacGregor's profile added to the other four, all of the major cultural groups in the United States were represented. The logo appeared prominently on their first flyer, a fold-out page, typed and photo off-set, with their philosophy, information about women's history week, and the beginnings of what they came to call the "Women's History Resource Service."[18]

Directly and indirectly each of the founding members came to an appreciation of their history as women and their determination to use it as feminists because of Alice Wexler's course at Sonoma State College. Though a rural area of northern California, by the early 1970s even Sonoma County had been affected by antiwar activism, agitation for migrant workers' rights, and feminism. Feminists on the faculty, like the literary critic J. J. Wilson, committed themselves to creating programs and activities. When students insisted on a course in United States women's history, Wexler, a Latin Americanist and the only female in the history department, was eager to teach it. Bette Morgan had four children to raise and support, her work as a Catholic activist for migrant women, and a major to complete in architectural history. She told a classmate who suggested she take Wexler's course that she "didn't really have time for it." An artist friend changed her mind; Wexler and women's history led her to change the direction of her life.

This was the era when each bit of women's history came as a surprise, each heroine's accomplishment as a personal discovery. Morgan remembered that Wexler always began by asking the students to name five women in history; "and, of course, no one could do it." For Morgan, the moment of "historical self-consciousness" came that spring of 1972 when she helped create a women's history slide show designed to be part of the campus celebrations for a visit from the French author Anaïs Nin. Morgan was part of the group who collected the pictures. She particularly admired Viola Liuzzo, a white civil rights volunteer from Detroit shot by the Ku Klux Klan in Mississippi. "I couldn't find her and that made me think. . . . I'd done enough history by then . . . I knew where things ought to be."

Although Nin became ill and never did speak on campus, the slide show almost overnight became part of an on-going effort by the college's feminists to publicize women's history throughout the whole community.[19] When in the spring of 1974 MacGregor came to take courses, she was recruited to help in the presentations. "We the Women: Advocates for Social Change," five reels of slides, taped music, and a script to be read by multiple voices, portrayed "the story of the common woman and how she has worked to create a better world for you and for me." To emphasize this point the first images were photographs of women from their own families, a particularly moving segment for Morgan, MacGregor, and the others who created the original sequence. In retrospect, however, for their audiences, for women who had never known about women's activities, who had never seen the faces of famous women and never heard their words, it would have been the procession of "stars" that elicited the biggest response: Anne Hutchinson's heresies, Sojourner Truth, Clara Lemlich, Ida Wells Barnett, Jeannette Rankin voting against war, Alice Paul, Margaret Sanger, Bessie Smith's singing, Dolores Huerta speaking, and many more. In its final version, the presentation ended with Helen Reddy's "I Am Woman," as the evocative background music for pictures of contemporary activists like Bella Abzug, Angela Davis, and Gloria Steinem.[20]

In subsequent years Morgan and MacGregor would speak and write with such intensity about the power of feminist history because of their own and other women's experiences. Morgan remembered, "We'd stand in the back of the room and read the script, do all the different parts, and the lights would go on, and women would be crying." Often, she and MacGregor recalled, "the women in those early audiences got angry. They felt they had been deprived." They wanted to act on this new-found awareness. As Morgan later explained, we saw "that history could do that, that history could have an impact . . . could reach out to certain women and really change their lives."

The slide show went with them in the mid 1970s to the Education Task Force of the Commission on the Status of Women. By this time it had been shown all over the county, even in San Francisco to a group of secretaries at the Standard Oil corporate headquarters. With the first celebration of Women's History Week in 1978, it was natural that the slide presentation should be the focal point of the Commission's annual dinner. This was the evening that made Mary Ruthsdotter a convert to and a proselytizer of women's history. She remembered that MacGregor kept ad-libbing because something happened to the projector, then to the tape recorder. "I was really glad for the equipment failures because I was just sitting there stunned. . . . All this was up there on the screen . . . Why hadn't I ever heard of any of this? I was amazed." Ruthsdotter described her schooling as a "sassy education," but knew that she had no idea who most of these women were.[21] Later she realized how much her own experience mirrored that of other women. Because her father was a pilot in the marines she always lived near the air fields. She remembered racing around her backyard pretending to be a plane, and the beautiful model jets she kept in her room, samples sent to her father by designers. She even had a biography of Amelia Earhart, but it never occurred to her that she could be a pilot.

Morgan, MacGregor, Ruthsdotter, and Cuevas had their own styles and perspectives, but they shared the same overriding goal—to promote multicultural women's history—and a willingness to do whatever worked. Morgan later remembered that the shift from a local initiative to a national project "just seemed a natural progression." Finding the ways to fund their activities and the most effective structure for their organization evolved in much the same way.[22] All of the original founders thought in terms of volunteering, sharing expenses, and doing as much as possible themselves. All except MacGregor had to have jobs outside of the Commission, adjunct teaching, historic preservation projects for local townships, campaign planning for local politicians, or working at the local unemployment office. Cuevas had formed a singing group called "De Colores" with a friend and was trying to make a living as an entertainer. Their first fundraising successes came from cookie sales at peace demonstrations and requests for donations.

The academy and the network of professional historians gave encouragement, but the NWHP soon discovered that state and federal agencies and departments would be the more valuable allies in promoting their multicultural vision of women's history. At the 1979 founding conference of the National Coalition for Sex Equity in Education they met Barbara Landers, who not only supported them through this organization ($3,000 to $4,000 worth of sales at the Coalition's yearly summer conferences), but also in her capacity as Director of the Title IX Assistance Office of the California State Department of Education. Landers saw women's history as a means to sex equity for young people, and the Project as an effective agent to bring women's history into the schools. She financed their first official teaching conference in 1983, and showed them how to write convincing grant proposals. In 1981 the Project was awarded $104,000 from Women's Educational Equity Act (WEEA) funds to make an in-service teacher-training slide-tape program.[23] The U.S. Department of Education subsequently funded K-4 curriculum units, an eleventh-grade United States women's history workbook, three program guides, and six women's history videos. State and city departments of education sometimes bought materials on a grand scale; in 1982 Vermont purchased information packets for all of its hundred social studies teachers.[24]

State and national equity and affirmative-action programs supported the project in other ways as well, with consultancies and money for training conferences. For example, Equal Employment Opportunity affirmative-action officers were responsible for the Workplace Organizers Conference in 1989. Ruthsdotter discovered that it was the Sex Desegregation Assistance Centers under Title IV of the Civil Rights Act that still had budgets for materials in 1991. Companies like Hewlett-Packard used NWHP videos in their employee training programs to satisfy government requirements for the encouragement of multicultural sensitivity and gender equity.

At first the group tried to maintain the feminist ideal of a women's collective, but the practical realities of their many tasks created a hierarchy with MacGregor as the leader despite their egalitarian intentions. Over the years, she had become a particularly good spokeswoman for them. Although an ardent feminist, MacGregor could walk into a room full of social studies teachers, most of them male team coaches, and put everyone at ease with anecdotes about her five brothers and growing up in a large Irish-Catholic family. Willing to use any teaching technique that proved effective, she intuitively developed an ingenuous, intense way of working with groups that combined an air of homespun with the confidence of an expert. Invariably when the meeting was over she had convinced the participants that they had always believed in the importance of women's history. In addition, it became obvious that MacGregor had not only become the public image of the Project, but the central figure for each of the other women founders as well. Over the next two difficult years of completing their first videos (no one knew how to make one), of trying to keep money coming in, juggling personalities and tasks, though they referred to MacGregor as "M3" and had their teasing stories—that "brown on brown" was her "favorite color scheme" for publications and posters or that she wore a heavy wool coat when she first moved north from southern California—each of the original members said that "Molly" was the reason she stayed on.[25]

With MacGregor as executive director, Ruthsdotter and Morgan developing materials, and Cuevas overseeing the business arrangements (she learned accounting as she went along), they made 1983 to 1984 the pivotal year of the NWHP. In this year they established sources of revenue other than government grants and stepped into their name, the National Women's History Project. Cuevas remembered the change in her own thinking. She had always seen her job as an interlude, something to do while her music career was beginning. Then in the mid 1980s she realized, "I can't leave because I have too much work to do."[26]

Together they learned successful small business tactics: loans to finance inventory for the Resource Service's peak sales period in January and February (with their houses as collateral), catalogue design, product development in new areas like the history videos and spin-offs from previous guides and curriculum units, the creation of new services like the Network and a newsletter. They wrote loan applications describing their "potential client pool," a "five-point program" for marketing, and explained with confidence that "direct market competition will not develop in the foreseeable future."[27] After Bonnie Eisenberg joined them, with experience not only as MacGregor's successor at the Commission on the Status of Women, but also with newspaper and small-press publishing (she founded and edited the Marin County *Women's News Journal*), they expanded the catalogue (to 48 pages in 1992), researched and wrote more guides and curriculum units, and took on new tasks like editing an elementary textbook series for McGraw-Hill. With each year the NWHP became more sophisticated and more efficient in every aspect of its operations: a glossier product delivered, faster and more varied services.

As in many effective enterprises, their enthusiasm, their optimism, and especially their ability to translate their own and others' experiences into general practice have been key reasons for their impact. When Ruthsdotter wrote a summary of their entrepreneurial services in 1990 she used the subheadings "successes" and "problems." Techniques that proved useful have been passed on requiring little or no change. From the beginning they included in their planning guides copies of all the letters, memos, press releases, banquet invitations, time lines and budgets, everything that they had used at the Commission in organizing their first women's history events. They even printed essay prize award certificates ready for duplication. The 1991 catalogue offered a "new" item for the novice organizer, a 20-minute keynote speech for $5.

A good idea will be expanded on and appear in a different form. Ruthsdotter's visit to a Santa Rosa classroom to talk about quilting turned into a kit with precut construction paper squares to piece and sew. By 1991 the original slide show had been transformed into five history videos; the 1978 elementary- and secondary-school curriculum packages with five topics for each of the five days of women's history week had become a variety of individual history units and three separate activities guides. One focused from a curricular point of view, one from a planner's perspective, and one emphasized "Creative Arts."

From the first observances around the country of National Women's History Week, the Project solicited participation and disseminated the responses. "Your

Help Is Needed," read the 1983 flyer, accompanied by a questionnaire. The NWHP promised to "pass on your ideas, experiences and suggestions" and sent thank you letters when people made contributions.[28] The "real women" essay-writing contest, now an event in many states, originated with the Title IX Resource Center in the Sacramento Unified School District. A play by four Minnesota high-school students found approval and was included in the 1991 catalogue. The activities of Barbara Tomin, a Santa Rosa second-grade teacher, are now like traditions in some school districts: celebration of Susan B. Anthony's birthday, costumes and banners for parades, and a kid's variant of Judy Chicago's Dinner Party. The "101 Wonderful Ways to Celebrate Women's History," a staple of the NWHP publications, originated because so many good ideas came into the Project from teachers and administrators. When a donor wrote that she had wished she had known of the Project in time for Mother's Day, the staff acted on the suggestion and turned their annual solicitation into a way of honoring someone for "Mother's Day." All of these mailings and answers to letters encouraged loyalty and the creation of an ever-expanding network and wider circles of dissemination.

In many ways the National Women's History Project in-service training video, "History Revisited," illustrates all of the strengths and the intuitive and purposeful techniques that explain the feminist impact of the organization in public school history classrooms. MacGregor remembered that her own education in women's history had begun when she was in her second year of teaching eleventh-grade United States history. A student asked, "What is the women's movement?"[29] Her own experiences became part of the video script: a male teacher confronted with a similar question, the interested look on his face, and then MacGregor's voice explaining, "It's time we opened our classroom doors to all the women in America." Every aspect of the video emphasizes the multicultural nature of the subjects, the revitalizing effects in the classroom of women's history, and the ways in which student attitudes will change as a result of its inclusion. There is a boy learning to appreciate his grandmother's stories and a girl admitting that she "never thought about my family having anything to do with history" and deciding that she liked the subject now.

True to their ideal that women's history can give a sense of power and purpose, the video declares that it will demonstrate "what human strength can accomplish." They make no effort at synthesis, at the formulation of a new history. Rather there is a positive, progressive view of events, and one that focuses on the biographical. From the perspective of the National Women's History Project, history has had its male heroes; now female ones will be lauded as well. The choices of the positive is intentional. In the spirit of Mary Beard the project through all of its materials shows "women as active participants in the events of our nation's past." Ruthsdotter explains the philosophy to workshop participants: "Yeah, it was bad, but what did we do?"[30]

The biographical happens with less conscious purpose. As in other instances choices have been made for practical reasons. Biographies sound more interesting than "history," and fit easily into slots in a curriculum. Portraits of individuals can be part of posters, displays and dramatizations. Concepts and trends are difficult to demonstrate in a 15- or 20-minute video, but a very careful selection of individual lives sounds the message of multiculturalism loud and strong, and offers real women that everyone can identify with.

This consistent simple message, the pragmatic, inventive choices, the energy and persistence of the leaders, the ability, as Cuevas phrased it, "to do what's in front of me," have had a direct impact on the way history is perceived both in and out of schools throughout the United States.[31] In addition, the National Women's History Project has fostered a more positive view among the general populace of what otherwise might be labeled, and even dismissed, as "feminist history." The NWHP uses the slogan from the first National Women's Conference in Houston in the early 1970s to describe its work: "We're here to move history forward."

The Project's impact exemplifies the ways in which women's history and feminism have come to intersect and interact. The National Women's History Project has affected one, then another, and another classroom generation. As early as 1984 a young supporter wrote: "I am a 11 year old girl concerned about women's rights. I am behind you 100%. Most of the girls in my 6th grade class are also fighting for you. But not as much as me." She described a successful draw "your favorite woman contest" that she and a friend had organized; "Even boys entered!" She concluded: "Well I just wanted to write this short letter (that could have been 9 pages long!) to tell you there's more people out there fighting! With you forever, Mary Alice Carter."[32]

Feminist historians in the academy also have a connection with this confident little girl. They have their own successes to applaud. With their research and their writing they have created the scholarship and professional authority that the NWHP has translated and promoted. They can count professorships and graduate programs opened to women at colleges and universities across the United States. They can cite publishers' lists filled with their books and professional journals edited and written by women historians. They have nominated and voted for feminist colleagues for campus offices and for jobs within professional associations. They have headed women's studies programs and institutes, committees and caucuses to ensure protection of the rights and opportunities already gained and the advancement of new generations of women scholars.

In addition, feminist historians have raised significant questions that challenge all in the discipline to consider the past and the present from new perspectives. They ask: When and why have sexual differences become culturally and politically significant? How have the meanings of being a woman and a man, of "feminine" and "masculine" been formulated? How have these meanings and differences, these gendered identities, been articulated and manipulated? How do they become part of institutional structures and strategies? Simply stated, how has gender, how have "sexual differences . . . operate[d] as a social force?"[33]

If members of the profession, both women and men, integrated these questions into their conceptual and analytical frameworks, they would be constructing the inclusive, multilayered narrative first imagined by women scholars at the beginning of the twentieth century and rearticulated by feminist historians in the 1960s. Then there would be no need to debate elderly, male scholars who see no value in women's history.

In the end, the transformation of the discipline and the profession that feminists within the academy have worked for requires the varied skills of both research scholars and gifted popularizers. All kinds of strengths and all kinds of strategies are necessary for such a commanding endeavor: the intellectual, the intuitive, the rational, and the pragmatic. As Bette Morgan explained, "We put our lives into changing people second by second." She illustrated this delicate balance between action and impact with a story from her own childhood. She recalled a walk on the beach with her father. He stopped in the midst of what he was telling her, took her hand, opened the fingers and filled her palm with sand. He told her to close her fingers as tight as she could. The harder she squeezed the more the sand pushed through and fell from her hand. Then her father told her to begin again, but this time to hold her hand open. The sand stayed still and heavy in her palm. Morgan thought of her work with the Project and the efforts of other feminists in the same way. It is as if "you just throw it there." "I know I can't control the change—control how it happens. I [just] know I can make a difference."[34]

NOTES AND REFERENCES

Section I

1. David Hackett Fischer, *Historians' Fallacies: Toward a Logic of Historical Thought* (New York: Harper & Row, 1970), 217.

2. The phrase is from Gerda Lerner, *Teaching Women's History* (Washington, DC: American Historical Association, 1981), 2. See Anne Firor Scott, *Making the Invisible Woman Visible* (Chicago: University of Illinois Press, 1984), 245.

Chapter 1

1. Francis Parkman, *Pioneers of France in the New World* (Boston: Little, Brown, & Co., 1925), xxv.

2. Theodore S. Hamerow, "The Bureaucratization of History," in "AHR Forum: The Old History and the New," *American Historical Review*, 94 (3), (June 1989): 659.

3. Voltaire, *The Age of Louis XIV*, trans. Martyn P. Pollack (New York: E. P. Dutton & Co., 1951), 1.

4. I have used the two-volume abridgement. Arnold J. Toynbee, *A Study of History* abridged by D. C. Somervell (New York: Oxford University Press, 1946, 1957), I, 211ff., and II, 320, 100, 101, 171. The philosophers of history have demonstrated the same gender blindness. Women disappear under the rubric "man." Friedrich Hegel's nineteenth-century *Lectures on the Philosophy of World History* (1822–23) described the evolution of society from "boyhood," through "manhood," to "perfect maturity and strength" as quoted in Robert Nisbet, *History of the Idea of Progress* (New York: Basic Books, 1980), 279. A century later R. G. Collingwood stated it even more blatantly: history is an exercise in "human self-knowledge" that teaches "what man has done and thus what man is." R. G. Collingwood, *The Idea of History* (New York: Oxford University Press, 1956), 10.

5. Edward Hallett Carr, *What Is History?* (New York: Alfred A. Knopf, 1963), 168.

6. Fernand Braudel, *On History*, trans. Sarah Matthews (Chicago: the University of Chicago Press, 1980), 8, 11. Gertrude Himmelfarb, the European intellectual historian, makes the clearest case for this kind of analysis and this narrow choice of subject: these men controlled events and created the context in which others had to act, therefore by understanding them and the world they created, one can understand the important aspects of the age. See her contribution to "AHR Forum: the Old History and the New," entitled "Some Reflections on the New History," *American Historical Review*, 94 (3), (June 1989): especially 662–63, 668–70. See also her book, *The New History and the Old: Critical Essays and Reappraisals* (Cambridge: Belknap Press of Harvard University Press, 1987).

7. Joan W. Scott explained this phenomenon: "They subsumed women, included them in a generalized, unified conception that was at once represented in the idea of Man,

but was always different from and subordinate to it. The feminine was but a particular instance; the masculine a universal signifier." Joan Wallach Scott, *Gender and the Politics of History* (New York: Columbia University Press, 1988), 183. David Hackett Fischer describes some of the logical devices that have been used in historical writing about women: the semantic fallacy of "synecdoche" when "a part is used for the whole, as 'bread' for 'food' or 'man' for 'people' "; "fallacies of substantive distraction" where the topic is denigrated by shifting the terms of argument rather than for reasons of fact; the "fallacy of racism" giving "a false explanation of culturally learned behavior in terms of a biological, physiological or hereditary cause." See David Hackett Fischer, *Historians' Fallacies: Toward a Logic of Historical Thought* (New York: Harper & Row, 1970), 236–242, 270, 283–85, 291–301, 232.

8. Voltaire, 25. See also 26.

9. Voltaire, 38. See also his description of another victim of affection, Queen Anne of England, "dominated" by the duke and duchess of Marlborough, 237, 192.

10. See Parkman, *Pioneers*, 245, 292, 287. Parkman disapproved of the Jesuits, which made Marie de' Medici's loyalties and activities even more reprehensible.

11. Jacob Burckhardt, *The Civilization of the Renaissance in Italy* (New York: Harper & Row, 1958), 390, 393.

12. Edward Gibbon, *The Portable Gibbon: The Decline and Fall of the Roman Empire*, ed. Dero A. Saunders (New York: Viking Press, 1953), 30. I have used the abridged version as it is more readily accessible than the multivolume, complete version.

13. Voltaire, 59.

14. Jules Michelet, *History of France*, trans. G. H. Smith (New York: D. Appleton & Co., 1865), vol. II, 159, 145.

15. Michelet, II, 169.

16. Michelet, II, 229. Stereotypical feminine qualities have been used in the nineteenth and twentieth centuries to create hierarchies among nations and peoples, the most feminine being the more inferior, the most masculine, the superior. I am grateful to John R. Gillis for suggesting that I mention this metaphorical continuity in Western culture.

17. For Comnena, see, for example, Toynbee, II, 197–99; the phrase "mischief makers" comes from II, 143.

18. Toynbee, I, 455ff.

19. See Toynbee, II, 77.

20. Toynbee, II, 347.

21. See Toynbee, II, 344–45, and 373–75 for the general description of the characteristics of declining civilizations.

22. Gibbon; see, for example, Lucilla, 117; Faustina, 114.

23. Gibbon, fn 633, 636.

24. See Michelet, II, 159, 145.

25. Both sets of images are as old as the written record of Western culture with precursors in Biblical, classical, and Germanic texts. For Voltaire, see descriptions of Anne of Austria, Henrietta, the Montespan sisters, and Mme. de Maintenon, 257, 268, 282, 293.

26. Burckhardt, 389, 390–91, 394, 391.

27. See description of Marie de l'Incarnation in Francis Parkman, *The Jesuits in North America in the Seventeenth Century* (Boston: Little, Brown, & Co., 1925), 278.

28. Francis Parkman, *The Old Regime in Canada* (Boston: Little, Brown, & Co., 1924), 407.

29. Parkman, *Jesuits*, 23, 20.

30. Parkman, *Old Regime*, 407.

31. Each textbook has had multiple editions. I chose the versions of the late 1960s. R. R. Palmer and Joel Colton, *A History of the Modern World* (New York: Alfred A.

Knopf, 1966); Thomas A. Bailey, *The American Pageant* (Boston: DC Heath & Co. 1966); William H. McNeill, *A World History* (New York: Oxford University Press, 1967). Palmer and Colton began their collaboration with the second edition of Palmer's textbook in 1956. With the exception of a longer section on Catherine the Great, the collaboration seems to have had no effect on the way in which women were portrayed. The sentences and phrases in the 1966 edition are the same as those in the first edition of 1950.

32. See McNeill's preface for a description of his "organizing idea." These phrases are from the third edition of 1978, v–vii.

33. See plates in McNeill's textbook; McNeill used these captions in the 1978 edition as well. Palmer and Colton did much the same with their illustrations. They wanted art to "give life and body to certain ideas that recur in the text." Like McNeill they used portraits of women as stereotypes to personify "the idea of 'class.' " Millet's "Gleaners" signified the peasantry, the Hon. Mrs. Graham and Mrs. Seymour Fort the aristocracy and bourgeoisie. Their caption for David's "Woman of the Revolution" reinforced the classic image of the aged hag: her expression of "interest mixed with suspicion . . . her air of determination and even of defiance," the "coarse garments and untended hair, the colorless lips, the lined forehead and the evidences of suffering in the eyes, all reveal a life of much labor and few amenities." See Palmer and Colton, preface, vi, and the plates.

34. Palmer and Colton, preface, vi.

35. Bailey, preface, v.

36. Palmer and Colton, 77, 296, 705, 710.

37. Palmer and Colton, 611.

38. Palmer and Colton, 314, 316.

39. See Palmer and Colton, 246, 246–47, 247. Palmer and Colton rarely comment on men's physiques. Marie Louise, Napoleon's second wife, was the other woman in their history to be noted for her breasts. See 387.

40. Bailey, 27, 614. Pocahantas also enjoyed this kind of description: "the dusky Indian maiden." See 15. Descriptions of men referred neither to the numbers of their children nor to their skin tone.

41. Bailey, 344, 585, 560.

42. Bailey, 344, 559, 665.

43. Bailey, 344.

44. Bailey, 394, 561, 666, 342, 987.

45. See Palmer and Colton, 96–97.

46. Bailey, 528, 304.

47. Palmer and Colton, 47; Bailey, 365–66.

48. Bailey, 814, 536, 560.

49. Palmer and Colton, 690, 428.

50. See Palmer and Colton, 563.

Chapter 2

1. Jacob Burckhardt as quoted in Edward Hallett Carr, *What Is History?* (New York: Alfred A. Knopf, 1963), 69. Carr, a historian of the twentieth century, called it "a process of selection in terms of historical significance" with historians deciding "the standard" by which that significance would be measured, see 138.

2. See Peter Gay, "History and the Facts," *Columbia Forum*, III (2), (Spring 1974), 13. For an explicit investigation of this function of "history as a legitimator of action and cement of group cohesion," see Eric Hobsbawm and Terrence Ranger, eds., *The Invention of Tradition* (New York: Cambridge University Press, 1983), 12–13. Joan W. Scott writes of "master narratives . . . based on the forcible exclusion of Others' stories." Joan W. Scott, "History in Crisis? The Others' Side of the Story," in "AHR

Forum: The Old History and the New," *American Historical Review*, 94(3) (June 1989): 690. In the late 1920s Virginia Woolf wrote about this exclusion and imagined what women's history might be like. See for example, chapter 5, *A Room of One's Own* (New York: Harcourt, Brace & World, 1957 ed.)

3. Beard had offered a compromise of sorts to his critics. He reconciled himself to the difficulties by suggesting that a semblance of "objectivity," and thus authority, came when historians acknowledged their limitations and thus their potential bias. See Peter Novick, *That Noble Dream: The 'Objectivity Question' and the American Historical Profession* (New York: Cambridge University Press, 1989), introduction, 1–2, for a clear definition of "objectivity," and all that it connoted in the United States. He called the problem "nailing jelly to the wall." See his choice of quotations from Becker and Beard on 278, 257, and his description of the arguments of the 1930s, particularly 141–67. Novick believed that "objectivity" for United States historians meant "consensus," not absence of subjectivity; see, for example, 320. John Higham took a contrasting view: that historians disagree with each other when they are under attack as a profession. See his description of the 1930s, John Higham, *History: Professional Scholarship in America* (Baltimore: The Johns Hopkins University Press, 1983 ed.), 125–29.

4. These kinds of ideas have been called the "conceptual underpinnings" of the discipline. See Allan Megill, "Recounting the Past: 'Description, Explanation, and Narrative' in Historiography," *American Historical Review* 94 (3) (June 1989): 628.

5. For example, as Judith Allen, an Australian historian, pointed out, they would assert that "it was not they but their objects of study which excluded women." Judith Allen, "Evidence and Silence: Feminism and the Limits of History," in *Feminist Challenges: Social and Political Theory*, eds. Carole Pateman and Elizabeth Gross (Boston: Northeastern University Press, 1987), 178. David Hackett Fischer identified the third premise as the "genetic fallacy" by which an underlying ethical system is proclaimed to be "the objective teaching of history itself." David Hackett Fischer, *Historians' Fallacies: Toward a Logic of Historical Thought* (New York: Harper & Row, 1970), 156.

6. See Allen, 178. Joan W. Scott described the way it appeared to feminists: "A particular approach to historical inquiry claim [ed] to embody the entire discipline by defining itself as 'History' and declaring challenges to it to be non-historical, unacceptable and irrelevant because outside the boundaries of the field." Scott, "AHR Forum," 681.

7. H. Stuart Hughes. *History As Art and As Science: Twin Vistas on the Past* (New York: Harper & Row, 1965), 71.

8. Howard Zinn, *The Politics of History* (Chicago: University of Illinois Press, 1990 ed.), 3. Robinson as quoted in Zinn, p. 19. See the article on the "New Left" historians by Jonathan M. Wiener, "Radical Historians and the Crisis in American History 1959–1980," *Journal of American History*, 76 (2) (September 1989), 399–434. The issue includes a useful series of historiographical articles as "A Round Table: What Has Changed and Not Changed in American Historical Practice?" I am grateful to Sandi E. Cooper for bringing this issue of the journal to my attention.

9. Interview with William Appleman Williams, MARHO, eds. Henry Abelove, Betsy Blackmar, Peter Dimock, and Jonathan Schneer, *Visions of History* (New York: Pantheon Books, 1983 ed.), 129. I am grateful to Joseph B. Broderick for bringing this book to my attention.

10. See Lynn Hunt's discussion of this evolution in her introduction to Lynn Hunt, ed., *The New Cultural History* (Berkeley: University of California Press, 1989), 1–4.

11. Febvre as quoted in Hughes, 28.

12. Geography gave the "constants" in the human experience, what the Annalistes refer to as the *longue durée*, such factors as climate that influenced history across many centuries; the second level, "social realities" measured in decades, described "all the major forms of collective life, economies, institutions, social structures"; traditional

political history, the individual decisions of a day or week, filled the last section of the study. See Fernand Braudel, *On History*, trans. Sarah Matthews (Chicago: The University of Chicago: Press, 1980), 4, 11, 27, 31–33 and Fernand Braudel, *The Mediterranean and the Mediterranean World in the Age of Philip II*, trans. Sïan Reynolds (New York: Harper & Row, 1972), II, 1243, 1240.

13. Marc Bloch, *The Historian's Craft*, trans. Peter Putnam (New York: Vintage Books, 1964), 155. Braudel called it a freeing of history by "accepting and absorbing all the successive definitions" that otherwise confined it. Braudel, *On History*, 18, 69.

14. I am grateful to Temma Kaplan for suggestions of titles for this section.

15. See Carroll Smith-Rosenberg's description in "Hearing Women's Words: A Feminist Reconstruction of History," in *Disorderly Conduct: Visions of Gender in Victorian America* (New York: Oxford University Press, 1985), 17. The article first appeared in the September/October 1983 issue of *Academe*.

16. Hughes, 20. Academic and scholarly validation from United States scholars came for these new techniques and this more inclusive history with the publication in 1971 of two issues of *Daedalus*, the journal of the American Academy of Arts and Sciences. The editors included articles by many of the Annalistes: Jacques Le Goff, Pierre Goubert, and Emmanuel Le Roy Ladurie; as well as by their English and United States counterparts: Eric Hobsbawm, Robert Darnton, and Lawrence Stone. These historians wrote on topics as diverse as the broader definitions of history, the uses of archaeology, psychology, and the new quantitative methods. *Daedalus*, 100(1–2), (Winter and Spring 1971), entitled *Historical Studies Today* (1), and *The Historian and the World of the Twentieth Century* (2). The two issues were reprinted: Felix Gilbert and Stephen R. Graubard, eds., *Historical Studies Today* (New York: W. W. Norton & Co., 1972).

17. See, for example, the collection of Gutman's articles *Work, Culture, and Society in Industrializing America: Essays in American Working-Class History* (1976). See Novick on the evolution of African-American history, 475–87.

18. See Wiener on the acceptance of the radicals' views, 430–31.

19. Fischer, 64.

20. Hughes, 76.

21. Carr, 26, 43. Carr, however, hoped for unanimity: "Somewhere between these two poles—the north pole of valueless facts and the south pole of value judgments still struggling to transform themselves into facts—lies the realm of historical truth." Carr, 175.

22. See his essays, "What Is Radical History?" and "The Historians" in Zinn. For the question, see 303.

23. Lemisch as quoted in Wiener, 421. See also Lemisch's own essay in the "Roundtable" where he acknowledged the "blind spot" about women in Marxist history, but then chose the title: "Who Will Write a Left History of Art While We Are All Putting Our Balls on the Line?" *Journal of American History*, 76(2), (September 1989): 485–86.

24. Throughout the book the term "men's history" is used to signify those histories that "take men as the universal model for all human activity." This term acquired another meaning in the 1980s when social and cultural historians began to study ideas of the "masculine" as an influence on male experience. John R. Gillis suggested this clarification and offered the definition. John R. Gillis to Judith P. Zinsser, 24 February 1992.

25. Bloch, 25, 66.

26. Febvre wrote a history of Marguerite of Navarre, Georges Duby wrote about Joan of Arc, yet neither thought to study these women in the same way that they defined, researched, and wrote the history of men. Duby and Le Roy Ladurie are considered members of the second Annales generation. Both used the functionalist theories of the anthropologist Claude Levi-Strauss in their work. See Christine Fauré, "Absent from History," trans. Lillian S. Robinson, *Signs*, 7(3), (Autumn 1981): 74. See Susan Mosher

Stuard, "Viewpoint: The Annales School and Feminist History: Opening Dialogue with the American Stepchild," *Signs*, 7(1), (Autumn 1981): 141, 143.

27. See Braudel, *Mediterranean*, for example, on: Mary of Hungary, II, 923; Margaret of Parma, II, 1040; Mary Tudor, 930; Elizabeth Tudor, II, 840, 1044, 1197; Catherine de' Medici, II, 686, 1022, 1106.

28. Braudel, *On History*, viii.

29. Stuard, "Annales," 142.

30. Ann J. Lane commenting on Thompson, as quoted in Mari Jo Buhle, "Gender and Labor History," in J. Carroll Moody and Alice Kessler-Harris, eds., *Perspectives on American Labor History: the Problems of Synthesis* (DeKalb: Northern Illinois University Press, 1989), 67.

31. See Joan W. Scott, *Gender and the Politics of History* (New York: Columbia University Press, 1988), "Women's History," 21–22; "American Women Historians: 1884–1984," 197; "Women in *The Making of the English Working Class*," 72–77. See in E. P. Thompson. *The Making of the English Working Class* (New York: Vintage Books, 1963), for example, 201–3, 234, 265, 413–16, 730. For a recent critique of U.S. historians' work see Susan Levine, "Class and Gender: Herbert Gutman and the Women of 'Shoe City,' " *Labor History*, 29, (summer 1988).

32. Smith-Rosenberg, "Words," 18; Carroll Smith-Rosenberg, "The New Woman and the New History," *Feminist Studies*, 3 (1 and 2), (Fall 1975): 189. On inclusion as persons "in their own right," see Gerda Lerner, *Teaching Women's History* (Washington, DC: American Historical Association, 1981), 6. See also Mary Beth Norton, "Review Essay: American History," *Signs*, 5 (2), (Winter 1979): 324. Barbara Sicherman first pointed out that "when social historians are hoping to rewrite history 'from the bottom up,' the study of women has an undeniable legitimacy." Barbara Sicherman. "Review Essay: American History," *Signs*, I (2), (Winter 1975): 461. Family history flourished as a new specialty in the 1970s and 1980s but almost by definition had to keep women in traditional roles. See, for a recent assessment of the field, Judith E. Smith, "Review Essay: Family History and Feminist History," *Feminist Studies*, 17 (2), (Summer 1991): 349–64.

33. For a similar analysis of the cause and effect relationship between the radicalism of the 1960s and black feminist historians' ability to gain a hearing see Jacquelyn Dowd Hall, "Partial Truths," *Signs*, 14 (4), (Summer 1989), 903–4.

34. See Herbert Gutman's interview, *Visions*, 204. David Potter made his case for the study of women's as distinct from men's history in the early 1960s. See his essay "National Character," *American History and the Social Sciences*, ed. Edward N. Saveth (New York: Free Press, 1964), especially, 430–32, 437–39, 445. Carl N. Degler, "What the Women's Movement Has Done to American History," eds. Elizabeth Langland and Walter Gove, *A Feminist Perspective in the Academy: The Difference It Makes* (Chicago: The University of Chicago Press, 1981), 82–83. I am grateful to Suzanne Lebsock for the reference to Potter's essay.

35. Carr, 26.

Section II

1. Gerda Lerner, *The Origins of Patriarchy* (New York: Oxford University Press, 1986), 6.

2. The fact that the collection was not published until 1976 is misleading. All of the articles were written between 1969 and 1973. Most were well-known to other feminist scholars who had heard them as papers at professional conferences or seen them published in local or specialized journals like the *Massachusetts Review* and *Radical America*. Berenice A. Carroll to Judith P. Zinsser, 3 March 1992.

3. Joan Kelly, "The Social Relations of the Sexes: Methodological Implications of

Women's History," in *Women, History and Theory: The Essays of Joan Kelly* (Chicago: The University of Chicago Press, 1984), 15.

Chapter 3

1. See Gutman's description of these significant shifts in thought and action; Herbert Gutman interview, in MARHO, *Visions of History*, eds. Henry Abelove, Betsy Blackmar, Peter Dimock, and Jonathan Schneer (New York: Pantheon Books, 1983 ed.), 203, 202.

2. Joan W. Scott, "Women's History and the Rewriting of History," in *The Impact of Feminist Research in the Academy*, ed. Christie Farnham (Bloomington: Indiana University Press, 1987), 390.

3. Susan M. Stuard, "Viewpoint: The Annales School and Feminist History: Opening Dialogue with the American Stepchild," *Signs*, 7(1), (Autumn 1981): 136.

4. On the interrelationship between feminism and feminist scholarship, see Ellen DuBois as quoted in Louise A. Tilly, "Gender, Women's History, and Social History," *Social Science History*, 13(4), (Winter 1989): 441. See Gerda Lerner, *Teaching Women's History* (Washington, DC: American Historical Association, 1981) for the significance of Mead's books, and of *Patterns of Culture* (1934) by another anthropologist, Ruth Benedict. Mead had first suggested these ideas in her books on South Pacific cultures, for example, *Coming of Age in Samoa* (1928) and *Sex and Temperament in Three Primitive Societies* (1935).

5. See, for a discussion of de Beauvoir's approach, *New French Feminisms*, eds., Elaine Marks and Isabelle de Curtivron (New York: Schocken Books, 1981), 7. They have a selection from the introduction to *The Second Sex*, 46–48.

6. Sheila Rowbotham, *Woman's Consciousness, Man's World* (New York: Penguin Books, 1987 ed.), 28. See also Hilda Smith, "Feminism and the Methodology of Women's History," *Liberating Women's History: Theoretical and Critical Essays*, ed. Berenice A. Carroll (Urbana: University of Illinois Press, 1976), 371. See also Sheila Ryan Johansson, " 'Herstory' as History: A New Field or Another Fad?" in ed. Carroll, 427.

7. DuBois as quoted in Tilly, 441; Dolores Barracano Schmidt and Earl Robert Schmidt, "The Invisible Woman: The Historian as Professional Magician," in ed. Carroll, 54. Miriam Schneir, who compiled one of the first anthologies of feminist writings stated it with more militancy: "In short women have been deprived of their history—thus, their group identity." Miriam Schneir, ed., *Feminism: The Essential Historical Writings* (New York: Vintage Books, 1972 ed.), xi.

8. Linda Gordon, interview, *Visions*, 76.

9. Her full name was Elizabeth Fries Lummis Ellet. See Carol Ruth Berkin and Mary Beth Norton, *Women of America: A History* (Boston: Houghton Mifflin, 1979), 4–5. Historians speak of two "waves" of feminism: the first in the nineteenth century culminating in the 1920 women's suffrage amendment to the United States Constitution, the second originating in the 1960s and continuing to the present.

10. The document collection is Sophonisba Breckenridge's 1931 *Marriage and the Civil Rights of Women*; the bibliography is Eugenie A. Leonard, Sophie H. Drinker, and Miriam Y. Holden's *The American Woman in Colonial and Revolutionary Times: 1565–1800*, (1962). This list is by no means definitive. I have primarily chosen works by United States and European authors still central to historians' research. For fuller descriptions of earlier books in United States women's history see Berkin and Norton, introduction; Lerner, *Teaching*; Kathryn Kish Sklar, "American Female Historians in Context 1770–1930," *Feminist Studies*, 3(1 and 2), (Fall 1975). Sklar also discussed the lives of the authors. See Anne Firor Scott, *Making the Invisible Woman Visible* (Chicago: University of Illinois Press, 1984) for women historians in the 1960s, fn xxiii. For

European women historians, some of whom wrote on women, see Bonnie G. Smith, "The Contribution of Women to Modern Historiography in Great Britain, France, and the United States 1750–1940," *American Historical Review*, 89(3), (June 1984); Ellen Jacobs, "Writing the Record: Women in the Historical Profession in England: 1900–1940," Berkshire Conference on Women's History, Douglass College, New Brunswick, N.J. June 1990.

11. Gerda Lerner credited Beard with inventing the modern concept of women's history. Gerda Lerner, *The Majority Finds Its Past: Placing Women in History* (New York: Oxford University Press, 1979), introduction, xxii. Feminist scholars also cite Virgina Woolf's speculations on women's history in *A Room of One's Own* (1929), especially the description of Shakespeare's "wonderfully gifted sister, Judith." See 48–50 and also chapter 5 (New York: Harcourt, Brace & World, Inc., 1957 ed.).

12. Mary Ritter Beard as quoted in Barbara K. Turoff, *Mary Beard As a Force in History* (Dayton, Ohio: Wright State University, 1979), 16. While in England Beard worked with the English suffragist Emmeline Pankhurst.

13. Turoff, 2.

14. Mary R. and Charles A. Beard, *The Rise of American Civilization* (New York: Macmillan, 1937 ed.), 25, 601.

15. For this and others of her writings see the collection *Mary Ritter Beard: A Sourcebook*, ed. Ann J. Lane (New York: Schocken Books, 1977).

16. Beard as quoted in ed. Lane, 34. Miriam Y. Holden, one of Beard's principal allies, had a large private collection of women's history housed in her eastside brownstone in New York City. Beard, and later Gerda Lerner, used this collection when writing their histories of women.

17. See ed. Lane, 35, 46.

18. Mary Beard, *Woman as Force in History: A Study in Traditions and Realities* (New York: Macmillan, 1946), 37, 144, v.

19. Beard, *Force*, vi. See also 47, 331, and Turoff, 40, 41. For her ideas on law, see, for example, 171–72, 177 ff., 203, 204; some sample descriptions of medieval and early modern queens appear on 214 ff, 305 ff., of mystics on 264–66, of writers on 323.

20. See Beard, *Force*, 95, 115–16, 118–19 and ed. Lane, 2. In 1934 when asked about the ERA, Beard explained: "I simply regard it as inadequate today. Men are so incompetent and ridiculous when not base that I can't stomach the idea of equality as the ultimate goal any longer." Beard as quoted in Mary Beth Norton, "Teaching Women About Themselves" (review of Nancy Cott, ed., *"A Woman Making History: Mary Ritter Beard Through Her Letters,"* New York Times Book Review, (13 January 1991): 18.

21. Beard, *Force*, 276. For use of the phrase "man as the measure" see Berenice A. Carroll, "Mary Beard's *Woman As Force in History*: A Critique," ed. Carroll, 33.

22. Beard, *Force*, 147, 332. On this view of women as reformers see also Turoff, 38, 48, 51, and Lane, ed., 64–65.

23. See, on Hexter's attitudes, Peter Novick, *That Noble Dream: The "Objectivity Question" and the American Historical Profession* (New York: Cambridge University Press, 1989 ed.), 375, 394, 624; and John Higham, *History: Professional Scholarship in America* (Baltimore: The Johns Hopkins University Press, 1983 ed.), 133. For mention of the review see Johannson, and a full discussion in Carroll, 27–39, both in ed. Carroll, 416, The review appeared on 17 March 1946. Jeannette P. Nichols reviewed the book for the American Historical Association and described Beard as "scholarly in spite of herself." Nichols suggested a new version, "a small, paperbound, 'pocket-book-type' of book" that would be accessible to "many thousands of women" and thus accomplish Beard's purpose more effectively. Jeannette P. Nichols, *American Historical Review*, 52(2), (January 1947): 292–94.

24. For discussions of the book see Carroll, ed. Carroll, 26–41; and ed. Lane, especially 68.

25. Lerner, *Majority*, introduction, xxi. See also on the impact of first reading Beard's book, xxi, xxiii.

26. See Lerner, *Majority*, introduction, xxvi. Friedan's book described the dissatisfactions of educated, suburban women. The *President's Report* detailed women's disadvantaged circumstances, such as the relative inaccessibility of skilled and professional training and jobs, discriminatory pay, fewer employment opportunities, lower standards of living, and poorer health care.

27. For a historiographical analysis touching on many of these themes see Linda K. Kerber, "Separate Spheres, Female Worlds, Woman's Place: The Rhetoric of Women's History," *The Journal of American History*, 75(1), (June 1988): especially 28, 38–39.

28. See Lerner, *Majority*, 153. The list of publications in chronological order is: "The Lady and the Mill Girl: Changes in the Status of Women in the Age of Jackson" (Spring 1969); "New Approaches to the Study of Women in American History" (Fall 1969); *The Woman in American History* (1971); *Black Women in White America: A Documentary History* (1972); "Placing Women in History: Definitions and Challenges" (Fall 1975); "The Majority Finds Its Past" (May 1976); *The Female Experience: An American Documentary* (1977); *Teaching Women's History* (1981). All of these articles and some of her speeches are in the collection, *The Majority Finds Its Past: Placing Women in History* (1979).

29. Lerner, "The Lady," in *Majority*, 27–28. See also Lerner, "New Approaches," in *Majority*, 8.

30. Lerner, "Majority" in *Majority*, 167 and "Placing" in *Majority*, 159. It was in this last article that she assigned a new status to traditional accounts of the past: "History, as written and perceived up to now, is the history of a minority, who may well turn out to be a subgroup," 158.

31. Lerner, *Teaching*, 3; "Placing" in *Majority*, 149, 180.

32. Gerda Lerner, *The Origins of Patriarchy* (New York: Oxford University Press, 1986), 5. The fullest explanation of women's exclusion occurs in "The Challenge," in *Majority*. In the 1980s and 1990s black feminist historians have made a particular point of these differences in experience. Deborah K. King writes of "differences between blacks and whites, between black men and black women, between black women and white women." Deborah K. King, "Multiple Jeopardy, Multiple Consciousness: The Context of a Black Feminist" *Signs*, 14(1), (Autumn 1988), 45–46.

33. See Lerner, *Teaching*, 6; Lerner, "Majority" in *Majority*, 180; "The Challenge," in *Majority*, 171, 178–79.

34. Lerner, *Teaching*, 57; see also Lerner, "Majority," in *Majority*, 164, and "The Challenge," in *Majority*, 170. Women's contributions to the process were described in "New Approaches," fn. 12, and in "Majority," 166, both in *Majority*.

35. Lerner, *Patriarchy*, 5; "Majority," in *Majority*, 159. *Ms.* magazine popularized Jane O'Reilly's way of characterizing this moment of identification. O'Reilly used the word "click" to indicate an instant, that point when a woman saw everything differently and understood what feminists had been talking about.

36. Lerner, "Placing," in *Majority*, 148; see also 145–147.

37. Lerner, "Majority," in *Majority*, 160; see "The Lady" in *Majority* for the first discussion of the need to write about women of different circumstances; see also the introduction to *Majority*, xxviii, and the three essays on black women's history in the collection: "Black Women in the United States: A Problem in Historiography and Interpretation," "The Community Work of Black Women," "Black and White Women in Interaction and Confrontation."

38. For a description of this phase and suggestions about how to write it, see Lerner, "Placing," in *Majority*, 158.

39. Lerner, "Majority," 162; introduction, xxxi; both in *Majority*.

40. See Lerner, introduction to *Majority* and "The Challenge," in *Majority*, 180.

41. Memo from Gerda Lerner to the Committee on Restructuring the College, 29 April 1971, 1. Letter "To All Women Faculty Members," September 1971, Amy Swerdlow files.

42. Kelly, *Essays*, introduction, xi.

43. Joan Kelly to Gerda Lerner, 6 October 1971, Amy Swerdlow files.

44. For the account of Kelly's discovery of women's history, see Kelly, *Essays*, introduction, xii–xiii, xiii.

45. Joan Kelly, "Early Feminist Theory and the *Querelle des Femmes*," in Kelly, *Essays*, 79.

46. Joan Kelly, "Did Women Have a Renaissance," in Kelly, *Essays*, 28, 20, 27. This essay first appeared in the 1977 collection of *Becoming Visible: Women in European History*, edited by Renate Bridenthal and Claudia Koonz. On the significance of Kelly's essay, see Carolyn Lougee, "Review Essay: Modern European History," *Signs*, 2(3), (Spring 1977): 632.

47. Kelly, *Essays*, introduction, xiii.

48. Kelly referring to Dow and Telle, two authorities on early modern literary texts, in "Early Feminist Theory and the *Querelle des Femmes*, in Kelly, *Essays*, fn. 24, 101.

49. See Joan Kelly, "The Social Relations of the Sexes: Methodological Implications of Women's History," in Kelly, *Essays*, 1. This essay was originally presented as a paper in 1973.

50. Lerner, "The Challenge," in *Majority*, 170.

51. Kelly, introduction, xix; "Relations," 9; both in Kelly. *Essays*. Hilda Smith at the University of Chicago was formulating similar ideas at the same time. See her essay "Feminism and the Methodology of Women's History" in ed. Carroll.

52. Joan Kelly, "Seminar and Course Evaluation," written for Sarah Lawrence College, n.d., 1, Amy Swerdlow files. For example, she named the members of the group who had particularly helped in the formulation of "The Social Relations of the Sexes": Marylin Arthur, Blanche Wiesen Cook, Pamella Farley, Mary Feldblum, Alice Kessler-Harris, Amy Swerdlow, Carole Turbin. See "Relations," in Kelly, *Essays*, fn. 1, 15.

53. Suzanne Lebsock, interview, 16 November 1990; Alice Kessler-Harris, interview, New Brunswick N.J., 10 April 1991.

54. Kelly, "Seminar and Course Evaluation," 1, Amy Swerdlow files.

55. See Turoff, 48, 51.

Chapter 4

1. Joan Kelly, "Seminar and Course Evaluation," written for Sarah Lawrence College, n.d. 1, 2, Amy Swerdlow files.

2. Temma Kaplan taught the first course offered by the UCLA history department in the 1971 winter quarter. It was entitled "Women and Capitalism." Temma Kaplan interview, New York City, 1 December 1991.

3. Anne Firor Scott, *Making the Invisible Woman Visible* (Chicago: University of Chicago Press, 1984), 364. Her early book was entitled *The Southern Lady: From Pedestal to Politics, 1830–1930* (1970).

4. Linda Gordon's group included Mari Jo Buhle, Ellen DuBois, Nancy Cott, Kathyrn Kish Sklar, and Lise Vogel. Linda Gordon interview, MARHO, *Visions of*

History, eds. Henry Abelove, Betsy Blackmar, Peter Dimock, and Jonathan Schneer (New York: Pantheon Books, 1983 ed.), 76.

5. Gerda Lerner, *Teaching Women's History* (Washington DC: American Historical Association, 1981), 3.

6. Carol Ruth Berkin and Mary Beth Norton, *Women of America: A History* (Boston: Houghton Mifflin, 1979), 15.

7. See, for example: Marilyn B. Young, ed., *Women in China: Studies in Social Change and Feminism* (1973); Roxane Witke and Margery Wolf, eds., *Women in Chinese Society* (1975); Nancy J. Hafkin and Edna G. Bay, eds., *Women in Africa: Studies in Social and Economic Change* (1976); Asunción Lavrin, ed., *Latin American Women: Historical Perspectives* (1978); June Hahner, *Women in Latin American History: Their Lives and Views* (1979); Lois Beck and Nikki Keddi, eds., *Women in the Muslim World* (1978). The Organization of American Historians's *Teaching Packets for Integrating Women's History into Courses on Africa, Asia, Latin America, the Caribbean, and the Middle East* (1988) gives an extensive series of bibliographies for women in these parts of the world and includes listings of monographs from the 1970s and early 1980s.

8. The principal bibliographic essays that appeared in the 1970s and give a sense of the new field were: (US women's history) Barbara Sicherman, "Review Essay: American History," *Signs*, 1 (2), (Winter 1975): 461–85, and Mary Beth Norton, "Review Essay: American History," *Signs* 5 (2), (Winter 1979): 324–37; (European women's history) Natalie Zemon Davis, "Women's History in Transition: the European Case," *Feminist Studies* 3 (3/4), (1976): 83–103 and Carolyn C. Lougee, "Review Essay: Modern European History," *Signs*, 2 (3), (Spring 1977), 628–50. Gerda Lerner and Carroll Smith-Rosenberg wrote more interpretive essays in the 1970s: "Placing Women in History: Definitions and Challenges" and "The New Woman and the New History," respectively. Both essays were reprinted in their collected essays. More specialized bibliographies began to appear as well; for example, by era, Kathleen Casey's and Carolly Erickson's "Women in the Middle Ages: A Working Bibliography," in *Medieval Studies*, 37, (1975); or by topic, Elizabeth Wood, "Review Essay: Women in Music," *Signs*, 6 (2), (Winter 1980). Gerda Lerner's pamphlet, *Teaching Women's History* was particularly inclusive with extensive listings on minority black, Hispanic, and Asian women in the United States. For other work on minority women, see also the special issue of *Frontiers* on Chicanas, 5 (2), (Summer 1980), and Rayna Green's "Review Essay: Native American Women," *Signs*, 6 (2), (Winter 1980). For listings of more recent works on minority women, see *Unequal Sisters: A Multicultural Reader in United States Women's History*, eds. Ellen Carol DuBois and Vicki L. Ruiz (New York: Routledge, 1990).

9. On the influence of other disciplines, see Sicherman, 462–63; Lougee, 628; Carroll Smith-Rosenberg, "The New Women and The New History," *Feminist Studies*, 3 (1/2), (Fall 1975): 188–91. The works most often referred to were: Tamara K. Hareven's article "Family Time and Industrial Time: Family and Work in a Planned Corporate Town, 1900–1924," *Journal of Urban History* 1, (May 1975): 365–89, and the following two collections of articles: Michelle Zimbalist Rosaldo and Louise Lamphere, eds., *Woman, Culture, & Society* (Stanford CA: Stanford University Press, 1974); and Rayna R. Reiter, ed., *Toward an Anthropology of Women* (New York: Monthly Review Press, 1975). Rosaldo, Rubin, and Ortner explored the origins and continuation of women's subordinate status within societies.

10. See introduction to the first edition of Renate Bridenthal and Claudia Koonz, eds., *Becoming Visible: Women in European History* (New York: Houghton Mifflin, 1977), 2; Nancy F. Cott, ed., *Root of Bitterness: Documents of the Social History of American Women* (New York: EP Dutton & Co., 1972), 5.

11. Eleanor S. Riemer and John C. Fout, eds., *European Women: A Documentary*

History 1789–1945 (New York: Schocken Books, 1980), xiii. See for a similar statement of purpose for the history of United States women, Anne Firor Scott, 368; Mary S. Hartman and Lois W. Banner, eds., *Clio's Consciousness Raised* (New York: Harper & Row Publishers, 1974), vii.

12. Lerner as quoted in Dorothy O. Helly, " 'Doing History Today' A Revolution in Knowledge: Feminist Scholarship Transforming the Discipline," unpublished, 15; see Davis, "Women's History," 86; Carol Hymnowitz and Michaele Weissman, *A History of Women in America* (New York: Bantam Books, Inc., 1978), xii; Lougee, 630.

13. Cott, ed., 28. In addition to Cott and Lerner, a number of historians from the 1970s on have commented on this commitment to write of many women's different experiences. See Berkin and Norton, 9; Barbara Sicherman, E. William Monter, Joan Wallach Scott, Kathryn Kish Sklar, *Recent United States Scholarship on the History of Women* (Washington DC: American Historical Association, 1980), ii; see Lise Vogel, "Telling Tales: Historians of Our Own Lives," *The Journal of Women's History*, 2 (3), (Winter 1991): 89–101, for a bibliography of articles on this subject.

14. Carroll Smith-Rosenberg, "Hearing Women's Words: A Feminist Reconstruction of History," in *Disorderly Conduct: Visions of Gender in Victorian America* (New York: Oxford University Press, 1985), 19. See also Sheila Ryan Johansson, " 'Herstory' as History: A New Field or Another Fad?" *Liberating Women's History: Theoretical and Critical Essays*, ed. Berenice A. Carroll (Urbana: University of Illinois Press, 1976), 409.

15. Women "fared better," feminist historians discovered, in "periods of social dysfunction," not in those eras praised for uniformity, order, and the formalization of political, legal, and economic institutions and practices. These ideas came from a number of works. Marilyn J. Boxer and Jean H. Quataert, *Connecting Spheres: Women in the Western World, 1500 to the Present* (New York: Oxford University Press, 1987), 6, 5. For the concept of a "re-vision" of history, see 12. See Renate Bridenthal as quoted in Sicherman, 484; Hilda Smith, "Feminism and the Methodology of Women's History, ed. Carroll, 382.

16. For Kelly's complete list, see Joan Kelly, "Did Women Have a Renaissance?" in eds. Bridenthal and Koonz, 20. See Lerner, *Teaching* for her questions, appendix, 67–68. Davis, "Women's History," 90. See for other approaches, Lois Banner, "On Writing Women's History," *Journal of Interdisciplinary History* II (2) (Autumn 1971), 352; Riemer and Fout, xiv–xv; Johansson, ed. Carroll, 406–8.

17. See Miriam Schneir, ed., *Feminism: The Essential Historical Writings* (New York: Vintage Books, 1972 ed.), xv, xix; Sicherman, 464; Cott, ed., 3. See also Susan Groag Bell, *Women: From the Greeks to the French Revolution: An Historical Anthology* (Belmont, Calif.: Wadsworth Publishing Co., 1973), 1.

18. Kathryn Kish Sklar, *Catharine Beecher: A Study in American Domesticity* (1973); Judith R. Walkowitz, *Prostitution and Victorian Society: Women, Class and the State* (1980); Ruth Rosen, *The Lost Sisterhood: Prostitution in America, 1900–1918* (1980).

19. Linda Gordon, "A Socialist View of Women's Studies: A Reply to the Editorial," *Signs*, 1(2), (Winter 1975): 563.

20. For these works, see *Signs*, 2, (1976): 293–303 for Pagels's article; Olwen Huften's is entitled "Women in the French Revolution," *Past and Present*, 53, (November 1971): 90–108; Angela Davis's article appeared in *Black Scholar* 3, (December 1971): 3–15; and Julie Roy Jeffrey's book is entitled *Frontier Women: the Trans-Mississippi West, 1840–1880* (Hill and Wang, 1979).

21. See Hartman and Banner, eds., vii; *Recent US Scholarship*, i.

22. The ideas came from a variety of sources. See Smith, ed. Carroll, 370, 369; Bridenthal and Koonz, 2; Carroll Smith-Rosenberg, "Words," 12. See also for this sense

of scholarly and political "mission," Marilyn J. Boxer, "For and About Women: The Theory and Practice of Women's Studies," *Signs*, 7(3), (Spring 1982): 693.

23. Ellen Carol DuBois, Gail Paradise Kelly, Elizabeth Lapovsky Kennedy, Carolyn W. Korsmeyer, and Lillian S. Robinson, *Feminist Scholarship: Kindling in the Groves of Academe* (Urbana: University of Illinois Press, 1985), 8. Joan W. Scott, "American Women Historians: 1884–1984," *Gender and the Politics of History* (New York: University of Columbia Press, 1988), 192–93. On "masculinist" history see also Vinnie Thom, ed., *The Effects of Feminist Approaches on Research Methodologies* (Waterloo, Ontario: Wilfrid Laurier University Press, 1989), 2–3, 6. Mary Field Belenky, Blythe McVicker Clinchy, Nancy Rule Goldberger, and Jill Mattuck Tarule, *Women's Ways of Knowing: The Development of Self, Voice, and Mind* (New York: Basic Books, 1986) explored this kind of thinking and called it "disciplined subjectivity." See chapter 10.

24. Bridenthal and Koonz, eds., 10; Cott, ed., 28, Riemer and Fout, xxi; Gordon, "A Socialist View," 564.

25. Berkin and Norton, 3; Smith on "non-feminists," "feminists," and history, ed. Carroll, 371–372.

26. For Carroll's view and the question, see Berenice A. Carroll, "Introduction," v, x–xi. See also Smith, 369, both in ed. Carroll. Carroll describes her purpose in this way: "She believed that women's history needed no proof of its legitimacy, but had its own specific needs, namely: conceptual clarification, a critical historiography, and a testing of theories on a comparative basis. Carroll looked to a time when all historians would recognize the hidden biases in asking of women's history such questions as . . ." Berenice A. Carroll to Judith P. Zinsser, 28 April 1992, 2.

27. J. W. Scott, "Women Historians," *Gender*, 195.

28. For these criticisms, see Judith Shapiro as quoted in Elizabeth Langland and Walter Gore, eds. *A Feminist Perspective in the Academy: The Difference It Makes* (Chicago: University of Chicago Press, 1981), 2; Carl N. Degler, "What the Women's Movement Has Done to American History," eds. Langland and Gore, 82; Adrienne Rich, "Toward a Woman-Centered University," *On Lies, Secrets, and Silence: Selected Prose 1966–1978* (New York: WW Norton & Company, 1979), 135–36; A. F. Scott, 366. See also Boxer, "For and About Women," as printed in eds. Minnich et. al., 100.

29. For the views of women's historians, see Sicherman, 461, 468–69, 472–75; Kathryn Kish Sklar, "Comment: A Call for Comparisons" *American Historical Review*, 95(4), (October 1990), 1110. See also Smith-Rosenberg, "Words," 11.

30. This way of thinking has been called "integrationist." See, for example, Degler, ed. Langland. For criticisms, see: Marilyn J. Boxer, "Book Review," *Signs*, 10 (4), (Summer 1985), 806; Doroles Barracano Schmidt and Earl Robert Schmidt, "The Invisible Woman: The Historian As Professional Magician," ed. Carroll, 43–44; J. W. Scott, "Women Historians," *Gender*, 16–17; K. Daniels as quoted in Judith Allen, "Evidence and Silence: Feminism and the Limits of History," *Feminist Challenges: Social and Political Theory*, eds. Carole Pateman and Elizabeth Gross (Boston: Northeastern University Press, 1987), 181.

31. Elizabeth Minnich, *New York Times*, 23 November 1981, AHA Commission on Women Historians files. Many feminist historians have written of this need not just to enlarge but to transform traditional histories. See Ann D. Gordon, Mari Jo Buhle, and Nancy Schrom Dye, "The Problem of Women's History" in ed. Carroll, 89; and J. W. Scott, "Gender: A Useful Category of Historical Analysis," *Gender*, 30. Linda K. Kerber, "Separate Spheres, Female Worlds, Woman's Place: The Rhetoric of Women's History," *Journal of American History*, 75(1), (June 1988), suggested the idea of thinking of these approaches as "bridges" between women's and traditional histories; see, for example, 38–39. For a similar summary of the various syntheses formulated by women's

historians, see Phyllis Stock-Morton, "Finding Our Own Ways: Different Paths to Women's History in the United States," in *Writing Women's History: International Perspectives*, eds. Karen Offen, Ruth Roach Pierson, and Jane Rendall (Bloomington: Indiana University Press, 1991), 59–77. For a very complete bibliography of articles and books exploring these theoretical approaches, see *Journal of Women's History*, 2(3), (Winter 1991): 147–57.

32. The best known of these new publications is *History Workshop*, founded in England in the late 1970s. This periodical now describes itself as the "Journal of Socialism and Feminism." The equivalent journal in the United States is *Radical History Review* founded in the early 1970s.

33. David Montgomery, interview, *Visions*, 177. The editor of *Radical America* described "Women in American Society: An Historical Contribution" by Mari Jo Buhle, Ann G. Gordon, and Nancy Schrom as their "most important [and most often reprinted] single article" in the 1970s.

34. See on Beard, Ann J. Lane, ed., *Mary Ritter Beard: A Sourcebook* (New York: Schocken Books, 1977), 66–67; Bridenthal and Koonz, 5. Catharine A. MacKinnon the legal theorist questioned the interrelationship in yet another way: "Is male dominance a creation of capitalism or is capitalism one expression of male dominance?" See her "Feminism, Marxism, Method, and the State: An Agenda for Theory," *Signs*, 7(3), (Spring 1982): 517. Gordon, *Visions*, 78, 79.

35. For this approach, see, for example, Temma Kaplan's essay "Female Consciousness and Collective Action: the Case of Barcelona, 1910–1918," *Signs*, 7(3), (1982).

36. Bridenthal's article appeared in *Radical America* 10 (March–April 1976): 3–11; Linda Gordon's was published in *Marxist Perspectives*, 1 (Fall 1978): 128–35; MacKinnon's article appeared in *Signs*, 7 (3), (Spring 1982): 515–44. For more recent commentaries by Marxist-feminists, see Liz Stanley, "Recovering *Women* in History from Feminist Deconstructionism," *Women's Studies International Forum*, 13(1/2), (1990); and Elizabeth Fox-Genovese, "Socialist-Feminist American Women's History," *Journal of Women's History*, 1(3), (Winter 1990).

37. I am grateful to Temma Kaplan and Renate Bridenthal for their help in separating out the key characteristics of this synthesis. On these ideas and those in the next paragraph, see Gisela Bock, "Women's History and Gender History: Aspects of an International Debate," *Gender and History*, 1(1), (Spring 1989): 19; Gordon, *Visions*, 83; Kerber, 28. For an understanding of how feminist historians discovered these distinctions for women in the United States, see Alice Kessler-Harris, *Out to Work: A History of Wage-Earning Women in the United States* (New York: Oxford University Press, 1982). Scholars of black history discovered that black men were the exception. They have been even more vulnerable at the lowest paid levels of employment than black women.

38. Joan Kelly, "The Doubled Vision of Feminist Theory," in *Women, History and Theory: The Essays of Joan Kelly* (Chicago: The University of Chicago Press, 1984), 52.

39. See for early descriptions of this approach: Temma Kaplan, "A Marxist Analysis of Women and Capitalism," *Women in Politics*, ed. Jane S. Jaquette (New York: John Wiley & Sons, 1974); Sicherman, 462.

40. For the criticisms of Marxism when applied to women's history, see: Joan W. Scott, "Women's History and the Rewriting of History" *The Impact of Feminist Research in the Academy*, ed. Christie Farnham (Bloomington: Indiana University Press, 1987), 41; Sicherman, 463–64; Smith, ed. Carroll, 383; Mari Jo Buhle, "Gender and Labor History," *Perspectives on American Labor History: the Problems of Synthesis*, eds. J. Carroll Moody and Alice Kessler-Harris (DeKalb: Northern Illinois University Press, 1989), 67–68.

41. Barbara Welter's article appeared in *American Quarterly*, 18 (2, Part 1), (Summer 1976): 151–74. See, for example, the work of Aileen Kraditor, Carroll Smith-

Rosenberg, Nancy Cott, and Estelle Freedman. By the 1980s writings on women in many periods used this dichotomy. The seventh Berkshire Conference in Women's History in 1988 continued to use the idea, as a foil if nothing else. The book of articles collected from the proceedings and edited by Dorothy O. Helly and Susan Reverby was entitled *Beyond Dichotomy: Public & Private Spheres in Historical Perspective.* In addition, scholars in other disciplines explored the idea in their feminist analyses. For example, Linda Nicholson used it for her book on political theory, *Gender and History: The Limits of Social Theory in the Age of the Family* (1986).

42. Carroll Smith-Rosenberg, "Words," 27.

43. See *Disorderly Conduct* for Smith-Rosenberg's article. See Ellen DuBois, "Politics and Culture in Women's History: A Symposium," *Feminist Studies,* 6 (1) (Spring 1980), 29–31; Mary Maples Dunn, "Women of Light," eds. Norton and Berkin, 114–33; Nancy Cott, *The Grounding of Modern Feminism* (New Haven: Yale University Press, 1987), and Estelle Freedman, "Separatism as Strategy: Female Institution Building and American Feminism 1870–1930," *Feminist Studies,* 5 (3) (Fall 1979), 513–14. Carl Degler used this concept of separate spheres as the organizing principle for his analysis of the women's rights movement, *At Odds: Women and the Family in America from the Revolution to the Present* (New York: Oxford University Press, 1980). He argued that men acquiesced when feminist demands reinforced the separation and resisted when they did not. See Kerber 16–17 and her review, *Signs,* 8 (1) (Autumn 1982): 138–43. Lillian Faderman's *Surpassing the Love of Men: Romantic Friendship and Love Between Women from the Renaissance to the Present* (1981) explored the whole range of women's loving relationships that became highlighted as a result of Smith-Rosenberg's original insight.

44. Gordon, *Visions,* 91. See Kerber's historiographical article, "Separate Spheres," 9–39, especially 28, 38–39. For other criticisms, see the "Symposium" published in *Feminist Studies* cited previously with contributions by Ellen DuBois, Mari Jo Buhle, Temma Kaplan, Gerda Lerner, and Carroll Smith-Rosenberg. Judith R. Walkowitz introduced the discussion.

45. Kelly, "Doubled Vision," *Essays,* 57. See also Paula Baker, "The Domestication of Politics: Women and American Political Society 1780–1920," *Unequal Sisters: A Multicultural Reader in U.S. Women's History,* eds. Ellen Carol DuBois and Vicki L. Ruiz (New York: Routledge, 1990).

46. See for Smith-Rosenberg's approach, "Words," 16. See Allen, 181 and Vogel, 3–4 for discussion of the limitations and the subsequent criticisms. Nancy A. Hewitt, "Beyond the Search for Sisterhood: American Women's History in the 1980s," *Social History,* 10 (3), (October 1985), especially 315. Michelle Zimbalist Rosaldo, an anthropologist, wrote one of the most influential descriptions of this concept of "public" and "private." In 1980 she also modified her view to emphasize women's diverse and random social interactions. See "The Use and Abuse of Anthropology: Reflections on Feminism and Cross-cultural Understanding," *Signs,* 5 (3) (Spring 1980): 389–417.

47. Scott, in ed. Farnham, 41. For a recent discussion of the advantages and disadvantages of this approach see Lenore Davidoff, "Beyond the Public and Private: Thoughts on Feminist History in the 1990s," *Past and Present,* forthcoming (1992). Davidoff argues that "public" and "private" can still be useful if understood as intentionally gendered constructions not as fixed spheres of activity for women and men.

48. On the acceptance of the idea, see Lerner, *Teaching,* 15, and *Recent US Scholarship,* ii. Judith Bennett, "Feminism and History," *Gender and History,* 1 (3), (Autumn 1989): 258. Davis, "Women's History," 90. See for a more recent statement Micheline Dumont, "The Influence of Feminist Perspectives on Historical Research Methodology," *The Effects of Feminist Approaches on Research Methodologies,* ed. Vinnie Thomm (Waterloo, Ont.: Wilfred Laurier University Press, 1989), 112.

49. See Bock, 11, 17, 20, 21; and J. W. Scott, "Women Historians," *Gender*, 197. See also Smith, ed. Carroll, 373, on the need for studies of "society's concept of masculinity." In her essay on "The Social Relations of the Sexes," Joan Kelly began to explore what she called "the social formation of 'femininity,' " 6.

50. Natalie Zemon Davis, *Visions*, 118. See also J. W. Scott, "Gender" in *Gender*, 31.

51. J. W. Scott, "Gender," 42; and introduction, 2, *Gender*.

52. On these influences, see James Clifford, "Introduction: Partial Truths," *Writing Culture: The Poetics and Politics of Ethnography*, eds. James Clifford and George E. Marcus (Berkeley: University of California Press, 1986), 10; Rosaldo as quoted in J. W. Scott, "Gender," *Gender*, 42. On the potential effects on historiography generally, see James T. Kloppenberg, "Objectivity and Historicism: A Century of American Historical Writing," *American Historical Review*, 94 (4), (October 1989): 1026. Writers of more traditional histories, like Gertrude Himmelfarb, take a contrary position fearing that "deconstructionism" would make any interpretation valid. See Gertrude Himmelfarb, "Some Reflections on the New History," in "AHR Forum: The Old History and the New," *American Historical Review*, 94 (3), (June 1989): 665.

53. See Lynn Hunt for a description of the evolution of this approach within the context of cultural history, Lynn Hunt, ed., *The New Cultural History* (Berkeley: University of California Press, 1989), especially 17, 20. On the French feminists, see Elaine Marks and Isabelle de Courtivron, eds., *New French Feminisms* (New York: Schocken Books, 1981), especially xii–xiii. For analyses of the ways in which historians use these approaches, see Jane Caplan, "The End of Grand Theory? Notes on Post Modernism, Post Structuralism, Deconstruction," unpublished, October 1989; T. J. Jackson Lears, "The Concept of Cultural Hegemony: Problems and Possibilities," *American Historical Review*, 90 (3), (June 1985): 567–93, especially, 593. The Columbia Seminar on Women and Society devoted its February 1988 session to this intersection of disciplines, this "collapsing" of "analytical and spatial boundaries" when writing from a feminist perspective. See Judith Walkowitz, Myra Jehlen, and Bell Chevigny, "Patrolling the Borders: Feminist Historiography and the New Historicism," *Radical History Review*, 43, (1989). For a discussion of "deconstruction" by a literary critic, see Terry Eagleton, *Literary Theory: An Introduction* (Minneapolis: University of Minnesota Press, 1983).

54. J. W. Scott, "Women Historians," *Gender*, 27; Gay L. Gullickson, "Comment" on Louise Tilly's "Women's History, Social History, and Deconstruction," *Social Science History*, 13 (4), (Winter 1989): 469: One feminist scholar went further and described gender as "fundamental to the articulation of knowledge in Western thought." Its use throughout the disciplines, she argued, would constitute a "multidimensional reconstruction of knowledge." See Andersen, in eds. Minnich et. al., 39.

55. The works referred to were: *The Spinners and Weavers of Auffay* by Gay L. Gullickson (1986); Lenore Davidoff and Catherine Hall's *Family Fortunes: Men and Women of the English Middle Class 1780–1850* (1989); *Gender at Work: The Dynamics of Job Segregation by Sex during World War II* by Ruth Milkman (1987). On the French Revolution, for example, see Joan Wallach Scott, "French Feminists and the Rights of 'Man': Olympe de Gouges's Declarations," *History Workshop*, 28, (Autumn 1989): 1–21; Lynn Hunt, *Politics, Culture, and Class in the French Revolution* (Berkeley: University of California Press, 1986 ed.), Part I; Louise A. Tilly, "Gender, Women's History, and Social History," *Social Science History*, 13 (4), (Winter 1989): 459–60. For reservations about the use of deconstructionist techniques, see: Tilly, 452; Linda Alcoff, "Cultural Feminism versus Post-Structuralism: The Identity Crisis in Feminist Theory," in eds. Minnich et. al., 283; Catherine Hall, "Politics, Post-Structuralism and Feminist History," *Gender and History*, 3 (2) (Summer 1991): 204–10; and Joan Hoff, *Law*

Gender, and Injustice: A Legal History of U.S. Women (New York: New York University Press, 1991), 350–56.

Section III

1. Susan Hardy Aiken, Karen Anderson, Myra Dinnerstein, Judy Lensink, and Patricia MacCorquodale, "Trying Transformations: Curriculum Integration and the Problem of Resistance," *Reconstructing the Academy: Women's Education and Women's Studies*, eds., Elizabeth Minnich, Jean O'Barr, and Rachel Rosenfeld (Chicago: The University of Chicago Press, 1988), 110.

2. Gerda Lerner, introduction, *The Majority Finds Its Past: Placing Women in History* (New York: Oxford University Press, 1979), xxiv.

Chapter 5

1. Fernand Braudel, *On History*, trans. Sarah Matthews (Chicago: The University of Chicago Press, 1980), 62. See also, for example, Edward Hallett Carr, *What Is History?* (New York: Alfred A. Knopf, 1963), 34–35.

2. John Higham, *History: Professional Scholarship in America* (Baltimore: The Johns Hopkins University Press, 1983 ed.), fn. on 259.

3. The scholar was Bernard Bailyn, see Higham, 251, 193. Donnan was, in fact, an economist. Others have written criticism of Higham's work. See, for example, Peter Novick, *That Noble Dream: The 'Objectivity Question' and the American Historical Profession* (New York: Cambridge University Press, 1989 ed.), 13; Joan W. Scott, "American Women Historians, 1884–1984," in *Gender and the Politics of History* (New York: Columbia University Press, 1988), 189. I am indebted to Dorothy O. Helly for initially drawing my attention to his omissions. See her article, "Doing History Today (A Revolution in Knowledge: Feminist Scholarship Transforming the Discipline)," (unpublished, 1989), 29.

4. Theodore Hamerow, "The Bureaucratization of History," in "AHR Forum: The Old History and the New," *American Historical Review*, 94 (3), (June 1989), 656–57. Higham, 66. See also Novick on this evolution, 50–59; and Gisela Bock, "Women's History and Gender History: Aspects of an International Debate," *Gender & History*, 1 (1), (Spring 1989):7.

5. The uncooperative scholar was Roger Merriman. Margaret A. Judson, *Breaking the Barrier: A Professional Autobiography by a Woman Educator and Historian Before the Women's Movement* (New Brunswick, N.J.: Rutgers, The State University of New Jersey, 1984), 34, 35.

6. Judson, 109, 110.

7. Novick, 367.

8. Douglass College interview with Elizabeth Kimball, New Brunswick, N.J., 17 November 1976.

9. Judson, 110, 121.

10. Beatrice Hyslop, "Letter to the Editor," *American Historical Review*, LXII (1) (October 1956): 289. The letter is quoted in Joan W. Scott, "History and Difference," eds. Jill K. Conway, Susan C. Bourque, and Joan W. Scott, *Learning About Women: Gender, Politics, and Power* (Ann Arbor: The University of Michigan Press), 107.

11. Douglass College interview with Margaret Judson, New Brunswick, N.J., 17 November 1976. See also Judson, 79.

12. Adrienne Rich, "Toward a Woman-Centered University," *On Lies, Secrets and Silence: Selected Prose 1966–1978* (New York: W. W Norton & Co., 1979), 141.

13. Judson interview.

14. The study as quoted by Joyce Antler, *Personal Lives and Professional Careers:*

The Uneasy Balance by the Women's Committee of the American Studies Association
(College Park, Md.: American Studies Association, 1988), 27.

15. Margaret Judson gave a long list of her contemporaries and their writings in her
autobiography. See 82–85. See also Bonnie Smith, "The Contribution of Women to
Modern Historiography in Great Britain, France and the United States 1750–1940,"
American Historical Review, 89 (3), (June 1984): 712 and fn. Other information in this
and the following paragraph came from Kathryn Kish Sklar, "American Female Historians
in Context 1770–1930," *Feminist Studies*, 3(1/2), (Fall 1975); Scott, ed. Conway; see
also entries in Edward T. James, Janet Wilson James, Paul S. Boyer, eds., *Notable
American Women 1607–1950: A Biographical Dictionary* (Cambridge: Cambridge University
Press, 1971), 3 vols.; Barbara Sicherman, Carol Hurd Green, Ilene Kantrou, and
Harriette Walker, eds., *The Modern Period* (Cambridge: Harvard University Press, 1980).
Jacqueline Goggin has made an extensive study of the papers of the American Historical
Association and the Jameson Papers. She is in the process of writing a history of the
women Ph.D.s from the 1890s to the 1940s. She mentions many of the women historians
cited in this chapter and in chapter 7. See Jacqueline Goggin, "Challenging Sexual
Discrimination in the Historical Profession: Women Historians in the American Historical
Association: 1890–1940," *American Historical Review*, 97 (3), (June 1992).

16. For a discussion of the strategies used by academic women, see the article by
Miriam Slater and Penina Migdal Glazer "Prescriptions for Professional Survival," in
ed. Conway, especially 102; chapter 2 of their book *Unequal Colleagues: The Entrance
of Women Into the Professions 1980–1940* (New Brunswick, N.J., Rutgers University
Press, 1987).

17. Novick, 367.

18. See Willie Lee Rose, "Rose Committee Report" (Washington DC: American
Historical Association, 1970), the summaries on 11–12, the tables in appendix A.

19. Blanche Wiesen Cook speaking about Charles A. Barker, Fiftieth Anniversary
Program Tape, Berkshire Conference of Women Historians, South Egremont, Mass., 13
May 1979, Douglass College Archives and Blanche Wiesen Cook to Judith P. Zinsser,
24 February 1992. Barker subsequently supported Cook's work and apologized after she
described the incident in public. Sandi E. Cooper interview, New York City, 14 April
1991.

20. Jane S. DeHart, "Reflections on the Twenty Years After the Rose Report and
Beyond: Women Historians in the Twenty-First Century" (unpublished, 1990), 1–2.

21. Marilyn B. Young as quoted in Sara M. Evans, *Born for Liberty: A History of
Women in America* (New York: The Free Press, 1989), 279. For a narrative of the
Women's Movement, see Flora Davis, *Moving the Mountain: The Women's Movement
in America Since 1960* (New York: Simon & Schuster, 1991).

22. For the ways in which "contradictions" moved women to activism on their own
behalf, see Sara M. Evans, *Personal Politics: The Roots of Women's Liberation in the
Civil Rights Movement and in The New Left* (New York: Vintage Books, 1980 ed.),
212–32. See also Ellen Carol DuBois, Gail Paradise Kelly, Elizabeth Lapovsky Kennedy,
Carolyn W. Korsmeyer, and Lillian S. Robinson, *Feminist Scholarship: Kindling in the
Groves of Academe* (Urbana: University of Illinois Press, 1985), 18, 36; see Gerda Lerner,
"The Feminists: A Second Look" in *The Majority Finds Its Past: Placing Women in
History* (New York: Oxford University Press, 1979), 43. For examples of women historians
first active in civil rights and anti-war groups and then within the profession, see
Debra L. Schultz, *Women Historians As a Force in History: The Activist Roots of Women
Historians* (New York: Master's Essay for New York University: May 1990).

23. The details of Scott's career came from her own account, "A Historian's Odyssey,"
in Anne Firor Scott, *Making The Invisible Woman Visible* (Chicago: University of
Illinois Press, 1984). See xxi for the quotation. Her advisor at Harvard was Oscar Handlin.

24. Natalie Zemon Davis interview, MARHO, *Visions of History*, eds. Henry Abe-love, Betsy Blackmar, Peter Dimock, and Jonathan Schneer (New York: Pantheon Books, 1983 ed.), 104. Subsequent quotations come from 102, 103, 105, 108.

25. Ellen Furlough, "Future Trends in the Profession" (unpublished), American Historical Association Annual Meeting, December 1984, 7 CWH files. See, for examples of this thinking, Scott, "Historians," in J. W. Scott *Gender*, fn. on 227; Ann Snitow, "A Gender Diary," *Conflicts in Feminism*, eds. Marianne Hirsch and Evelyn Fox Keller (New York: Routledge, Chapman and Hall, Inc.), 19–20.

26. A study done in 1980 on "productivity" showed no distinction on the basis of whether or not scholars had remained single. Married women were actually more productive than unmarried women. Rank was the significant variable. Mariam K. Chamberlain, ed., *Women in Academe: Progress and Prospects* (New York: Russell Sage Foundation, 1988), 265.

27. The Committee on Women Historians has made periodic studies of women's professional status and recommended three sets of hiring and promotion guidelines. See the "Guidelines on Hiring Women Historians in Academia," American Historical Association, *Newsletter*, 19(6), (September 1981), 7; 2nd ed., 1984, 2. AHA *Perspectives*, 29(2), (February 1991): 17–18. See also for discussion of women's situation: "Survey of the Historical Profession: Academia: Summary Report 1981–1982" (Washington DC: American Historical Association, 1984), 36–39 (462 departments responded); Kathryn Kish Sklar, "The Status of Women in the Historical Profession—Updating the Rose Report" (unpublished, 1980), 3–5, CWH files. Her report included a breakdown of the thirty universities surveyed in the original Rose Report, 3; CWH 1983 Annual Report, unpublished, 3–4 and Tables. The Organization of American Historians also established a Committee on the Status of Women. See its report in May 1986. The pattern described in this chapter is also characteristic of other academic disciplines as of studies made to 1987. See Jessie Bernard's foreword in Angela Simeone, *Academic Women Working Toward Equality* (So. Hadley, Mass: Bergin & Garvey Publishers, 1987), xi; and Chamberlain, especially the Tables on 262.

28. Sklar, "Update," 7.

29. AHA 1991 Guidelines, 17–18. For more on this phenomenon, what Joan W. Scott called "hierarchically differentiated systems," see Scott, in ed. Conway, 93, 113; Carl N. Degler, "On Rereading 'The Woman in America'," ed. Conway, 202–4; Slater and Glazer, ed. Conway Chamberlain, v–vi, 29–30.

30. Rose Report 1968–1969, tables, appendix A; Patricia Albjerg Graham, "Revisiting the Rose Reports (unpublished, 29 Dec. 1986), 1, CWH files. (Note that I have corrected the percentage for all ranks at Coeducational Liberal Arts Colleges. I am grateful to Joseph B. Broderick for bringing the error in the original calculations to my attention.) The American Historical Association defines "equity" in the following way: "When a department has the same proportion of women in its tenured ranks as available in the pool of women Ph.D.s in cohorts of tenure ages." All comparisons between women and men are made for these cohorts. The 1991 Guidelines gave the following cohorts and percentages of women Ph.D.s in each group:

1930–59	13%	1975–80 26%
1960–69	10.4%	1982–88 33%
1970–74	15.8%	

See 1991 Guidelines, 17.

31. See Glazer and Slater, ed. Conway, 123; see also their book, 14, and Nadya Aisenberg and Mona Harrington, *Women of Academe: Outsiders in the Sacred Grove*

(Amherst: The University of Massachusetts Press, 1988), 38, 42–43, 50–53. These scholars suggested that all women academics had to be "superperformers" given the persistent inequalities of their circumstances in comparison to men.

32. The CWH used the phrase in the first *Survival Manual for Women (and Other) Historians*, and in subsequent editions. See Melanie Gustafson, ed., *Becoming a Historian: Survival Manual for Women and Men* (Washington DC: Committee on Women Historians and American Historical Association, 1991 ed.), vii.

33. Gordon, *Visions*, 75.

34. See *Survival Manual*, 1975 ed., 5, 4; 1980 ed., 19, 14; also 1991 ed., 18. The Hilda Smith anecdote is from an interview with Berenice A. Carroll, 23 April 1991. On graduate student experiences, see also D'Ann Campbell, "Women Historians Attend Graduate School: Emotional, Financial and Peer Group Support," *CCWHP Newsletter*, (March 1975): 1–4.

35. See for all the cautions on this, *Survival Manual*, 1991 ed., 29–30; Joan Jensen, "Committee on Women Historians: 1970–1990 A Twenty-Year Report," *AHA Perspectives*, 29(3), (March 1991): 9. The CWH statement on sexual harassment became part of the AHA "Statement on Standards of Professional Conduct" issued in 1987.

36. *Survival Manual,*, 1975 ed., 19, 5, 10; 1991 ed., 52.

37. DeHart, 4.

38. The American Studies Association report, *Personal Lives*, documented many of these pressures: choices made between completing a dissertation and having children; careers influenced by responsibilities to husband, children, parents; "competitive tensions" with a spouse who was also an academic. See especially 3–4, 9–10, 11. The student as quoted in *Personal Lives*, 5. DeHart, 4. See also Aisenberg and Harrington, 117.

39. Gordon, *Vision*, 88, 89, 94.

40. *Survival Manual*, 1991 ed., 71, 69. Judith Bennett, "Feminism and History," *Gender & History*, 1(3), (Autumn 1989): 252–53. Aisenberg and Harrington described ways in which women scholars' choice of research topics and different approaches to teaching and writing made them suspect in traditional academic departments; see especially 78–80, 86–87, 96–99.

41. Virginia Woolf as quoted in Rich, *Lies*, 133, and Rich, *Lies*, 134.

42. Information came from a variety of sources: Cooper interview; Annette Kolodny, "Dancing Between Left and Right: Feminism and the Academic Minefield in the 1980's," *Feminist Studies*, 14(3), (February 1988), 464, 462. Bennett, 254, 256. For more on these divisions, see also: Kathryn Pyne Addelson, "A Comment on Ringelheim's 'Women and The Holocaust: A Reconsideration of Research,' " *Signs*, 12(4), (Summer 1987): 833; introduction, Minnich, eds. and passim. Berenice A. Carroll, interview, 1 March 1992. On divisions within academic feminism, see eds. Hirsch and Fox Keller. On divisions within the feminist movement as a whole, see: Alice Echols, *Daring to Be Bad: Radical Feminism in America 1967–1975* (Minneapolis: University of Minnesota Press, 1989) and Davis, *Moving the Mountain*.

43. Deborah Gray White finished her doctorate in 1979 but could not find a publisher for her dissertation, the first full-length study of black women under slavery. Scott heard of her work in October 1982, recommended the book to W. W. Norton, and White had a contract by December. Deborah Gray White interview, 23 February 1992.

44. See Evelyn Fox Keller and Helene Moglen, "Viewpoint: Competition and Feminism: Conflicts for Academic Women," *Signs*, 12(3), (Spring 1987): 495, 497–99; Marilyn J. Boxer, "For and About Women: The Theory and Practice of Women's Studies in the United States," eds. Minnich, 76–77; Kolodny, 464–65; Jensen, "Twenty-Year Report," 9.

45. Ann Ferguson, commenting on an Adrienne Rich article, "On 'Compulsory

Heterosexuality and Lesbian Existence': Defining the Issues," *Signs*, 7(1), (Autumn 1981): 158–59. See also Blanche Wiesen Cook, "Viewpoint: 'Women Alone Stir My Imagination': Lesbianism and the Cultural Tradition," *Signs*, 4(4), (Summer 1979), and Boxer, "For and About Women." For a description of the proliferation and elaboration of feminist theory by lesbian scholars since 1982, see: Katie King, "Producing Sex, Theory, and Culture: Gay/Straight Remappings in Contemporary Feminism," in eds. Hirsch and Fox Keller, 82–101.

46. The sociologist Deborah K. King described this phenomenon as "multiple jeopardy" with African-American women disadvantaged because of race, class, and gender, "three, interdependent control systems." See "Multiple Jeopardy, Multiple Consciousness: The Context of a Black Feminist Ideology," *Signs*, 14(1), (Autumn 1988): 42–72.

47. 1991 Guidelines, 18. For totals for the years 1986–90, see Jensen, "Twenty-Year Report," 8.

48. White interview. I am grateful to Deborah Gray White for suggestions in the formulation of this section.

49. Biographical data for Berry came from the Organization of American Historians. Subsequent biographies came from *Who's Who of American Women*.

50. Deena González, "Twenty Years After the Rose Report and Beyond: Women Historians in The Twenty-First Century," American Historical Association Annual Meeting, New York City, 28 December 1990.

51. Darlene Clark Hine, *Personal Lives*, 18, 19. She was also quoted in *Survival Manual*, 1991 ed., 69. See also Phyllis Marnick Palmer, "White Women/Black Women: The Dualism of Feminist Ideology and Experience in the United States," *Feminist Studies*, 9(1),(Spring 1983); Elizabeth Higginbotham, "Review Essay: Feminism and the Academy," *NWSA Journal*, 2(1), (Winter 1990); Evelyn Brooks Higginbotham, "Beyond the Sound of Silence: Afro-American Women in History," *Gender & History*, 1, (Spring 1989). African Americanists sometimes shared these reservations about black women's history. In the late 1970s White had to justify writing and teaching her specialty to her new department head at the University of Wisconsin-Milwaukee. The male scholar finally conceded that black women's history might be useful, for while black men discovered their heritage, black women could learn how better to raise their sons for the twenty-first century. White interview.

52. Nancy A. Hewitt, "Beyond the Search for Sisterhood: American Women's History in the 1980s," *Social History*, 10(3), (October 1985): 300. Rosalyn Terborg-Penn, "The Status of Black Women in the Historical Profession: 1979–1989," Association of Black Women Historian's Newsletter *Truth*, December 1989. See for criticism of the women's movement in general Rosalyn Terborg-Penn, "Discrimination against Afro-American Women in the Woman's Movement 1830–1920," *The Afro-American Woman: Struggles and Images*, eds., Rosalyn Terborg-Penn and Sharon Harley (Port Washington, NY: Kennikat Press, 1978); and for bibliographies of articles critical of white women historians in particular, Hewitt cited above, and Lise Vogel, "Telling Tales: Historians of Our Own Lives," *The Journal of Women's History*, 2(3), (Winter 1991).

53. King, and Fannie Lou Hamer as quoted in King, 43. See also on black feminist thought in general, Patricia Hill Collins, "The Social Construction of Black Feminist Thought," *Signs*, 14(4), (Summer 1989), especially 753.

54. Maxine Baca Zinn, Lynn Weber Cannon, Elizabeth Higginbotham and Bonnie Thornton Dill, "The Costs of Exclusionary Practices in Women's Studies," in eds. Minnich, especially 128, 131; the central argument appears on 128–35.

55. See Elizabeth V. Spelman, *The Inessential Woman* (Boston: Beacon Press, 1988), 165–66, 163; I have adapted her general argument from 169 to the situation in history. See also Elsa Barkley Brown, "African-American Women's Quilting: A Frame-

work for Conceptualizing and Teaching African-American Women's History," *Signs*, 14(4), (Summer 1989).

56. Johnella E. Butler as quoted in Elsa Barkley Brown, "Womanist Consciousness: Maggie Lena Walker and the Independent Order of Saint Luke," *Signs*, 14(3), (Spring 1989): 632. See also 611–13.

57. Evelyn Higginbotham, 50; Paula Giddings made the same point about minority women and men in *When and Where I Enter: The Impact of Black Women on Race and Sex in America* (New York: Bantam, 1988 ed.). See the preface for her thesis.

58. Flo Kennedy, Cherrie Moraga, Julia Perez, Barbara Smith, and Bevery Smith as quoted in Teresa de Lauretis, ed., *Feminist Studies/Critical Studies* (Bloomington: Indiana University Press, 1986), 7, 18. For similar thoughts, see eds. Hirsch and Fox Keller, 379. On the inherent contradictions, see also Nancy Cott, *The Grounding of Modern Feminism* (New Haven: Yale University Press, 1987), especially 282–83. The activist lawyer Flo Kennedy called it "horizontal violence" when feminists fought with each other. Alice Kessler-Harris and Amy Swerdlow in their report on the Sarah Lawrence conference noted the numbers of women of color participating and the "recognition of the politics of difference and the tension it created" as "perhaps the most important outcome" of the meetings. See "Report on the First Conference on Women's History and Public Policy," *AHA Perspectives*, 28(5), (May/June 1990): 10–11. When in 1991 the CWH approached the Ford Foundation, a major funder of the Sarah Lawrence conference, with its proposal for a second meeting, this time for black women, the Foundation responded that it was "not interested in a conference on Afro-American women and public policy." Rosalyn Terborg-Penn, "1991 Committee on Women Historians Report," *AHA Perspectives*, 30(3), (March 1992): 3.

Chapter 6

1. See, on the reciprocal success of women's history and women historians, Noralee Frankel and William Chafe, "The Present Status of Women in the Historical Profession" (unpublished, American Historical Association Convention, 29 December 1984), 11, Committee on Women Historians files.

2. See Elizabeth Minnich, Jean O'Barr, and Rachel Rosenfeld, eds., *Reconstructing the Academy: Women's Education and Women's Studies* (Chicago: The University of Chicago Press, 1988), especially the chapter on the University of Arizona for the interrelationship between women's studies and the separate disciplines. Florence Howe as quoted in Margaret L. Andersen, "Changing the Curriculum in Higher Education," eds. Minnich et al., 39. Linda Gordon, "A Socialist View of Women's Studies: A Reply to the Editorial, Volume 1, Number 1," *Signs*, 1 (2), (Winter 1975): 559. See also Nadya Aisenberg and Mona Harrington, *Women of Academe: Outsiders in the Sacred Grove* (Amherst: The University of Massachusetts Press, 1988), 105.

3. Gordon, "A Socialist View," 562; Joan W. Scott, "History and Difference," *Learning About Women: Gender, Politics, and Power* eds. Jill K. Conway, Susan C. Bourque, and Joan W. Scott (Ann Arbor: The University of Michigan Press, 1989), 108.

4. Gordon, "A Socialist View," 565. The other concepts came from Andersen, in eds. Minnich et al., 39 and Ellen Carol DuBois, Gail Paradise Kelly, Elizabeth Lapovsky Kennedy, Carolyn W. Korsmeyer, and Lillian Robinson, *Feminist Scholarship: Kindling in the Groves of Academe* (Urbana: University of Illinois Press, 1985), 197. A number of other scholars have written on the political aspects of teaching and research. See Marilyn J. Boxer, "For and About Women: The Theory and Practice of Women's Studies in the United States," *Signs*, 7(3), (Spring 1982): 661, 674–75 (reprinted in eds. Minnich et al.). On the ways in which all "knowledge is culturally constructed" and thus the gendered politics of the scholarly process, see Jean F. O'Barr, *Women and A New Academy* (Madison: The University of Wisconsin Press, 1989), 5.

5. Temma Kaplan, interview, New York City, 1 December 1991.

6. Cathy Cade and Peggy Dobbins developed the course in New Orleans, Naomi Weisstein, the one at Chicago. Boxer, "For and About Women," in eds. Minnich et al., 70, 75, and passim. For Beard, see Adrienne Rich, "Toward a Woman-Centered University," *On Lies, Secrets, and Silence: Selected Prose 1966–1978* (New York: W. W. Norton & Co., 1979), 126. These were not the first courses in women's history. Mary W. Williams (1878–1944), a Latin Americanist at Goucher, had taught one in the 1930s; Alma Lutz, a friend of Mary Beard's, did one at Radcliffe in the 1950s; Annette K. Baxter taught one at Barnard and Gerda Lerner at the New School in New York City in the 1960s. Mary Beard wrote the first syllabus in women's studies in 1936. See Kathryn Kish Sklar, "American Female Historians in Context 1770–1930," *Feminist Studies* 3(1/2), (Fall 1975): J. W. Scott in ed. Conway; appropriate entries in *Notable American Women*.

7. Anne Firor Scott, *Making the Invisible Woman Visible* (Chicago: University of Illinois Press, 1984), xxiii–xxiv, xxiii. Jesse Bernard's foreword to Angela Simeone, *Academic Women: Working Toward Equality* (So. Hadley, Mass.: Bergin & Garvey Publishers), xiii.

8. Alice Kessler-Harris, introduction, *Conceptual Frameworks for Studying Women's History* by Marylin Arthur, Renate Bridenthal, Joan Kelly-Gadol, and Gerda Lerner (Bronxville, N.Y.: Sarah Lawrence College Women's Studies, 1975).

9. See Boxer, "For and About Women." Sara M. Evans estimated the number as 30,000 in 1980; see her *Born for Liberty: A History of Women in America* (New York: The Free Press), 300. Florence Howe and Paul Lauter wrote for NIE, *The Impact of Women's Studies on the Campus and the Disciplines* (1980); *Men's Studies Modified: The Impact of Feminism on the Academic Disciplines,* ed. Dale Spender, appeared in 1981. Another indication of the increasing significance was publication of directories and guides on how to integrate women into traditional programs, for example, in 1981 from the Wellesley Center for Research on Women, the University of Arizona's Southwest Institute for Research on Women, and from a 1983 Wheaton College conference.

10. Gerda Lerner, *Teaching Women's History* (Washington DC: American Historical Association: 1981), 1; Mariam Chamberlain, ed., *Women in Academe: Program and Prospects* (New York: Russell Sage Foundation, 1988), 144.

11. The University of California at Santa Barbara produced the first such bibliography in 1978; Ballou wrote a bibliographic essay in 1977, "Bibliographies for Research on Women," *Signs,* 3 (2), (Winter 1977). In 1989 Oryx Press issued a *Directory of Women's Studies Programs and Library Resources* edited by Beth Stafford with profiles of over four hundred programs and library collections.

12. For the complete list of research centers as of 1988, see ed. Chamberlain, 297, 308–9; for the list of women's studies programs, see 133, 136–38.

13. Chamberlain ed., 296.

14. Elsa Barkley Brown, "Womanist Consciousness: Maggie Lena Walker and the Independent Order of Saint Luke," *Signs,* 14 (3), (Spring 1989): 611. Deborah Gray White interview, 23 February 1992. Rosalyn Terborg-Penn, "The Status of Black Women in the Historical Profession: 1979–1989," *Truth,* (December 1989), 8. Much of the description that follows of African-American women's activities came from Terborg-Penn's article. I am grateful to Deborah Gray White for her help in formulating this section of the chapter.

15. See Evelyn Brooks Higginbotham, "Beyond the Sound of Silence: African-American Women in History," *Gender & History* 1 (1), (Spring 1989), 50–67. Elizabeth Fox-Genovese emphasized that black women historians see their history as a "distinct paradigm." Elizabeth Fox-Genovese, "Socialist-Feminist American Women's History," *Journal of Women's History,* 1 (3), (Winter 1990): fn 5, 202. See also her bibliography

of recent articles on this subject, fn 8, 208. For a theoretical work that offers methodological models and language, see Patricia Hill Collins, *Black Feminist Thought: Knowledge,
Consciousness and the Politics of Empowerment* (Boston: Unwin Hyman, 1990).

16. The historian Lois Banner was one of the editors of the study. See Chamberlain
ed., 156.

17. Berenice A. Carroll, introduction, *Liberating Women's History: Theoretical and
Critical Essays* (Urbana: University of Illinois Press, 1976), ix.

18. See, for example, Glenda Riley's and Abby Wettan Kleinbaum's article on
teaching in *The History Teacher*, 12(4), (August 1979). Markus Wiener published compilations of course outlines in 1984 and 1988 covering women's history in the major regions
of the world. The contributors came from every kind of college and university, for
example: Oberlin, Morgan State University, Cornell, the University of California-Davis,
Hofstra, the University of Iowa, and Duke.

19. For the information on the funding of this and other projects, see, for example,
Betty Schmitz, *Integrating Women's Studies into the Curriculum: A Guide and Bibliography* (Old Westbury, N.Y.: The Feminist Press, 1985), 2–3; Chamberlain ed., 295–96,
141–42.

20. Amy Swerdlow, later director of the program at Sarah Lawrence, received one
of the first degrees awarded. The information on graduate programs came from a variety
of sources. Amy Swerdlow, interview, New York City, 19 April 1991; Alice Kessler-
Harris, interview, New Brunswick, N.J., 10 April 1991; Gerda Lerner and Amy Swerdlow, *Evaluation Report: Women Studies Program 1972–1976* (unpublished), Amy Swerdlow private files, ii, 1, 4. See also "Report to the President," n.d., Swerdlow private
files and Teaching, 1.

21. See NEH Wingspread conference report, *Graduate Training in United States
Women's History* (Racine, Wisc.: National Endowment for the Humanities for the Johnson
Foundation, 1989), 49–51. Of the institutions represented, fifty-four granted the Ph.D.
and M.A.; nine granted the M.A. only, 29. See also, Gerda Lerner, "A View from the
Women's Side," *Journal of American History*, 76(2), (September 1989): 454.

22. The editor was Robert K. Webb. The article appeared in the *Journal of Contemporary History* (1971). Temma Kaplan, interview, New York City, 1 December 1991.

23. Berenice A. Carroll has written on the ways in which the concept of "originality" has been used to establish what she called "the class system of the intellect." See
"The Politics of 'Originality': Women and the Class System of the Intellect," *Journal
of Women's History*, 2(2), (Fall 1990): 136, 138, 139–40. Note that the phrasing in this
section is the author's, not Carroll's.

24. See *A Survival Manual for Women (and other) Historians* (Washington DC:
Committee on Women Historians and American Historical Association, 1980 ed.), 44,
45. These circumstances applied doubly to minority women in the academic community
who were identified with multiple constituencies.

25. See the Committee on Women Historians Annual Report 1973, CWH files;
American Historical Association, *Survey of the Historical Profession: Academia 1981–82
Summary Report* (Washington DC: American Historical Association, 1984), table 4, 15;
the explanation of priorities was Mary Beth Norton's, 1985 Annual Report of the Committee on Women Historians, *AHA Perspectives*, 24(2), (February 1986): 9.

26. The results of the journals study appeared in Dolores Barracano Schmidt and
Earl Robert Schmidt, "The Invisible Woman: The Historian as Professional Magician,"
in ed. Carroll, 43. On grants and awards, see *Survival Manual*, 1975 ed., 5, 13; 1991
ed., 35–36; CWH 1985 Annual Report, *AHA Perspectives*, 9 on NEH in particular (the
scholar was Clara Lovat); Minutes of Committee on Women Historians, 27–29 December
1977, 1, CWH files.

27. Mary Beard to Margaret Grierson as quoted in Ann J. Lane, ed., *Mary Ritter Beard: A Sourcebook* (New York: Schocken Books, 1977), 57.

28. Barbara Sicherman, "Review Essay: American History," *Signs*, 1(2), (Winter 1975): 461.

29. This and other stories about Harper Collins came from an interview with Hugh Van Dusen, 15 November 1990, New York City; Karen Petersen and J. J. Wilson were also interviewed, 18 May 1991, Santa Rosa, Calif. In the late 1970s the college became part of Sonoma State University.

30. The *Handbook* (New York: Garland Pub., 1990) was by Angela Howard Zophy and Frances M. Kavenik. Patricia K. Ballou edited the *Bibliography of Bibliographies* (Boston: G. K. Hall & Co., 1986). There are bibliographies for United States and European women's history, both revised in 1985–86: Cynthia E. Harrison, Anne Firor Scott, and Pamela R. Byrne, *Women in American History: A Bibliography* (2 Vols., 1979, 1985); Linda Frey, Marsha Frey, and Joanne Schneider, *Women in Western European History: A Select Chronological, Geographical, and Topical Bibliography From Antiquity to the French Revolution* (Westport, Conn: Greenwood Press, 1982), and the *First Supplement* (1986) bringing the list up through the twentieth century. Similar guides for women in other parts of the world have not been so formalized. The best overall bibliography remains the collection of review articles and book lists done by the Organization of American Historians: *Restoring Women to History: Teaching Packets for Integrating Women's History into Courses on Africa, Asia, Latin America, the Caribbean, and the Middle East* (1988). The *Journal of Women's History* has begun publishing review articles for different regions. See 2(1) for additional titles published from 1988–90.

31. DuBois et al., 157.

32. The five disciplines were history, philosophy, education, anthropology, and literature. Anthropology and literature had the best records. In 1969 the figure for all disciplines combined was 2.24%. In 1980 the equivalent figure for all disciplines was 5.31%. See DuBois et al., 158–60, 163, and Table III, 166–69; see also Table II with statistics for all disciplines, 165. 1973–74 had an unusually high percentage for history: 11.76%. DuBois and her colleagues suggested that this higher percentage was because so many first research questions were analyzed and ready for publication at the same time, 179. The ten history journals surveyed were: *American Historical Review; French Historical Studies; Historian; Journal of American History; Journal of the History of Ideas; Journal of Modern History; Journal of Negro History; Journal of Social History; Pacific Historical Quarterly*; and *William and Mary Quarterly*.

33. Linda Gordon's early theoretical suggestions on "What Women Historians Should Do" appeared in *Marxist Perspectives*; Ann D. Gordon, Mari Jo Buhle, and Nancy Schrom Dye's critique of male historians' writings on women was first published by *Radical America*. See for listings of articles and receptive journals in the 1970s, Sicherman, 462; and Barbara Sicherman, E. William Monter, Joan Wallach Scott, and Kathryn Kish Sklar, *Recent United States Scholarship on the History of Women* (Washington DC: American Historical Association, 1980), 29–53.

34. The *American Historical Review* first published an issue on women's history in 1984.

35. The quotations came from the first issues of the journals, in the following order: *Women's Studies*, 1(1), (1972): 1–2; *Frontiers: A Journal of Women's Studies*, 1(1), (Fall 1975): iv; "Statement of Purpose," *Feminist Studies*, 1(1), (Summer 1972); *Signs: A Journal of Women in Society*, 1(1) (Autumn 1975): v.

36. *Feminist Periodicals* is edited by Susan Searing. The listings include the tables of contents for each of the journals.

37. "Editors' Note and Acknowledgement," *Journal of Women's History*, 1(1),

(1989): 11; "Statement of Purpose," 7, 8–9. DuBois et al. expressed similar fears of marginalization at the end of their study; see 177, 186, 187, 188–89, 192.

38. The program chairman was Raymond Grew. Berenice A. Carroll interview, 23 April 1991.

39. Accounts came from Mary Hartman, interview, 4 April 1991, New Brunswick, N.J. and Louise Dalby's reminiscences, Berkshire Conference of Women Historians, Fiftieth Anniversary Panel, 13 May 1979, So. Egremont, Mass., Douglas College Archives.

40. For attendance estimates, see, for example, Sicherman, 462, A. F. Scott, xxiii. In 1973 *Feminist Studies* devoted a double issue of its second volume to publication of papers from this first conference. Harper and Row subsequently published them as *Clio's Consciousness Raised* (edited by Lois Banner and Mary Hartman, the conference co-chairs), as its second major women's history title.

41. Estelle Freedman, "Separatism as Strategy: Female Institution Building and American Feminism 1870–1930," *Feminist Studies*, 5(3), (Fall 1979): 518, 525–26. Peter Novick also identified this strategy but ascribed it only to blacks and leftists in the 1960s and 1970s. See Peter Novick, *That Noble Dream: The 'Objectivity Question' and the American Historical Profession* (New York: Cambridge University Press, 1989 ed.), 160.

Chapter 7

1. Beginning in 1994 the convention is scheduled for the end of the first week in January; the result of a suggestion put forward by women historians who argued that family obligations made the meeting between Christmas and New Year's difficult.

2. Women represented 3.7% of the total participants (402). The following women gave papers: Ruth Pike Hunter, Elizabeth A. R. Brown, Gertrude Himmelfarb, Penina Migdal Glazer, Claire Sprague, Nancy Roelker, Miriam Usher, and Natalie Zemon Davis. Barbara Solomon chaired the session. The statistical information in this chapter came from AHA studies done by the Committee on Women Historians and was supplied by Noralee Frankel, Assistant Director on Women and Minorities.

3. Women chaired 31% of the sessions; gave 38% of the papers; made 37% of the comments. Committee on Women Historians files; Noralee Frankel, interview, 25 February 1991.

4. See Louis Harlan's presidential address, "The Future of the AHA," *American Historical Review*, 95(1), (February 1990): 1.

5. See Willie Lee Rose, "Rose Report" (Washington DC: American Historical Association, 1970), appendix C; statistical studies done for the Committee on Women Historians for 1969 and 1990. In 1969 two of the women sat on book prize committees, one on the Committee on Committees, one on the Committee on International Historical Activities, and one on the joint AHA–Canadian Studies Association Committee.

6. See Theodore S. Hamerow, "The Bureaucratization of History," in "AHR Forum: The Old History and the New," 94(3), (June 1989): 654; John Higham, *History: Professional Scholarship in America* (Baltimore: The Johns Hopkins University Press, 1983 ed.), 8. See Joan W. Scott, "American Women Historians, 1884–1984," *Gender and the Politics of History* (New York: Columbia University Press, 1988), 179; see also her address "Politics in the Profession of History," Committee on Women Historians, Breakfast Meeting, December, 1988, unpublished. Peter Novick's *That Noble Dream: The 'Objectivity Question' and the American Historical Profession* (New York: Cambridge University Press, 1989 ed.) described this aspect of the profession at length.

7. Elizabeth Kimball, interview, 17 November 1976, New Brunswick, N.J., Douglass College Archives. On women historians see J. W. Scott, "Women Historians," *Gender*, 183–4 and Joan W. Scott, "History and Difference," *Learning About Women:*

Gender, Politics, and Power, eds. Jill K. Conway, Susan C. Bourque, and Joan W. Scott (Ann Arbor: University of Michigan Press, 1989), 106. For more details of women's efforts within the AHA, see Jacqueline Goggin, "Challenging Sexual Discrimination in the Historical Profession: Women Historians and the American Historical Association: 1890–1940," *American Historical Review*, 97(3), (June 1992).

8. Kimball, interview. Neilson studied with F. W. Maitland and Sir Paul Vinogradoff in England. Merle Curti chaired the Program Committee in 1940 and used the convention to focus attention on the relatively new field of social history. This was also the year in which Mildred Thompson gave the first AHA panel on women's history. See J. W. Scott, "Women Historians," *Gender*, 185–90; Novick, 100–101. On Neilson, see Edward T. James, Janet Wilson James, Paul S. Boyer, eds., *Notable American Women: 1607–1950: A Biographical Dictionary* (Cambridge MA: Harvard University Press, 1971).

9. Dorothy Ganfield Fowler, Berkshire Conference of Women Historians, Fiftieth Anniversary Berkshire Panel, So. Egremont, Mass., 13 May 1979, Douglass College Archives.

10. Louise R. Loomis as quoted in J. W. Scott, "Women Historians," *Gender*, 190. See also J. W. Scott, ed. Conway, 105–6. The group was originally called the Lakeville History Conference and changed to the present title in 1935. See Kathryn Kish Sklar, American Female Historians in Context 1770–1930," *Feminist Studies*, 3(1/2), (Fall 1975): 181. There has been some uncertainty about the date of the first meeting. Margaret Judson wanted the record straight and insisted to a friend visiting her in the hospital just before her death that it was the spring of 1929. Mary Hartman interview, New Brunswick, NJ, 4 April 1991. Events within the AHA make 1930 the more likely date.

11. Kimball, interview; also, Ganfield Fowler, Berkshire Anniversary Panel. They particularly liked the Red Lion Inn in South Egremont, Mass. Emily Hickman had met the manager on the trans-Siberian Railroad. He gave them special rates and a "luncheon picnic with lobster salad" in the woods about three miles from the inn. Margaret A. Judson, *Breaking the Barrier: A Professional Autobiography by a Woman Educator and Historian Before the Women's Movement* (New Brunswick, N.J.: Rutgers The State University of New Jersey, 1984), 81.

12. Judson, 78–79.

13. Margaret Judson, interview, 17 November 1976, New Brunswick, N.J., Douglass College Archives.

14. Judson, 80; Judson, interview.

15. Ganfield Fowler, Emiliana Noether, and Mary Beth Norton, Fiftieth Anniversary Berkshire Panel.

16. Though the two groups had members in common and maintained contact, each worked for its own agenda at the Convention. This was also the meeting when Jesse Lemisch inaugurated the attack on the "objectivity" of traditional histories of the United States and of the Cold War, especially the work of Allen Nevins, Daniel Boorstin, Arthur Schlesinger, Jr., and Oscar Handlin. Gerda Lerner, "A View from the Women's Side," *Journal of American History*, 76(2), (September 1989): 449–50. See Novick for a description of the radical and leftist activities, especially 435; and Jonathan A. Wiener, "Radical Historians and the Crisis in American History," *Journal of American History*, 76(2), (September 1989): 422.

17. The information in this and subsequent paragraphs about Carroll's career and her activities with the AHA comes from: Berenice A. Carroll, interview, 23 April 1991 and 8 June 1991; Sandi E. Cooper, interview, New York City, 18 December 1990; Berenice A. Carroll to Judith P. Zinsser, 2 March 1992. The head of department was Margaret Judson.

18. Berenice A. Carroll as quoted in Hilda Smith, Nupur Chaudhuri, and Gerda Lerner, *A History of the Coordinating Committee on Women in Historical Profession—Conference Group on Women's History* (Oak Park IL: CCWHP–CGWH, 1989), 7. In 1968 and 1969 feminists in academic fields other than political science and history organized caucuses and pressured their professional associations for studies on the status of women (for example, Florence Howe in the Modern Language Association). In addition, between 1966 and 1979 almost thirty studies of the status of academic and professional women appeared, for example, the sociologist Jessie Bernard's *Academic Women* (1966), and the article by Alice S. Rossi in the *American Sociologist* (Fall, 1969). All clearly demonstrated patterns of gender discrimination. See Mariam K. Chamberlain, ed., *Women in Academe: Progress and Prospects* (New York: Russell Sage Foundation, 1988), 277; and Ellen Carol DuBois, Gail Paradise Kelly, Elizabeth Lapovsky Kennedy, Carolyn W. Korsmeyer and Lillian S. Robinson, eds., *Feminist Scholarship: Kindling in the Groves of Academe* (Urbana IL: University of Illinois Press, 1985) for discussion of the phenomenon.

19. "Petition to the Council of the American Historical Association"; Paul L. Ward (executive secretary to the AHA) to Mrs. Carroll, 2 December 1969. I am grateful to Berenice A. Carroll for copies of these documents. The Council initially asked Mary Wright, a professor of Chinese history at Yale, to chair the committee but she declined because of illness. Jane S. DeHart, interview, 3 January 1992.

20. The meeting took place after an unofficial session on the status of women in the profession. Carroll and Gerda Lerner co-chaired the steering committee of the CCWHP for the first few months; then Lerner resigned and Carroll served alone until 1972. See Smith, CCWHP, 8–9; and Lerner, "Women's Side," 448. Smith's original version of the CCWHP history described the panel, comprised of Emiliana Noether, Hanna Holborn Gray, Jo Tice Bloom, Hilda Smith, and Christopher Lasch. In this version, she gave the number at the original caucus meeting as twenty-five. See this version in the CCWHP files, 1–2. The wording of the 1969 resolution came from a copy in Suzanne Lebsock's private files.

21. The AHA published the entire amended petition in *AHA Perspectives*, 8(5), (June 1970): 12–14.

22. The members were: Willie Lee Rose (chair), Patricia Albjerg Graham, Hanna Holborn-Gray, Carl Schorske, and Page Smith. See "Rose Report", 6, 12–13, 9.

23. See, for the recommendations, "Rose Report," 2–5; for the overall policy statement, 1.

24. Carroll, interview.

25. Emiliana Noether and Dalby at Berkshire Anniversary Panel. Linda K. Kerber was the nominee.

26. See, for example, American Historical Association, "1972 Annual Report," 116. See, for an example of the response rate, Committee on Women Historians, "1983 Annual Report," 7. The report appeared in *AHA Perspectives*, 22(3), (March 1984).

27. Committee on Women Historians, "1981 Annual Report," 3.

28. "Rose Report," 10.

29. Committee on Women Historians, "1974 Annual Report," 2. See CWH to Committee on the Profession, 30 April 1974; and Eleanor Straub to CWH, 15 October 1974, from Lebsock files.

30. Committee on Women Historians, *A Survival Manual for Women (and other) Historians* (Washington DC: Committee on Women Historians and American Historical Association, 1980 ed.), 48.

31. See forewords of 1975 and 1980 editions of *Survival Manual* for almost identical wording. Note that with each edition, while continuing to address specific women's concerns, the tone became more gender neutral. The 1991 edition was entitled: *Becoming

An Historian: Survival Manual for Women and Men. A number of historians contributed to the first manual, for example: the chair of the CWH Jane S. DeHart who initiated the project; Linda K. Kerber; Carl Degler; Dorothy Ross; and Otis Graham. DeHart, interview.

32. *Survival Manual,* 1975 ed., 21; see also 1980 ed., 55–56; 1991 ed., 78. In 1986 the Committee submitted a formal definition of and statement on sexual harassment to the Professional Division for adoption by the AHA. See AHA "Statement on Standards of Professional Conduct," section 4 on Employment, *AHA Perspectives,* 25(6) (September 1987): 3.

33. The idea for a panel on women in the profession was part of the original Council resolution establishing the Rose Committee in 1969. Members of the Committee and of the CCWHP took the initiative at organizing panels on this subject and on women's history. The CCWHP organized the 1970 AHA panel at which Hilda Smith, later president of the CGWH, gave the first version of "Feminism and the Methodology of Women's History." At the same meeting, the Rose Committee held an open session on its recommendations. Program of 1970 annual meeting and Carroll to Zinsser, 3 March 1992.

34. See Kathryn Kish Sklar, "The Status of Women in the Historical Profession–Updating the Rose Report" (unpublished, 1980), 2, CWH files.

35. Committee on Women Historians, 1983 Annual Report, 8.

36. Alice Kessler-Harris interview, 10 April 1991, New Brunswick, N.J.; Noralee Frankel comments on the chapter; author's files as a member of the 1990 program committee. See Minutes of CWH: 27–28 December 1977, 2; Minutes of CWH, 20–31 March 1980; Minutes of CWH, 28 December 1981, 2, for AHA resistance to and final acceptance of "gender balancing," CWH files. For recent discussions, see, *AHA Perspectives,* 30 (4), (April 1992): 13–16.

37. For statistical summaries, see, for example, the work of William Monter, William Chafe, and Melanie Gustafson, Committee on Women Historians, 1979 and 1983 Annual Reports. The current editor, David L. Ransel, was a professor of women's history when he took on the editorship. It has been his policy to have four of the ten members of the editorial board be women and to solicit papers by women. He reports that "this and other actions . . . have had the intended effect of attracting a larger proportion of manuscript submissions from women." David L. Ransel to Judith P. Zinsser, 18 May 1992.

38. The Kelly Prize was first awarded in 1984. All statistics are from AHA lists of prize winners.

39. Feminists have noted the ways in which even after women's salaries have been brought in line with men's, in a few years they tend to lag behind again, by as much as $2,000 for individuals at the same rank (example given was the University of Maryland–College Park). Discussion, "Twenty Years After the Rose Report and Beyond: Women Historians in the Twenty-First Century," American Historical Association Convention, New York, N.Y., 28 December 1990. See "AHA Guidelines," *AHA Perspectives,* 29 (2), (February 1991): 7–18. See Joan M. Jensen, "Committee on Women Historians: 1970–1990 A Twenty-Year Report," *AHA Perspectives,* 29 (3), (March 1991):9.

40. National Research Council figures for doctorates awarded to women and men of color from 1975 to 1988 were: total—700; women—192; men—508. "1990 Guidelines," *AHA Perspectives,* 29(2), (February 1991): 18.

41. "1990 Guidelines." See *Survival Manual,* 1980 ed. for early awareness of these problems, 49–50; see CWH 1983 Annual Report, *AHA Perspectives,* 12; Jensen, "Twenty-Year Report," 8. See on hiring practices: CWH Minutes, 28 December 1983, 28 December 1986, 8 April 1988; and Committee on Women Historians, 1988 and 1989 Annual Reports, CWH files.

42. Carroll and Cooper as quoted in Smith, CCWHP, 7, 12.

43. Cooper, interview; Sandi E. Cooper to Steering Committee, 27 June 1973, 3, Lebsock files.

44. Suzanne Lebsock, interview, 19 November 1990.

45. The April 1972 Council meeting discussed the need for CWH staff support: objections ranged from Sylvia L. Thrupp's interjection that women's history did not warrant separate status because it would be included when "better social history" was written to John Higham's recommendation that the AHA should not just respond to the most vocal (i.e., women) but rather should consider appointing someone who would "cooperate with all agencies that are working towards solutions of problems in social justice for minorities [sic]." Report of 7 April 1972 Minutes of Council Meeting, "Association Items," *AHA Newsletter,* X (4), (September 1972): 7.

46. The CCWHP had a sister organization, the Conference Group On Women's History, which worked to advance this aspect of the original resolutions. The CGWH, as it came to be called, cosponsored panels at the AHA conventions and made a particular point of organizing sessions which included the history of Third World Women. CCWHP-CGWH newsletters regularly carried bibliographies of women's history.

47. Lebsock, interview, 19 November 1990. Smith, CCWHP, 19. See also December 1972 CCWHP Statement of Purpose, Lebsock files. For example, the CCWHP wrote resolutions pressing for the graduate student member of the CWH called for in the Rose Report recommendations.

48. Cooper's list included Gerda Lerner, Natalie Zemon Davis, Joan Kelly, Mary Frances Berry, and Berenice A. Carroll. Cooper to Brison D. Gooch, 10 April 1972. Sandi E. Cooper, "Supporting Statement for Resolution," AHA Annual Meeting, 29 December 1972, 2; Cooper to Steering Committee, 21 August 1972. All documents are from Lebsock files.

49. As quoted in Chaudhuri, CCWHP, 31. The candidates were Gordon Craig and Lawrence Stone.

50. Statistics supplied by Frankel, Committee on Women Historians.

51. Two graduate students worked with both the CCWHP and the CWH: Suzanne Lebsock was the first graduate student to serve on an AHA committee; Noralee Frankel became the Assistant Director for the CWH after serving with the CCWHP. The affiliates are: The Berkshire Conference of Women Historians; West Coast Association of Women Historians; New England Area Women Historians; Task Force on Ancient History; Washington DC Area Women Historians; Women Historians of the Midwest; Southern Association for Women Historians; New York Metropolitan Region CCWHP; Chicago Area Women's History Conference Group; Upstate New York Coalition for Women's History; Women Historians of Greater Cleveland Ohio; National Women's History Project; Chesapeake Area Group of Women Historians; St. Louis Women Historians. See Chaudhuri, CCWHP, 24, and *AHA Newsletter,* 115 (6) (September 1977): 16–17.

52. Cooper to Steering Committee, 8 March 1972, 3, and Cooper "Supporting Statement," AHA Convention, 29 December 1972, Lebsock files. See also *Survival Manual,* 1975 ed., 3. Lawrence Stone as quoted in Sandi E. Cooper, "Role of the Committee on Women Historians—A Few Ideas on Its Direction," 1 November 1973, 1, Lebsock files.

53. See Chaudhuri, CCWHP, 23; Committee on Women Historians Minutes, 10–11 October 1975, CWH files, for discussion of the policy and support for the resolution. Also Cooper interview.

54. In choosing the AHA, I have omitted the accomplishments of feminists (both women and men) in other professional groups such as the Organization of American Historians and the American Studies Association. The Organization of American Histori-

ans (OAH) is the specialist group for historians of the United States. In the 1970s it was more responsive than the AHA to women's issues. For example, Gerda Lerner served as president in 1979.

55. There were precedents for this kind of resolution from the 1960s and 1970s. In 1968, the annual meeting was moved from Chicago to New York as a result of protests from members after the events of the summer. A number of resolutions opposing United States policies in Vietnam were passed at annual meetings in the early 1970s. On the petition, see Linda K. Kerber to historians, 24 August 1978, Lebsock files. See for discussion among women historians, *CCWHP Newsletter*, 9 (3), (December 1978): 4. The CWH assumed primary sponsorship of a breakfast meeting at the 1974 AHA Convention. Originally it had been under the aegis of the Berkshire Conference. The CWH chair now gives the annual report at this meeting. The CCWHP has continued its advocacy for women outside the academy. For example, it filed an amicus brief in the Supreme Court hearing of *Webster v. Reproductive Health Services*. See "Abstract" *Journal of Women's History*, 2 (3), (Winter 1991): 145.

56. Kessler-Harris, interview.

57. Cooper, interview; Kessler-Harris, interview. See also Linda K. Kerber as quoted in *Graduate Training in United States Women's History: A Conference Report* (Racine, WI: National Endowment for the Humanities and the Johnson Foundation, 1989), 52.

Chapter 8

1. Alice Kessler-Harris, Berkshire Conference of Women Historians, panel discussion, 13 May 1991, New Paltz, N.Y.; Judith Bennett, "Comment," *Social Science History*, 13(4), (Winter 1989), 472.

2. Ellen Carol DuBois, Gail Paradise Kelly, Elizabeth Lapovsky Kennedy, Carolyn W. Korsmeyer, and Lillian S. Robinson, eds., *Feminist Scholarship: Kindling in the Groves of Academe* (Urbana, Ill.: University of Illinois Press, 1985), 158, 180.

3. Carl N. Degler, "What the Women's Movement Has Done to American History," *A Feminist Perspective in the Academy: The Difference It Makes*, eds. Elizabeth Langland and Walter Gove (Chicago: The University of Chicago Press, 1981), 77, 68, 69. The phrase "personal sources" is from Louise A. Tilly, "Gender, Women's History, and Social History," *Social Science History*, 13(4), (Winter 1989), 458.

4. See on this reciprocity, Lynn Hunt, "Introduction," *The New Cultural History* (Berkeley: University of California Press, 1989), 18–19. On the two historical periods mentioned, see for example: Linda K. Kerber, *Women of the Republic: Intellect and Ideology in Revolutionary America* (1980); the first collection of documents edited by Darline Gay Levy, Harriet Branson Applewhite, and Mary Durham Johnson, *Women in Revolutionary Paris 1789–1795* (1979); Lynn Hunt's essay on "The Imagery of Radicalism" in her *Politics, Culture, and Class in the French Revolution* (1984); and Joan B. Landes, *Women and the Public Sphere in the Age of the French Revolution* (1988).

5. Linda Gordon, *Heroes of Their Own Lives: The Politics and History of Family Violence: Boston 1880-1960* (1988); Elaine Tyler May, *Homeward Bound: American Families in the Cold War Era* (1988). On the integration of women and gender into family history, see Judith E. Smith, "Review Essay: Family History and Feminist History," *Feminist Studies*, 17(2), (Summer 1991). On family history in general, see the review article by Tamara K. Hareven, "The History of the Family and the Complexity of Social Change," *American Historical Review*, 96(1), (February 1991): especially 118 on women. Bonnie G. Smith has written on the ways in which demographic considerations can be made an integral part of a European history survey course. See *AHA Perspectives*, 29 (6), (September 1991): 22–24.

6. Suzanne Lebsock as quoted in Martha Howell, "A Feminist Historian Looks at the New Historicism: What's So Historical About It?" (New York: Columbia Seminar on Women and Society, unpublished, 8 January 1991), 3.

7. The term "re-visioning" was from Marilyn J. Boxer and Jean H. Quataert, *Connecting Spheres: Women in the Western World, 1500 to the Present* (New York: Oxford University Press, 1987); see the introduction. James T. Kloppenberg, "Objectivity and Historicism: A Century of American Historical Writing," *American Historical Review*, 94(4), (October 1989): 1026. See also Peter Novick, *That Noble Dream: The 'Objectivity Question' and the American Historical Profession* (New York: Cambridge University Press, 1989 ed.), 579, 578–80. Mary Hartman, interview, New Brunswick, N.J., 4 April 1991.

8. For examples of these views, see: Gerda Lerner, *Teaching Women's History*, (Washington DC: American Historical Association, 1981), 4; Gisela Bock, "Women's History and Gender History: Aspects of an International Debate," *Gender & History*, 1(1), (Spring 1989): 1; Carol Gruber spoke of "ghettoization" at the evening panel, Berkshire Conference of Women Historians, New Paltz, N.Y., 13 May 1989; Annette Kolodny used the ideas of "containment" and "appropriation" about women's studies in "Dancing Between Left and Right: Feminism and the Academic Minefield in the 1980s," *Feminist Studies*, 14(3), (Fall 1988), 460; Judith Bennett, "Feminism and History," *Gender & History*, 1(3), (Autumn 1989): 252. See also Joan W. Scott on separate status and uses of "gender" in "Gender: A Useful Category of Historical Analysis," *Gender and the Politics of History* (New York: Columbia University Press, 1988), 30, 31–32. Gay Gullickson, "Comment," *Social Science History*, 13(4), (Winter 1989): 464.

9. Alice Kessler-Harris interview, New Brunswick, N.J., 10 April 1991. Gullickson, 464.

10. Alice Kessler-Harris and Isabel Hull, evening panel, Berkshire Conference of Women Historians, New Paltz, N.Y., 10 April 1991. Berenice A. Carroll interview, 23 April 1991. See also her article, "The Politics of 'Originality': Women and the Class System of the Intellect," *Journal of Women's History*, 2(2), (Fall 1990). As an example of the persistence of the sexist images, a 1989 *New York Times* reviewer turned a woman scholar into a "research assistant" even though she and her male colleague had clearly "cooperated as coeditors." Gregory M. Britton to *New York Times*, 6 August 1989, Book Review Section, 30.

11. Melanie Gustafson, ed., *Becoming a Historian: A Survival Manual for Women and Men* (Washington, D.C.: Committee on Women Historians and American Historical Association, 1991 ed.), 28.

12. Linda Gordon, interview, MARHO, *Visions of History* eds. Henry Abelove, Betsy Blackmar, Peter Dimock, and Jonathan Schneer (New York: Pantheon Books, 1983 ed.), 93.

13. See the study by Sydney Stahl Weinberg, "The Role of Women in Immigration History" (New York: Columbia Seminar on Women and Society, unpublished, 29 November 1989), 2, 9–10, 18–22.

14. See for this discussion of labor history the study by Ava Baron, "Gender and Labor History: Learning from the Past, Looking to the Future," in *Work Engendered: Toward a New History of American Labor*, ed. Ava Baron (Ithaca: Cornell University Press, 1991), especially 2–8, 15–16, 21, 37. I am grateful to Elaine Abelson for bringing this collection to my attention.

15. Lawrence Stone, "Only Women," *The New York Review of Books*, 32(6), (11 April 1985): 21; Joan Wallach Scott, "American Women Historians," *Gender*, 196. Other feminist scholars have written on this inability to see particularity in men's history. Judith Allen called it the "phallocentric" configuration of the discipline. Judith Allen, "Evidence and Silence: Feminism and the Limits of History," *Feminist Challenges:*

Social and Political Theory, eds. Carole Pateman and Elizabeth Gross (Boston: Northeastern University Press, 1987), 188. See also Susan Hardy Aiken, Karen Anderson, Myra Dinnerstein, Judy Leasink, and Patricia MacCorquodale, "Trying Transformations: Curriculum Integration and the Problem of Resistance," *Reconstructing the Academy: Women's Education and Women's Studies*, eds. Elizabeth Minnich, Jean O'Barr, and Rachel Rosenfeld (Chicago: The University of Chicago Press, 1988), 113.

16. Alice Kessler-Harris, "The Just Price, the Free Market, and the Value of Women," *Feminist Studies*, 14(2), (Summer 1988): 235. J. W. Scott has written extensively on this interplay between politics, the multiplicity of interpretations and constructions of the past, and criticism of women historians. See, for example, hers and the other articles in "AHR Forum: The Old History and the New," *American Historical Review*, 94(3), (June 1989), 680–81.

17. The reviewers of *Woman's Body, Woman's Right: Birth Control in America* were respectively: Edward Shorter, J. Stanley Lemons, and David M. Kennedy. See Jonathan N. Wiener, "Radical Historians and the Crisis in American History: 1959–1980," *Journal of American History*, 76(2), (September 1989): 426–27.

18. G. R. Elton, "History According to Saint Joan," *The American Scholar*, 54, (1985). The quotations came from throughout the text in the following order: 549, 554, 555, 550, 549, 555.

19. See, for this reasoning, Gertrude Himmelfarb, "Some Reflections on the New History," in "AHR Forum: The Old History and the New," *American Historical Review*, 94(3), (June 1989): 662, 670. Alice Kessler-Harris contributed the hypothetical question, interview. J. W. Scott, "Introduction," *Gender*, 3. There is also a discussion of this way of thinking in Novick, 610–11.

20. The study of women in this period of French history continues to expand. In April of 1989 five hundred scholars and activists met in Toulouse, France, as part of the bicentennial celebration of the French Revolution. They came together to report on their research and to commemorate all that women had done in the Revolution. See for a description of the significance of this scholarship to French feminists, Karen Offen, "Women's Memory, Women's History, Women's Political Action: The French Revolution in Retrospect 1789–1889–1989," *Journal of Women's History*, 1(3), (Winter 1990): 211–30.

21. Tilly, 439; Gullickson, 465.

22. Bock, 8. See for the same suggestion by Bonnie S. Anderson and Judith P. Zinsser, in Nancy Wartik, "So Long, Robespierre," *Ms* (October 1988), 68.

23. In contrast, although not a textbook, Bonnie S. Anderson's and Judith P. Zinsser's *A History of Their Own: Women in Europe from Prehistory to the Present* (1988) presents European women's experiences from the perspective of "place" and "function," concepts borrowed from feminist anthropology and sociology. The volumes divide into sections on peasant women from 800 to 1980, women of the churches from 800 to 1750, sixteenth- to nineteenth-century women of the courts and salons, nineteenth- and twentieth-century women of the cities, and so on. See, for justification of traditional approaches in European history, the introduction to Renate Bridenthal, Claudia Koonz, and Susan Mosher Stuard, *Becoming Visible: Women in European History* (1977, 1987 eds.). For textbook examples of conventional periodization, see Bonnie G. Smith, *Changing Lives: Women in European History Since 1700* (1989); see, for United States history: Sara M. Evans, *Born for Liberty: A History of Women in America* (1989); and the series edited by Mary Beth Norton, *Major Problems in American Women's History: Documents and Essays* (1989).

24. See, for example, one of the first articles, Betty Levy, "The School's Role in the Sex-Role Stereotyping of Girls: A Feminist Review of the Literature," *Feminist Studies*, 1(1), (Summer 1972).

25. See "National Women's History Week: Academic Rationale" (Santa Rosa, Calif.: National Women's History Project); the statistics come from *Stereotypes, Distortions, and Omissions in United States History Textbooks* (New York: The Council on Interracial Books for Children, 1977); The Council of the Great City Schools, "Draft Report Prepared for the American History Textbook Commission" (Washington, D.C.: 30 January 1989). Most educators use the checklist for bias formulated by Myra Pollack Sadker and David Miller Sadker in their *Sex Equity Handbook for Schools* (New York: Longman, 1982).

26. See, for many of these points, Carole Srole, "Intersections and Differences: Integration of Women into the United States Survey Course, Part I," *The History Teacher*, 23(3), (May 1990), 264, 260. See also the study done by Mary Kay Thompson Tetreault: "Integrating Women's History: The Case of United States History Textbooks," *The History Teacher*, 19(2), (February 1986). *Women in World Area Studies* is from Glenhorst Publications, Inc.

27. Minnich et al., eds., 43.

28. Paul Gagnon, *Democracy's Half-Told Story: What American History Textbooks Should Add* (Washington DC: American Federation of Teachers, 1989); National Commission on Social Studies in the Schools, *Charting a Course: Social Studies for the 21st Century* (November 1989); see 26, 15, 10, 8.

29. The secondary-school teacher was Marjorie Wall Bingham. Commentators on the Commission's report have praised the suggestions for historical topics in the primary grades, the inclusion of more "world history," and the sequencing of courses as the innovative aspects of the recommendations. See, for examples cited, Bradley Commission, *Building a History Curriculum: Guidelines for Teaching History in Schools* (USA: Educational Excellence Network, 1988), "Vital Themes and Narratives," "Topics" in United States and World History: 12, 25, 11, 14. The *Guidelines* were also reprinted in *Historical Literacy: The Case for History in American Education*, eds. Paul Gagnon and the Bradley Commission on History in Schools (New York: Macmillan, 1989). For reviews critical of this book, see *The History Teacher*, 23(3), (May 1990).

30. J. W. Scott has identified this as a "conceptual and structural phenomenon." See "Women Historians," *Gender*, 196.

31. The information on testing came from an interview with Despina Danos, Group Head and Senior Examiner in the History–Social Studies Group of the College Board Test Division of the Educational Testing Service, 21 June 1991, and Bonnie G. Smith, New Brunswick, N.J., 7 October 1991 and 5 March 1992.

32. *Practicing to Take the GRE History Test* (Princeton, N.J.: Educational Testing Service in association with Warner Books, 1986). For a discussion of department problems using the GRE multiple-choice examinations for evaluation of college majors, see Robert V. Schnucker, "Preliminary Report for a History Assessment Test," *The History Teacher*, 24(4), (August 1991): 425–26. The multiple-choice questions of the United States and European advanced placement tests from the 1970s showed more change. Approximately 10% of the test questions related to women's experience directly or indirectly.

33. Danos, interview; Smith interview, 5 March 1992.

34. For many of the points in this paragraph, see Kathryn Pyne Addelson, "Comment," *Signs*, 12(4), (summer 1987): 831.

35. Bennett, "Feminism," 266. For an example of the feminist argument favoring women's historians initiating the "dialogue" with traditional histories, see Tilly, 474–76.

36. The phrase "Consciousness raising to social change," is Hester Eisenstein's: "Introductory Remarks," Columbia Seminar on Women and Society, New York, N.Y., 15 April 1991.

CHAPTER 9

1. In 1990 the NWHP realized net sales of its own and others' books, curriculum materials, and videos of over $713,000, with 64% from out-of-state orders. The leaders run yearly training conferences in California and six other states. Maria E. Cuevas, speech for International Coeducation Conference, University of Valencia, Spain, 3 November 1989, 6; and published in edited form in *Women of Power*, 16, (Spring 1990). See also Maria E. Cuevas, interview, Santa Rosa, Calif., 15 May 1991; Net Operating Profit Worksheet, June 1990, Maria E. Cuevas files. Mary Ruthsdotter, notes, May 1991.

2. The college became part of Sonoma State University in the late 1970s.

3. Molly Murphy MacGregor, Bette Morgan Patterson, and Evelyn Truman, "Proposal for Women's History Week," 19 October 1977, Molly Murphy MacGregor private papers. The information on the Commission came from Elizabeth Bock's files on the Sonoma County Commission on the Status of Women.

4. Information on the first year's activities came from the Sonoma County Commission on the Status of Women, Annual Report 1977, Bock files.

5. At first the city refused to close Main Street for them, so all the groups marched on the sidewalk. On these first years, see, for example, the Board of Supervisor's "Resolution" proclaiming March 6–10 as women's history week, National Women's History Project Archives and NWHP Celebratory Program, video, Santa Rosa, Calif., 18 May 1991.

6. Molly Murphy MacGregor, "Annual Report 1979–1980" to the Sonoma County Commission on the Status of Women, Bock files. Sacramento Press Conference, 4 March 1980, tape, NWHP Archives. This reasoning is a staple of all NWHP publications; see, for example, "Academic Rationale," 1982, 2–3 and flyer for Women's History Week, 1981. See also Elizabeth Fox-Genovese, *Feminism Without Illusions: A Critique of Individualism* (1991), 3, 2, where she explained that "Young women must be trained to support themselves, preferably by work that draws upon their talents and enhances their self respect," for "marriage is no longer a viable career". Other feminist historians have written on the debilitating and denigrating effects of the omissions and illusions of traditional histories. See Gerda Lerner, preface, *The Majority Finds Its Past: Placing Women in History* (New York: Oxford University Press, 1979), xvii; Lerner, "The Majority Finds Its Past," *Majority*, 163–164; Dolores Barracano Schmidt and Earl Robert Schmidt, "The Invisible Woman: The Historian as Professional Magician," *Liberating Women's History: Theoretical and Critical Essays*, ed. Berenice A. Carroll, (Urbana: University of Illinois Press, 1976), 53.

7. Alice Kessler-Harris, evening panel discussion, Berkshire Conference of Women Historians, 13 May 1989, New Paltz, N.Y.

8. Gerda Lerner, "Report on Summer Institute for High School Teachers," 13 November 1976, 3, Amy Swerdlow private files.

9. Mary Ruthsdotter interview, Santa Rosa, Calif., 13 May 1991.

10. Molly Murphy MacGregor, "History Revisited," video, National Women's History Project; 1987 Congressional Resolution, NWHP Archives.

11. Descriptions of events came from NWHP Archives.

12. MacGregor, interview, 18 May 1991. For a description of the "Send-Off Party" and the plan to make T-shirts like those sold at the parade for all of the Institute participants, see "Status Quotes: News from the Sonoma County Commission on the Status of Women," (July 1979), 1, Bock files.

13. In 1976 as part of this broader commitment Sarah Lawrence in cooperation with the American Historical Association had run the first National Endowment for the Humanities teacher training institute. See Gerda Lerner to Committee on Restructuring the College, 29 April 1971, 1–2; "Minutes of Feminist Studies Committee," 3 April

1973; "Call for Planning," March 1977; "Evaluation Report: Women Studies Program," 6; Swerdlow private files.

14. See *New Directions for Women*, 8 (4), (Autumn 1979): 12–13, 23.

15. By coincidence MacGregor was in Washington in July of 1981 to report on a federal grant her group had received. A message from Elam told her to rush to the capitol building where she heard the votes for the joint resolution officially designating a National Women's History Week. The account of the events came from interviews: MacGregor, 15 May 1991; MacGregor and Pam Elam interview, New York N.Y., 7 July 1991. The lobbying continued because the resolution has had to be repassed first every year and now every two years. Mikulski was the sponsor in the House of Representatives, Orrin Hatch in the Senate. Passage has become more, not less, difficult over the years because of general congressional annoyance with this type of commemorative resolution. For 1990 MacGregor remembered that it was harder than ever. She had to involve the NWHP network, six hundred subscribers to the NWHP resource newsletter, asking for telegrams and phone calls to representatives. She just went down the list and matched the NWHP network mailing list with the states that had not become cosponsors. This kind of strategy had been used previously. After the declaration of Black History Month MacGregor and her colleagues realized that women could have a month as well. Alaska, Colorado, New York, and Michigan expanded their women's commemoration from a week to a month even before the change in the congressional resolution.

16. NWHP video #1, May 1984, NWHP Archives.

17. Initially, the Project had nonprofit status as part of the Women's Support Network that they had founded to raise money for specific programs that were outside the more general mandate of the Commission. Hammett worked with them at the Commission and at their first offices from 1977–83. Though she made significant contributions to all of their activities during this period, she chose to remain a volunteer and never took a leading role.

18. The first flyer for the National Women's History Project offered three guides: one on how to initiate celebrations, one on activities, and one giving elementary and secondary materials (much of it taken from curriculum units developed for the Berkeley public schools). To raise money to finance their continuing efforts they sold T-shirts, buttons, a tote bag, and their first commemorative poster. Descriptions of these early years in this and subsequent paragraphs came from interviews with MacGregor, 15 and 18 May 1991; Cuevas, 15 May 1991; Morgan, 25 June 1991; NWHP Video #1, May 1984, NWHP Archives.

19. Wilson took the slide show to Nin in the hospital, so she did see it. Morgan, interview.

20. See "We the Women: Advocates for Social Change," slide–tape program, NWHP Archives.

21. This account came from NWHP Video #1, May 1984, NWHP Archives; Ruthsdotter interview, 13 May 1991. Ruthsdotter and her family moved to Santa Rosa from Los Angeles in the summer of 1977, primarily to have a better place to raise their daughter. Trained in urban planning at UCLA, Ruthsdotter had also made time to be active in political campaigns, in antiwar and abortion rights groups. She was looking for a group to work with and having heard of the Commission, she, her husband, and daughter went to one of their evening meetings. She volunteered and eventually became chair of the Commission. On her marriage she had taken her husband's name, Dawson, but subsequently changed it in the early 1980s to a version of "Ruth's daughter."

22. Morgan interview.

23. The Project had already been funded under Title IX with a more modest grant of $25,000 in 1980 to replicate a project MacGregor had done with students to evaluate gender bias in their textbooks and classes.

24. Notes on 1982 Celebrations, NWHP Archives. Information also came from MacGregor, interview, 15 May 1991; Ruthsdotter, notes, May 1991.

25. As Morgan explained it: "In order for things to move forward . . . there was a distinct need for the buck to stop somewhere." Information about this period came from Cuevas, interview; Bonnie Eisenberg, interview, 18 May 1991; Ruthsdotter notes, May 1991; Morgan, interview.

26. Cuevas, interview. In June of 1982 they made approximately $26,000 in sales of materials they had created themselves, and others they had chosen from educational and trade sources, the equivalent figure by June of 1984 was $106,000.

27. NWHP, n.d., information sheet for bank loan, 2–3, Cuevas files.

28. 1983 flyer and form, and postcard for 1986, NWHP Archives.

29. MacGregor, interview, 15 May 1991.

30. Cuevas, speech, 8; video script quotations all come from 1990 workshop video #1, Santa Rosa, Calif., NWHP Archives.

31. Cuevas, interview.

32. Mary Alice Carter to NWHP, 26 November 1984, NWHP Archives.

33. These questions are paraphrased from Ava Baron, "Gender and Labor History: Learning from the Past, Looking to the Future," *Work Engendered: Toward a New History of American Labor* (Ithaca: Cornell University Press, 1991), 21, 26, 32.

34. Morgan, interview.

SUGGESTIONS FOR FURTHER READING

Rather than present long lists of books and articles, I offer this bibliographical essay. I am assuming that the extensive endnotes will give specialists and those with very specific interests the detailed references they require. In contrast these suggestions have a different purpose. They should help readers reconstruct the principal concepts and general conclusions of the different sections: Men's History, Women's History, and the Impact of Feminism.

AN INTRODUCTION

To begin, for those who want to think about "feminism," about how to define the idea and the movement it inspired, I recommend the article by Karen Offen, "Defining Feminism: A Comparative Historical Approach," *Signs*, 14(1), (Autumn 1988). Two very good surveys deal with this whole question of "impact" in the academy: Ellen Carol DuBois, Gail Paradise Kelly, Elizabeth Lapovsky Kennedy, Carolyn W. Korsmeyer, and Lillian S. Robinson, *Feminist Scholarship: Kindling in the Groves of Academe* (Urbana: University of Illinois Press, 1985); and Elizabeth Minnich, Jean O'Barr, and Rachel Rosenfeld, eds., *Reconstructing the Academy: Women's Education and Women's Studies* (Chicago: The University of Chicago Press, 1988). In addition, there is now a collection of articles about the ways in which feminist history evolved in other countries: *Writing Women's History: International Perspectives*, eds. Karen Offen, Ruth Roach Pierson, and Jane Rendall (Bloomington: University of Indiana Press, 1991). Minnich's recent book, *Transforming Knowledge* (Philadelphia: Temple University Press, 1990), untangles the 'knots' in our culture's gendered ways of reasoning and describes what the transformation would mean.

MEN'S HISTORY

Those interested in "men's history," in how its underlying premises, methodologies, and politics have been described and challenged can consult a variety of works. Edward H. Carr's *What Is History?* (New York: Alfred A. Knopf, 1963) is beautifully written and remains the classic statement of what history was like at the beginning of the 1960s. *Historians' Fallacies: Toward a Logic of Historical Thought* by David Hackett Fischer (New York: Harper & Row, 1970), though denser in style, fully explores all of the logical implications of traditional constructions of the past. For a set of short articles that together give a picture of both the "new" and the "old" historical perspectives and theoretical approaches, look at the "AHR Forum" by Theodore S. Hamerow, Gertrude Himmelfarb, and Joan W. Scott in the *American Historical Review*, 94(3), (June 1989).

Although Peter Novick barely considered gender in his analysis of the historical profession, he chronicled every other source of discrimination. Novick entitled his book *That Noble Dream: The "Objectivity Question" and the American Historical Profession* to highlight the inherent subjectivity of what even the best-intentioned historians have written. The collection of essays edited by Eric Hobsbawm and Terrence Ranger, *The Invention of Tradition* (New York: Cambridge University Press) takes a different perspective on the writing of history, but also provides valuable insights into the contributions historians have made to the creation and legitimation of "tradition."

Of the new historical approaches popularized in the United States in the 1960s, I suggest reading the Europeans first. For many in the profession the French Annales School inspired the most dramatic rethinking in the 1960s and 1970s. A collection of Fernand Braudel's (the best known Annaliste) reviews and articles has been translated and published: *On History* (Chicago: The University of Chicago Press, 1980). It includes a selection from the last pages of *The Mediterranean and the Mediterranean World in the Age of Philip II* (New York: Harper & Row, 1972) that explains his approach to historical reconstruction.

Jonathan A. Wiener has written about the "radical" historians in the United States, "Radical Historians and the Crisis in American History: 1959–1980," (*Journal of American History*, 76 (2), (September 1989). He gives a clear overall sense of how historical interpretations have and have not changed in the United States as a result of their challenges. To hear the voices of these historians themselves go to the interviews done by MARHO (The Radical Historians Organization) and published as *Visions of History* edited by Henry Abelove, Betsy Blackmar, Peter Dimock, and Jonathan Schneer (New York: Pantheon Books, 1983).

WOMEN'S HISTORY

It may not be possible to recreate the feelings of disbelief, outrage, and righteous commitment that characterized the first generation of 1960s feminist historians. Those who want to try, however, might read two works often mentioned as having been significant in feminists' coming to "historical self-consciousness": Virginia Woolf's essay *A Room of One's Own* (New York: Harcourt, Brace & World, reprint of 1929 ed.) and Sheila Rowbotham's *Woman's Consciousness, Man's World* (New York: Penguin Books, 1987 ed.)

Although Gerda Lerner and Joan Kelly's writings represent in many ways a collective statement rather than individual formulation of feminist historians' thoughts in the 1970s, their essays have become "classics." See the collections: *The Majority Finds Its Past: Placing Women in History* (New York: Oxford University Press, 1979) and *Women, History and Theory: The Essays of Joan Kelly* (Chicago: The University of Chicago Press, 1984). Also revealing from the historiographical perspective is Berenice A. Carroll's collection *Liberating Women's History: Theoretical and Critical Essays* (Urbana: University of Illinois Press, 1976). Although not published until the later part of the 1970s, most of the essays are versions of papers given and published in the first years of feminist efforts to change how history was written and taught.

To explore the three "bridges" formulated to bring women's and traditional histories together the reader should go to some of the best-known formulations of the different approaches: Sheila Rowbotham's *Hidden from History: 300 Years of Women's Oppression and the Fight Against It* (London: Pluto Press, 1989 ed.) for the Marxist perspective; the collection of Carroll Smith-Rosenberg's essays *Disorderly Conduct: Visions of Gender in Victorian America* (New York: Oxford University Press, 1985) for the explication and illustration of a separate "women's culture"; Joan Wallach Scott's collected essays *Gender and the Politics of History* (New York: Columbia University Press, 1988) for the application of literary "deconstructionist" techniques and for examples of "gender" used as a category of analysis, the approach first enunciated by Kelly and Natalie Zemon Davis.

THE IMPACT OF FEMINISM

It would probably be most interesting to read first about the experiences of the women scholars of the 1930s and 1940s to gain a sense of what the profession was like before the renewed feminism of the late 1960s. See, as an introduction, Kathryn Kish Sklar's article "American Female Historians in Context

1770–1930," *Feminist Studies*, 3(1/2), (Fall 1975). To learn about a particular scholar, consult the four volume collection of women's biographies *Notable American Women*, eds. Edward T. James, Janet Wilson James, Paul S. Boyer; and Barbara Sicherman and Carol Hurd Green (Cambridge, Mass.: Harvard University Press, 1971 and 1980). The editors have written full, detailed entries that end with bibliographical information. For an understanding of women and the professions in general, see Penina Migdal Glazer and Miriam Slater, *Unequal Colleagues: The Entrance of Women into the Professions 1890–1940* (New Brunswick, N.J.: Rutgers University Press, 1987). They have a chapter specifically on historians at Mt. Holyoke. The best introduction to Mary Beard is her own writings. Ann J. Lane's *Mary Ritter Beard: A Sourcebook* (New York: Schocken Books, 1977) has a biographical introduction and selections from her speeches and articles.

Aside from the few pages in Peter Novick's book, until 1992 only Joan W. Scott had written about the interaction between women historians and the American Historical Association in "American Women Historians 1884–1984" (reprinted in the collection of her essays). Interested readers may now consult Jacqueline Goggin, "Challenging Sexual Discrimination in the Historical Profession," in the *American Historical Review*, 97(3), (June, 1992). The women's caucus, the CCWHP–CGWH, has its own history, a pamphlet done by Hilda Smith, Nupur Chaudhuri, and Gerda Lerner, *A History of the Coordinating Committee on Women in the Historical Profession-Conference Group on Women's History* (available through the organization, 1989).

Two recent collections of articles give a particularly vivid sense of what has happened to history, in this case United States history, as a result of the new scholarship on women and the application of gender as a category of analysis. For a sense of the variety of women's experiences, see *Unequal Sisters: A Multicultural Reader in U.S. Women's History*, edited by Ellen Carol DuBois and Vicki L. Ruiz. For the effects of gender, see Ava Baron's *Work Engendered: Toward a New History of American Labor* (Ithaca: Cornell University Press, 1991). Baron's own introductory essay "Gender and Labor History: Learning from the Past, Looking to the Future" describes the new kinds of questions historians are asking. For a sense of the initial excitement with gender as an analytical approach and of the ways in which it illuminated traditional topics in European history, see the collection of Natalie Zemon Davis's articles, *Society and Culture in Early Modern France* (Stanford: Stanford University Press, 1975).

The ways in which women scholars in the United States describe, experience, and act on their different feminisms is as diverse as women's circumstances. The reader might like to look through the journals that publish many of the most important theoretical articles (in alphabetical order): *Feminist Studies; Gender*

& *History*; the *Journal of Women's History*; and *Signs*. Deborah K. King's essay "Multiple Jeopardy, Multiple Consciousness: The Context of a Black Feminist Ideology," in *Signs*, 14 (1), (Autumn 1988), explains black women's perspective with particular clarity. Judith Bennett issued a new call for activism in "Feminism and History," *Gender & History*, 1 (3), (Autumn 1989); in "The Politics of 'Originality': Women and the Class System of the Intellect," *Journal of Women's History*, 2 (2), (Fall 1990), Berenice A. Carroll described how decisions about what is and is not "original" have affected women scholars.

The easiest way to gain a sense of the popular, "grassroots" initiatives is to write or call for the National Women's History Project catalogue: 7738 Bell Road, Windsor CA 95492-8518 (tel. 707–838–6000) and to celebrate Women's History Month.

INDEX

Abzug, Bella, 135
academic conferences, 89–90, 93–94,
    96–97; discrimination in, 105–6
academic equity, publication and, 85
academic historians, 17–18
academic journals, 89–93; feminist,
    92–93; publishing decisions, 86
academic programs, funding for, 83
academic women, feminism and, 41
academy, historical, 47–56, 59–60;
    acceptance by, 72; discrimination in,
    70; languages of, 59; politics of, 56
accuracy of history, 18
achievement testing, 123–25
activism: of Lerner, 38; of minority
    women scholars, 75
actor, historian as, 19
Addams, Jane, 32
advanced placement testing, 123–25
advisors to graduate students, 70
advocacy groups, Beard and, 31
affirmative-action programs: and National
    Women's History Month, 131; and
    NWHP projects, 137
affirmative-action policies, 68
African-American women scholars,
    73–74, 81–82. *See also* black
    women
Alexandra, Tsarina of Russia, 12
America: History and Life, 90
American Dream, Friedan and, 29–30
American Historical Association, 48,
    97–99, 100–112; annual
    conventions, 94–97, 106, 107,
    168n1; book exhibits, 87–88;
    CCWHP and, 109–11; Committee

on Women Historians, 68–69, 75,
    133; and discrimination, 104–5,
    107–8; feminist caucus, 79, 82,
    101–2; feminist impact, 94, 96–98;
    funding survey, 86; and gender
    studies, 54; pamphlet on teaching,
    83; "Recent United States
    Scholarship on the History of
    Women," 59; Rose Committee,
    64–66, 68, 101–5, 171n33; women
    as president, 66, 67, 99, 110
American Historical Review (AHR), 85,
    91; inequities in publication, 106–7;
    review of Gordon's work, 118
American Political Science Association
    (APSA), 101
American Scholar, The, review of Kelly's
    work, 118–19
amnesia, collective, 17, 18
Anderson, Bonnie S., *A History of Their
    Own: Women in Europe from
    Prehistory to the Present*, 89,
    175n23
androcentric bias of culture, 37: challenge
    of, 45
Angelou, Maya, 131
Annales d'histoire économique et sociale,
    20
Annales School, 20, 146–47n12, 147n16,
    147–48n26; feminist historians and,
    29; and gender, 23; research center,
    61
*Annales: Economies, Sociétés,
    Civilisations*, 20
Annalistes, 19, 20, 22–23
Anne of Austria, 7

187

204   INDEX

women's movement, 52; Beard and,
    33–34; Kelly and, 38; nineteenth
    century, 36
women's presses, 88
Women's Studies, 91–92
women's studies, 78–81; graduate
    programs, 83; institutionalization of,
    116; Lerner and, 38–39; Sarah
    Lawrence College, 41, 42
Woodbury, Helen Sumner, 64
Woodward, C. Vann, 96
Woolf, Virginia, 72, 150n11
work of women: historians' views,
    14–15; Marxism and, 51
working-class history, 23, 117–18
working-class women, 31, 53; labor
    historians and, 49
Workplace Organizers Conference, 137

World Center for Women's Archives, 32
World War II, and women historians, 64
Wright, Mary, 170n19
writing: of history, 16–18, 21; by women
    historians 43–44
writing contests, 131; NWHP, 139

Yale University, 64
Yale University Press, 88
Young, Marilyn B., 65; *The Vietnam
    Wars*, 87

Zinn, Howard, 22
Zinsser, Judith P., *A History of Their
    Own: Women in Europe from
    Prehistory to the Present*, 89,
    175n23

Judith P. Zinsser is the co-author of *A History of Their Own: Women in History from Prehistory to the Present* (Harper & Row, 1988). She has also written on the international feminist movement for *Women's Studies International Forum* and *New Directions for Women*. She has been a member of the Humanities Department of the United Nations International School since 1969 and has conducted workshops on integrating women into multinational history throughout the United States and Canada.